ARIZONA BOOTS AND BURGERS

Arizona Boots and Burgers

A Guide for Hungry Hikers

NEW AND EXPANDED EDITION

ROGER NAYLOR

University of New Mexico Press • Albuquerque

Printed in the United States of America

ISBN 978-0-8263-6907-9 (paper)
ISBN 978-0-8263-6908-6 (ePub)

Library of Congress Control Number: 2025944334

Founded in 1889, the University of New Mexico sits on the traditional homelands of the Pueblo of Sandia. The original peoples of New Mexico—Pueblo, Navajo, and Apache—since time immemorial have deep connections to the land and have made significant contributions to the broader community statewide. We honor the land itself and those who remain stewards of this land throughout the generations and also acknowledge our committed relationship to Indigenous peoples. We gratefully recognize our history.

Cover illustration: by Felicia Cedillos
Designed by Felicia Cedillos
Composed in Minion Pro

To my father, James Naylor, who taught me many valuable life lessons, not least of which is that there are few things in this world better than a good hamburger.

And to my sister, Susan Mortensen, who brightens my life, and the lives of so many others, every single day.

Contents

RIM COUNTRY AND THE WHITE MOUNTAINS

ARIZONA'S WEST COAST

PHOENIX AND THE VALLEY OF THE SUN: WEST VALLEY

PHOENIX AND THE VALLEY OF THE SUN: EAST VALLEY

CENTRAL HIGHLANDS

SEDONA AND THE VERDE VALLEY

FLAGSTAFF

GRAND CANYON

ARIZONA STRIP AND NAVAJO NATION

Preface

The first incarnation of this book was *Boots and Burgers: An Arizona Handbook for Hungry Hikers*, released by Rio Nuevo Publishers in 2014. It garnered a lot of media attention and enthusiastic responses from readers. That book helped many people in Arizona discover my work. I envisioned putting out multiple volumes, but it was not to be. Sadly (or perhaps happily), the book went out of print during the pandemic.

That allowed me to reclaim the rights to republish. Always a favorite of mine, I wanted the book to be readily available again. But I also didn't want to just release the same volume. I was thrilled when the University of New Mexico Press, publishers of my last four books, jumped at the chance to create a new edition of *Boots and Burgers*.

I salvaged a big chunk of the original *Boots and Burgers*, because most of those eateries are still going strong. No doubt aided by the stamp of approval they received in 2014 when a dusty hiker so poetically sang the praises of their food. Of course, most of the trails from the first book were intact as well. Thus, I started with about 30 hiking trails and restaurants, all spiffed up with fresh prose and updated information.

From there I spent several weeks rambling around Arizona on an epic fact-finding mission. Meaning I did what I do every summer—I hiked and I ate.

If you thought I wouldn't jump at the chance to gobble dozens of burgers all over the state, then obviously you and I have never met. In the end, I added another 40 or so trails and eateries to the book—more than 70 of each. Essentially, this is two books in one, a blast from the past combined with plenty of current favorites. Within these pages you'll find some of Arizona's best hiking trails paired with the most delicious burgers ever touched by a spatula.

Go ahead. Dig in.

Introduction

In your hands you hold my love letter to Arizona, artfully disguised as a hiking and dining guide. If this doesn't inspire some legendary Arizona road trips, I honestly don't know what will.

There's no better way to experience this magnificent state than to walk all across it. Explore every corner, moving slow and quiet, reveling in the ever-changing beauty, and reflecting upon the rich history. Then stop at a locally owned gem of a restaurant and chow down. It's a chance to experience solitude, scenery, and hot salty fries all in one memorable outing.

This book combines two of my great life passions—hiking and hamburgers.

Here's the scenario. I hike into the Arizona outback. I walk through pine-scented forests or alongside rivers and lakes, scramble in and out of steep-walled canyons, climb mountain summits, cross rolling grasslands, or explore lonely deserts beneath a red-eyed rage-ball of a sun. Doesn't matter where I hike. I adore every square inch of this heart-lifting, soul-freeing state.

Then afterward I stop at a diner or café, a mom-and-pop place where no one bats an eye at my dusty boots and sweat-streaked shirt. I don't need a menu because I know exactly what I want. I chug ice water and my stomach rumbles until my burger arrives. I bite into the juicy wheel of beef.

Right there, that's my favorite day of all. That's Halloween, Christmas, and the spring equinox all rolled into one. Walk off a few calories and then pack them on again. I admire the Zen-like simplicity of it. I'll take a boots-and-burgers day anytime I can get it.

So here I've amassed a whole bunch of boots-and-burgers days—hiking trails paired with nearby eateries. More than 70 of each are spread all across this state that I adore.

(*opposite page*) Hikers can walk on golden carpets across Arizona mountains in the autumn. Courtesy of Mike Koopsen, Sedona.

Burgers

Burgers have been my favorite food since childhood. I was such a picky eater as a kid they were nearly the only thing that kept me alive. I was also the last generation to grow up mostly eating burgers at mom-and-pop establishments. I ate burgers at lunch counters, the way God intended.

I ate burgers at short-order restaurants, snack bars, coffee shops, country markets, greasy spoons, hash houses, pool halls, and roadside shacks. Fast-food chains did not yet dominate the landscape. Drive-thrus were a rarity. You sat inside and ordered and watched your food being made. Acclaimed chefs had not yet taken notice of the humble hamburger. It was grill men and line cooks, tossing balls of fresh beef supplied by the neighborhood butcher onto the flat-top. It all started with that dragon hiss—sputter and sizzle and popping grease—the universal language of a busy griddle. The meat was flattened with the spatula but nobody knew at the time they were inventing smashburger style. They were just burgers cooked fast because orders kept coming.

My burger credentials are impeccable. Still, I may not be the most qualified guy to write a book about those iconic sandwiches. I don't have what you call a sophisticated palate to begin with. I'm not adventurous. Trying new things exhausts me. Seldom do I even put cheese on a burger. And don't get me started on the creeping infestation of mayo. It disgusts me in all its incarnations.

To be honest, I'm not a fan of fussy, over-produced burgers. It feels like the chef harbors secret dreams of one day working as a choreographer for lavish musicals. You know the burgers I mean. They sometimes appear as a towering, stacked pinnacle with more meat and topping layers than the Grand Canyon has strata of rock. Burgers are meant to be eaten by hand. Here's a tip: If your burger achieves so much elevation that the weather around the top bun is different than at the bottom, dial it back, Busby Berkley.

Wait a minute.

Hold on. That sounds cranky and this is the most joy-filled book I've ever written. Let me start again.

This book is a celebration of Arizona's remarkable diversity in all forms, scenic trails *and* juicy burgers. It shouldn't be surprising that we are a hotbed of fantastic burger spots. Beef has long been a foundation of Arizona commerce.

A rainbow arches above the iconic Bright Angel Trail. Courtesy of Mike Koopsen, Sedona.

It's one of the five C's our economy is based on: cattle, climate, codgers, and cactus candy—or whatever. One *c* definitely stands for cattle.*

For me an ideal burger tends to be understated. That's what I grew up with. The heart wants what the heart wants. And the stomach wants what isn't always good for the heart. The stomach wants what it remembers with joy. For me, a hamburger is the ultimate in comfort food because it is a flashback on a bun. My tastes still harken back to burgers from childhood. Good quality meat, freshly made, carefully cooked, and garnished with a smear of mustard and a small combo of extras. Heavenly! A burger gives us everything we desire, a concerto of flavors and textures in one simple yet surprisingly complex package. When done right, a burger is poetry on a plate.

Yet I do evolve. I've also developed a taste for plant-based Impossible and Beyond Beef patties. Now some of my favorites are those cooked at home by my vegetarian wife. That's why I also include vegan and vegetarian options from each restaurant.

In the end, what I tried to do is include as many amazing burgers as I

* Don't write me an angry letter—cattle, climate, citrus, cotton, copper.

Not only delicious, burgers are cultural and culinary icons. Courtesy of Rick Mortensen, Phoenix.

could, of all shapes, sizes, and styles. Small or large, smashed or pub-style, cooked over an open flame or on a flattop, fancy or simple, fully dressed or plain, gourmet or old-school. They're all here. No food is as versatile as a burger.

So no matter what kind of burger you prefer—even if it is dipped in mayo and piled so tall it resembles a giraffe gazing across the savannah—it's fine by me. Burger how you burger. At the end of the trail, there is no wrong way to eat a burger. Of course, my way is more right. That's why my name is on the book.

Boots

Look in my closet and you'll find nothing but multiple pairs of hiking boots. They're all classic Merrell Moab low-cut, basic colors, identical except for the varying stages of wear and tear. No sneakers, sandals, or flip-flops, just boots. I live in hiking boots. And for many years that's been my Merrells. Comfortable, lightweight, and sturdy, they are on my feet every day. Technically, I suppose they're shoes, but I call all hiking footwear boots because back in the day they were—big, stiff high-tops that you actually had to break in before you could hit the trail.

It's always a good day for a hike in Arizona. Courtesy of Mike Koopsen, Sedona.

I'm an avid hiker, often topping 1,000 trail miles in a year. While I don't hike every day, I could. I'm always dressed for the trail. From my windows I see mountains, mesas, and red rock cliffs. This is no place to hunker indoors. Easy access to trails and user-friendly climate makes Arizona a biped's paradise. If hiking isn't our state pastime, it should be. A trail snatches you; steals you from the mundane. The common misnomer is that we take a trail. In reality, the trail takes us.

By putting boots to soil, pinning eyes on the horizon, and plunging into wild country, we reap benefits, both health and spiritual. Walking has been described as controlled falling. For me, hiking is controlled falling in love.

Here are a variety of trails for all abilities. A few are ADA accessible—either entirely or partially—and I've identified them. With each trail I've included a nearby restaurant, each locally owned. While burgers are my principal focus, many establishments have wide-ranging menus. I also include other favorite specialties like hot dogs, barbecue, pizza, tacos, burritos, and plenty more, even for vegetarians.

This book is your key to Arizona adventures. It is packed with great days, amazing days, my best days. Peel off a few for yourself. Lace up the boots and explore the scenic wonders of this epic landscape. Then unwind in a comfortable little sanctuary where burgers leap off the grill like trout from a stream. Let yourself be pampered by a spatula technician. Order a burger—cheese it if you want—and bite into your delicious past.

Want fries with that?

Hitting the Trail

First things first. Hiking isn't typically dangerous. Yet any type of recreation

A good burger joint can be a sanctuary, a safe harbor from the small storms of everyday life. Courtesy of Rick Mortensen, Phoenix.

carries certain risks. The very things that make it so enticing—you're outside, exposed to the elements, and removed from civilization—also add aspects of danger. To ensure your safety, be prepared ahead of time and always alert while on the trail. Here are a few tips to keep you healthy, happy, and coming back for more.

Don't kid yourself. Be honest when assessing your physical capabilities. Don't hoist yourself off the couch and attempt to hike the Grand Canyon. Especially if "hoist" is an accurate assessment of what it takes to get you off the sofa. I've rated trails as easy, moderate, or strenuous. That's a subjective ranking that factors in things like distance, terrain, and elevation gain. If you can manage a few laps around the mall without wheezing, you should be able to handle easy ones. Moderate trails require a higher level of fitness because you'll be making some climbs or racking up mileage. Strenuous trails are best suited for experienced hikers in good health.

Download the app. There are all sorts of hiking apps to help with navigation and mapping. They sound like a great idea even if I never got in the habit of using them. Do your research and pick one that's best for you. Just remember to never rely solely on a smartphone app. Batteries die. Carrying a paper map is always a good idea. And if it eases your mind to know, all trails in this book are well-marked day hikes requiring no special route-finding skills. So going astray shouldn't be an issue. If you do wander off trail, stop immediately. Relax, look around, and assess your situation. In most cases you should be able to backtrack to the trail.

West Mitten is the centerpiece formation of the Wildcat Trail in Monument Valley. Courtesy of Mike Koopsen, Sedona.

Get the 411. Each trail in the book comes with the basics to get you started, like directions to the trailhead, length of the trail, and difficulty rating. But it's important to acquire the latest information. That's why I include contact details for each hike. Check on current road and trail conditions, which can change over time or be impacted by the seasons. And always get a weather forecast.

Join a gang. Hike with others. This rule I almost always break because I'm a crotchety old coot who prefers solitude. Wiser and more sociable folks can recruit friends, family, or join a hiking club.

Spill the beans. This is important. Always let someone know your hiking plans, where you're going, and when you'll return.

Dress for success. Start with comfortable hiking boots. You want lightweight but sturdy, and suitable for the terrain you'll be traversing. Wear a wide-brimmed hat and slather on the sunscreen. Dress in layers. Temperatures can change dramatically through the day and at different elevations.

Drink up. By the time you feel thirsty you're already slightly dehydrated. Arizona's arid climate wrings you out quicker than you realize. I always hydrate thoroughly before starting and drink steadily on the hike. For desert hiking, carry at least a gallon per day. And not just water. Longer hikes

Simple or complex, a burger is a warm moment of joy wrapped in a bun. Courtesy of Rick Mortensen, Phoenix.

demand some electrolyte-replacement drinks. Even if you have a post-hike burger in your sights, munching a few salty snacks on the trail will keep your energy level up.

Walk the dog. I specify which trails welcome pooches, but that doesn't necessarily mean you should take them. Consider all conditions, length of the trail, age and health of your good boy or girl, and most importantly the temperature. Dogs are extremely prone to heat stroke in the Arizona sun. If you can't walk barefoot on pavement, your dog shouldn't either.

The right stuff. Carry a few essentials like a first aid kit, flashlight, compass, map, snacks, whistle, signal mirror, and knife. Plus tweezers, comb, and duct tape, which are the primary tools of removing an array of cactus spines.

You talking to me? Carry a cell phone, but don't rely on it. Getting a signal in the outback is never a sure thing. And don't be gabbing all loud and self-absorbed for no reason; just because you're outside doesn't mean other trail users want to hear your outside voice.

Weather

You can hike year-round in Arizona and, baby, that's just what I do. The best months for desert hiking are October through April. During the heat of summer, head for higher ground. Temperatures cool as elevation rises. While summer brutalizes the lower deserts, the forests of the high country stay ridiculously mild.

Arizona has two wet seasons. At least if our prayers are answered it does.

When the trail calls, be ready to answer. Photo by the author.

Winter brings gentle, widespread rains in the desert and snow in the high country. During the monsoon, or summer thunderstorm season, hard-pounding localized rains can erupt suddenly in afternoons. A shifting wind pattern draws warm, moist air from the Gulf of Mexico. Monsoon season begins on June 15 and ends on September 30 with storms peaking between mid-July and mid-August. Monsoon storms tend to form suddenly later in the day, so always pack rain gear in summer. Keep yourself warm and dry to avoid hypothermia. And don't hesitate to turn back if weather turns menacing.

Thunderstorms are often accompanied by seething clouds and sky-scorching lightning. If you are caught in a lightning storm, don't seek shelter under large trees or rock outcroppings. Avoid ridgelines, peaks, and open spaces. Head for a low spot and crouch down, making yourself a small, uninteresting target.

Flash floods are another danger in Arizona. Water levels can rise suddenly even if it's not raining on your location. Storms upstream can send a wall of water through narrow canyons, and turn dry washes into raging rivers. Stay out of such places if rain is possible. The fury of flash floods happens quickly but doesn't last. Wait for waters to recede before crossing flooded arroyos. Likewise, don't attempt to drive across flooded roadways.

Wildlife

The backcountry of Arizona is home to a few venomous creatures such as scorpions, black widow spiders, Gila monsters, and rattlesnakes. To avoid any unpleasant encounters, don't put your hands or feet anywhere you can't see. When you find a log or boulder in the trail, don't step over in a single stride, just in case something is snoozing on the other side. Step up onto the log and then over, landing clear of the base.

Chances are you won't run into a rattlesnake on the trail, and even if you do, they're not stalking you. Rattlers aren't aggressive and don't bite unless they feel threatened. If you are bitten, stay calm—which is easier said than done because you've just been bitten by a rattlesnake! Maybe this will help: Rattlesnake bites are a serious medical emergency, but generally not life threatening. Remove watches or rings, which may constrict swelling. Keep the wound below the heart and get to the hospital as quickly as possible.

The likelihood of meeting other potentially dangerous wildlife like black bears or mountain lions is even more remote. If you do come face-to-face with one of the big animals, always keep a safe distance. Keep children close and dogs under control. Do not run. Make noise. In the extremely rare case that you are attacked, fight back.

Trail Etiquette

- Pack out everything you pack in, no matter how small. If you happen to see trash left by some imbecile, don't just cluck your tongue in dismay. Haul it out with you.
- Stay on the trail. Shortcuts and stray paths speed erosion and trample fragile plants.
- Don't disturb anything. Leave rocks, plants, and artifacts just as you find them.

- Hikers yield to equestrians. Bicyclists are supposed to yield to everyone, but frankly, it's often easier for a hiker to step aside and let bikers breeze past. When approaching equestrians, speak up so the horse knows you're a person and not a well-disguised mountain lion. Ask the rider for instructions.
- Hikers traveling downhill should yield to uphill hikers. If the ascending hikers want to stop for a rest break, they can wave the downhillers through.
- Don't use a trail when it's wet. Trekking through mud is not much fun anyway and can begin a process of erosion that's difficult to reverse. It's Arizona—the sun will pop out and dry the trail soon enough.
- Respect wildlife. Never feed or disturb critters you might encounter.
- To dispose of human waste, dig a hole 4 to 6 inches deep and at least 100 yards from water sources and dry washes. Do not burn or bury toilet paper. Instead, pack it out in a plastic baggie.
- Before hiking with your dog make sure pooches are allowed on that particular trail. Carry extra water and snacks. Always keep Marmaduke on a leash and pick up any trail deposits he might make.

SOUTHEASTERN ARIZONA

The southeastern corner of Arizona is an intoxicating blend of rugged scenery, vibrant habitats, and bloody history. It exists at a rare ecological crossroads where desert grasslands break apart against the hard flank of tall mountain ranges. Low elevation and high elevation in such close proximity, the hot and the cool, is a defining feature of Arizona diversity.

This is the land of Sky Islands. Forested mountaintop islands float above a vast sea of range and desert, stacking ecosystems one on top of the other and attracting all manner of wildlife. Sky Islands are geographic outlaws, creating lush habitats where none should be.

Through the centuries, this corner of the world was once the frontier of New Spain, Old Mexico, and the Wild West. Coronado, Cochise, and Wyatt Earp all rode into battle here. Today, amid devastating scenery and small towns full of charm, it is a land of jaguars, volcanoes, and ghosts.

"An early morning walk is a blessing for the whole day."
HENRY DAVID THOREAU

Approaching Montezuma Pass, Joe's Canyon Trail winds along the base of Coronado Peak. Photo by the author.

Joe's Canyon Trail, Coronado National Memorial

From the visitor center of Coronado National Memorial, I walked across the road to the trailhead. The gobble of a wild turkey wafted downcanyon as I watched a couple of deer move through the brush. Not even on the trail yet and I was already enjoying this hike.

Two dozen steep switchbacks later, some of that good feeling had evaporated. But not entirely. After all, a little huffing and puffing builds character. Joe's Canyon Trail climbs more than 1,000 feet in the first mile and that's a lot of character. As I made my way up through the high-walled defile, views surrounded me. Montezuma Peak rose to my right and the San Pedro River Valley spread out below.

Sitting on the border with Mexico, south of Sierra Vista, the park was created to memorialize the 1540–1542 expedition of Francisco Vásquez de Coronado and his men who searched the Southwest for cities of gold. Most historians believe the Spaniards traveled through the San Pedro River Valley. Although recent archaeological finds along the Santa Cruz River continue to stir debate about Coronado's exact route.

After passing some final rock outcroppings, along with gaudy neon blooms of a rainbow cactus, I climbed out of the canyon and crossed the grassy slopes of Smuggler's Ridge. Views widen here, peering deep into the rolling green hills of Sonora, Mexico. This is not the dusty sunbaked borderlands people envision. It feels pastoral with soft valleys and hills dotted with oaks and agaves.

From here the trail winds across the ridge, with vistas of Mexico on one side and Montezuma Valley on the other. When you reach the junction with Yaqui Ridge Trail, this is more than just a crossroads. This marks the beginning of the Arizona National Scenic Trail (AZT). The 800-mile-long iconic trail stretches the length of the state from Mexico to Utah, and Yaqui Ridge is the southern terminus. If you decide to take that side trip, Yaqui Ridge Trail makes a steep descent to the border in 1 mile. Then turn around and climb back, leaving 799 more miles to Utah.

Or just finish up Joe's Canyon Trail, which twists across shaggy slopes for another 0.7 miles to Montezuma Pass, a high saddle with picnic tables and parking area. When you reach this point, you've traveled 3.1 miles from the visitor center. From here, you've still got options. Turn around and return to the trailhead, or during winter the park often runs a hiker's shuttle, so you can catch a ride back down the canyon.

Another option is to add one last climb to your already weary feet—hear me out—by heading up Coronado Peak. You're already on the shoulder of the distinctive hill and an interpretive trail guides you to the summit with informational signage about the Coronado expedition along the way. It's just 0.4 miles to the rounded top of Coronado Peak where you'll find shady benches and more astounding views. Sit there admiring the panoramas and be grateful that you're not walking all the way to Utah.

Where: From Sierra Vista, go south on AZ 92 for about 14 miles to S. Coronado Memorial Dr. Turn right and follow this road 5 miles to the park entrance. The trailhead is located just across the road from the visitor center.
Cost: Free.
Difficulty: Moderate.
Length: 6.2 miles round-trip, 7 miles to the top of Coronado Peak.
Dogs: No.
Details: (520) 366-5515, www.nps.gov/coro.

Bisbee Breakfast Club, Bisbee

The restaurant opened on a deserted street near a massive open-pit mine, which doesn't exactly sound like a can't-miss business model. Yet the place stays packed. People fill every seat in this funky, historic space with conversations bouncing from table to table, and the clatter of dishes adding a morning soundtrack.

The wait staff can forgo gym memberships because they receive a full workout hustling in and out of the kitchen toting plates creaking beneath the weight of massive meals. Chicken-fried steaks, three-egg omelets, pancake stacks, scratch-made Frisbee-sized biscuits smothered with sausage gravy, and the Copper Queen Skillet, which includes virtually every breakfast item known to humankind

Following the diner code, they serve breakfast all day. But here's a nice flip side to that—they also serve lunch all day. Soon as they open in the morning until closing in late afternoon, every menu item is up for grabs. So, naturally, there I am at 9 a.m., chin-deep in a juicy burger. That's when I notice I'm being side-eyed by the bacon-and-eggs crowd like I'm the weirdo. At least I'm planning to hike off a few of my calories. Meanwhile, they're already ordering homemade pie. That's right, Bisbee Breakfast Club sells big slices of pie and cheesecake too. Breakfast traditions are being shattered right before our eyes.

As for the burgers, they're 7 ounces of hand-pressed chuck on a fresh, doughy bun. Build

Fast Fact: Lowell is a suburb community of Bisbee that was mostly lost when open-pit mining began. But Erie Street was saved and in recent years has been preserved as a moment frozen in time, with vintage vehicles and antique signs highlighting the historic buildings around the Bisbee Breakfast Club.

The fully-loaded Miner Burger from Bisbee Breakfast Club comes topped with onion rings and Jim Beam barbecue sauce. Courtesy of Rick Mortensen, Phoenix.

your own or select a specialty like the Miner Burger, a classic bacon cheeseburger topped with onion rings and a generous dollop of their Jim Beam barbecue sauce.

Jim Beam—it's not just for breakfast anymore.

Vegetarian Options: Along with the black bean burger, veggie sandwich, and salads, multiple vegetarian breakfast items are available. And of course, the pies.

Don't Forget: If Bisbee isn't in your travel plans, don't fret. BBC has opened locations in Tucson and the Valley of the Sun, beginning their march toward total breakfast domination in Arizona.

Details: 75A Erie St., (520) 432-5885, www.bisbeebreakfastclub.com.

Ramsey Canyon, Sierra Vista

Normally I hike first, eat afterward, but not always. This is often a burger-then-boots trail, depending on the season. Parking spots are scarce at Ramsey Canyon Nature Preserve and quickly filled by eager birders before the preserve opens in the morning during spring and fall. Crowds thin out later in the day as the birds settle in for a siesta, so I roll up after lunch to find open parking spaces.

Ramsey Canyon is a lush defile cut from the east face of the Huachuca Mountains. This woody ravine shelters a perennial stream so, of course, it teems with life. Over 170 species of birds have been spotted in the high-walled canyon, along with a variety of other wildlife. The Nature Conservancy took control of Ramsey Canyon in 1975. In the ensuing years, the non-profit conservation group has worked to undo damage caused by humans, while continuing ecological research and monitoring rare species.

A single trail starts from the back door of the visitor center, past benches and hummingbird feeders, and moseys alongside Ramsey Creek. For almost the entire hike you stay beneath a rich shade canopy. Big sycamore trees drape the stream while oaks and pines fill the canyon. It is a gentle wood, a fragrant wood. On my late-spring hike, the stream was so small it could hold hands with a butterfly. A tiny gurgle of water could barely be heard. It felt as if the creek was tiptoeing down the canyon, like an introvert trying to sneak away from a party without being noticed.

The trail rises on a slight grade at first, passing several points of interest detailed in a guide handed out at the visitor center. There are a couple of historic cabins, a butterfly seep, and terraced ponds with tiny frog eyes peering from the water. Here The Nature Conservancy is working to reestablish a population of the endangered Chiricahua leopard frog.

A weathered cabin built in 1911—before Arizona was even a state—perches above the floodplain in Ramsey Canyon. Photo by the author.

Then just as you start thinking it's all butterfly baths and frog stare-downs, the trail gets serious. At the Hamburg Trail sign, the path bears left into the woods and begins switchbacking up the steep slope. It climbs 500 feet in a half mile, leaving the preserve and entering Coronado National Forest. At 6,200 feet elevation there's a rocky overlook showcasing expansive views. This high perch is a mile from the visitor center and most folks use it as a turnaround point. But if you've got a little gas left in your tank, continue on to enjoy more gorgeous woodland.

Past the overlook, the trail drops down to the creek that tumbles over boulders in a series of small cascades spilling through the forest. Thick stands of oak, maple, and sycamore mingle with pine and fir. You'll make several creek crossings as the Hamburg continues on a level grade and enters the network of Huachuca Mountain trails. Just be sure to allow yourself plenty of time to return before the nature preserve closes.

Where: From Sierra Vista, go south on AZ 92 for 6 miles, turning right on Ramsey Canyon Rd. The preserve is at the end of the road, 4 miles west of the highway. Parking is limited to 27 spaces on a first-come, first-served basis. There is no parking along the road below the preserve.

Cost: Admission fee.

Difficulty: Moderate.

Length: 2 miles round-trip.

Dogs: No.

Details: (520) 378-2785, www.nature.org/arizona.

Pit Stop Gourmet Burgers, Sierra Vista

Sitting back from the highway at the end of a gravel parking lot, Pit Stop gives off a roadhouse vibe. But don't be deterred. It's welcoming inside, with one dining room flowing into another. Walls are adorned with racing signs and colorful artwork full of burgers, sugar skulls, and hopped-up cars.

The friendly staff bubbles with energy. Even when the place is packed, they keep things running smoothly. Specialty burgers include Risk It for the Brisket, which comes with a choice of cheese, bacon, barbecue aioli, and strips of rich brisket. Pit Stop bakes their own brioche buns and makes all sauces in-house. The burgers are ground ribeye sculpted into a hefty one-third-pound patty.

I can't resist the Big Dill. It arrives buried beneath a tall Jenga-like stack of fried tabasco dill pickle chips, bacon, and ranch. Except I had them hold the ranch. Lettuce, tomato, onion, and pickle come on the side, but honestly, I'm not sure where to put them. This is a big vertical burger.

It's obviously a situation often encountered, because the waitress asks if I want a knife. A machete may be more practical, but I decline. As a purist, I believe hamburgers are the original handheld device. I eat them with my mitts or not at all. I remove a few levels of the dill chips to enjoy as a side dish, along with my mountain of fresh-cut fries. Then the burger all comes together.

The fried pickles add a spicy crunch and mix well with the bacon and veggies. It still feels like a lot to consume. From what I saw, most people can easily make two meals out of every burger. So maybe a knife isn't a bad idea. You also have several sides to choose from, including the golden crispy fried pickle chips that I found myself still thinking about days later.

Stacked with fried tobasco pickle chips, the Big Dill brings plenty of flavor and a spicy crunch. Photo by the author.

Vegetarian Options: All burgers can be made using a veggie patty.
Don't Forget: It's no surprise since the burgers are made with ribeye, that Pit Stop also serves hand-cut steaks.
Details: 4907 AZ 92, (520) 728-9240, www.pitstopgourmetburger.com.

"You can find your way across this country using burger joints the way a navigator uses stars."
CHARLES KURALT

Heart of Rocks Loop, Chiricahua National Monument

I'll come right out and say it: Chiricahua National Monument is the most unsung, unappreciated spot in Arizona. If it existed in another state, it would be featured on their license plate.

The 12,000-acre national monument shelters an exotic array of sculpted stone. This is the result of a massive volcanic event in the distant past. Tall columns, slender spires, and impossibly balanced boulders loom above the timber. The skyline seems to be built from the splintered remains of ancient castles.

A beautiful system of trails, many of them interconnected, create one of my favorite hiking areas in the state. Start by taking the scenic drive, a narrow winding road with hairpin curves and spectacular vistas. From here you can access a trail from one of the higher trailheads at Echo Canyon or Massai Point.

The short loop through Heart of Rocks is the craggy core of the park, where you'll find the most spectacular collection of formations. The easiest route to Heart of Rocks is via a trio of trails: Ed Riggs (0.9 miles), Mushroom Rock (1.2 miles), and Big Balanced Rock (1 mile). From the Echo Canyon parking lot start on Ed Riggs, which drops gradually into a finger canyon bracketed by fractured columns and thrusts of stone. The trail ends at a three-way junction. Jump on the Mushroom Rock Trail. You'll spot Mushroom Rock in a quarter mile above the trees on your right. If you're slightly underwhelmed by the flattop fungus of stone, don't sweat it; lots more drama lies ahead.

The trail climbs through a forested ravine, connecting with Big Balanced Rock Trail. Follow Big Balanced Rock across a high ridgeline with sweeping views. Look for Cochise Head, a striking mountain suggesting the noble

Pinnacle Balanced Rock is one of the distinctive formations found along the Heart of Rocks Loop. Photo by the author.

profile of the Apache leader. These mountains were once the beloved home of the Chiricahua Apache people until they were forcibly removed. Soon you pass through a corridor of stacked rocks and haunting hoodoos. Near the end of the trail, the namesake 1,000-ton boulder perches on a thimble of stone. From here a short spur trail leads to Heart of Rocks.

Take the 1.1-mile loop clockwise. Volcanic intensity still crackles within this twisty little labyrinth, undercut by a sneaky sense of whimsy. You're surrounded by tumbled, crumpled, otherworldly rock formations, like somebody busted up Stonehenge and the Easter Island heads for kindling.

From the chaos looms the familiar as you wind through the stone garden. Unexpected shapes suddenly burst into sight. Behold, Thor's Hammer! Hey, a

Duck on a Rock! Visions of Punch and Judy, Camel's Head, and the Totem Pole pull you along. I love the weird verticality of this place where the rocks seem so alert, so poised. I think it's quite likely that on one night each year, the formations come to life and interact with each other. Now I just need to figure out which night.

Reconnect with Big Balanced Rock Trail and return the way you came.

Where: Chiricahua National Monument is located 120 miles southeast of Tucson. From I-10 East take exit 340 in Willcox. Drive south on AZ 186 for 32 miles to the junction of AZ 181. Turn left and proceed 4 miles to the park.

Cost: Free.

Difficulty: Moderate.

Length: 7.3 miles round-trip.

Dogs: No.

Details: (520) 824-3560, www.nps.gov/chir.

Hot Tip: Every January, the Wings Over Willcox event offers a rare spectacle. Tens of thousands of sandhill cranes gather on the Willcox Playa. They feed and socialize during the day, roosting in shallow wetlands at night. Crowds gather at sunrise to watch the flock lift off in unison, a soft and elegant eruption. Additional tours and seminars are conducted throughout the event.

Dot's Diner, Bisbee

Retro barely begins to describe the experience of grabbing a burger at Dot's Diner. You're sitting in a vintage trailer park, outside a 1957 Valentine diner, about to bite into a fresh-made hamburger sandwich. The good old days aren't gone, they're just waiting in Bisbee, the nation's southernmost mile-high city.

Tiny Dot's Diner is hidden away in the Shady Dell, a mid-century trailer court that offers beautifully restored aluminum trailers for overnight accommodations. Little Dot's blends right in with the time capsule experience.

Arthur Valentine came up with the concept of small prefabricated mail-order diners in the 1930s. Business boomed following World War II as more Americans took to the road, getting their kicks on Route 66 and elsewhere. Before the golden arches loomed, little red-and-white Valentine diners pulled hungry travelers off the highway.

Vintage Dot's Diner exudes loads of charm and cooks up a tasty burger. Photo by the author.

You can't squeeze inside at Dot's to score one of the few stools anymore because they need the whole tiny diner space to prepare their elevated menu. Several tables flank the building, and it's almost always perfect weather to sit outside in Bisbee.

Don't expect a ton of options. Small diner, small menu. But every dish is significant. They use locally sourced ingredients whenever possible including organic free-range eggs and locally raised pork products. They grind their own pure Angus chuck for the burgers, and it creates an intensely flavorful package. It comes with American cheese, butter lettuce, tomato, pickled red onion, and a special sauce, which I skipped—mustard is plenty special, thank you. My favorite burger condiment is always plain mustard, preferably Heinz, yellow as a field of sunflowers, yellow as a canary orgy.

Dot's burger comes cupped in a cushiony brioche bun, and it delivers that soft burst of beefiness I craved after a long day on the trail. I felt my muscles begin to relax at the first bite.

Treat yourself soon to a meal at Dot's. Be sure to check for hours, which are mostly centered around weekends. Better still, spend a night or two in one of the restored vintage trailers of Shady Dell. It's a memory I still cherish.

Vegetarian Options: The tender veggie burger comes with siracha aioli and all the fixings.

Don't Forget: Right next to Dot's is Dashes, the 1955 Airstream trailer bar serving beer, wine, and cocktails on weekends. Did someone say tiki party?

Details: 1 Old Douglas Rd., (520) 346-1624, www.theshadydell.com.

South Fork Trail, Portal

This is the side of the Chiricahua Mountains I don't visit nearly enough. While I'm a regular guest of Chiricahua National Monument on the western end of the range, spectacular Cave Creek Canyon is cut from the eastern slope of the mountains. A dirt road crosses the mountains but it's often in poor condition, so I never attempt it.

The easiest access to this side of the Chiricahuas is from New Mexico. But it's worth the drive. Each time I return to Cave Creek Canyon, I'm smitten by the astounding, ethereal beauty. Tall cliffs rise above a magical forest filled with a chorus of birdsong.

The South Fork Trail starts at the end of a dirt road. If you see people walking along the road before reaching the trail, they're not lost and are probably not carjackers. They are birders. Notice the binoculars and giant camera lenses. This is a world-renowned birding destination with folks traveling from everywhere hoping to catch sight of elegant trogons, painted redstarts, blue-throated hummingbirds, or other colorful characters flitting among the branches. I love birds but can only identify about a dozen different species, and one is Foghorn Leghorn. I'm here for the hiking.

The trail traverses a riparian forest of pine, oak, walnut, cypress, and sycamore. It's a cheerful, sunlit wood filled with ferns and wildflowers. A deer watched me pass from just off trail, quite unconcerned. Cliff tops peek in above the treetops, reminding me that I'm in a deep defile.

The path stays close to the banks of the creek. It was a shy little stream in late May, vanishing underground occasionally then reemerging. There are a few creek

Fast Fact: Cave Creek Canyon is sometimes known as the "Yosemite of Arizona" due to the towering rhyolite walls and cliffs rising overhead.

Especially popular with birders, the South Fork Trail follows a stream into the forests of the Chiricahua Mountains. Photo by the author.

crossings, and the most prominent is almost a mile into the hike, known as the Bathtub. Here a large pool of water is ringed by boulders and a clutch of tall trees. A cascade spills down the rocks, arranging an entire splashy symphony. No one else was around and I plopped down on the creekbank wrapped in a medley of tiny falls and terraced trickles. The moving water throws graceful patterns against the boulders, a kaleidoscopic array of lace and light. Joining me in the audience for this captivating show were assorted dragonflies, butterflies, and bees. For a long time I was unable to move, paralyzed by contentment.

Finally, the forest beckoned and I continued for another mile or so, enjoying the scents and sounds, while also dodging poison ivy growing close to the path. Upon reaching the junction with the Burro Trail, I turned around. While South

Fast Fact: The Chiricahua Mountains are one of the "Sky Islands" of Southern Arizona. Sky Islands are forest-clad mountain ranges isolated from one another by expansive valleys of grasslands or desert. These vaults of biodiversity extend the territory of not just birds but other animals as well like ocelots and jaguars.

Fork Trail stretches for 6.8 miles, climbing higher into the mountains, I generally stop after a mile or two. I want to preserve the memory of South Fork as a gentle walk in the woods.

What should you do if you encounter a birder? First, don't panic. They can sense your fear. Or maybe that's bears. Try to appear larger than you really are. No, that's for mountain lions. Maybe just say hello and ask what they've seen. If you're lucky they'll direct your vision deep into the trees where you might get to catch a fleeting glimpse of Foghorn Leghorn.

Where: From Tucson, take I-10 east 139 miles to US 80, crossing into New Mexico. Turn south and drive 28 miles to Portal Road. Turn west and drive 7 miles, reentering Arizona. Continue driving west on FR 42 approximately 2 miles to the South Fork turnoff. Turn right and continue 1 mile to the parking area. All roads are suitable for passenger vehicles.

Cost: Free.

Difficulty: Easy.

Length: 4 miles round-trip to Burro Trail.

Dogs: Yes, on a leash.

Details: (520) 364-3468, www.fs.usda.gov/r03/coronado.

Portal Café, Portal

In remote Cave Creek Canyon, all social life revolves around this combination café, country store, and lodge. And it has ever since the place was built in 1934. Far from the trappings of civilization, you can still sit outside on a warm summer evening listening to a live band, sipping a cool drink, and biting into an authentic, delicious burger.

The Portal Café catches your eye as you drive through the canyon. This *is* the business district of Portal. A faded sedan parks near the entrance and there's an actual phone booth, minus the phone, which undoubtedly has gone to join all other old phones in landline heaven. Walk into the well-stocked store that carries beer, wine, fresh bread, produce, candy, sundries, and camping supplies. You don't find many country stores left, the kind that cater to an entire community. I always stop to buy something because these are exactly the kinds of places I want to support. Even more so when I can also grab a middle-of-nowhere, fresh-cooked burger.

Visitors to the small hamlet of Portal can find just about everything they need at the combination store and café. Photo by the author.

Small dining rooms are just off the market. There's also a large patio beneath big shade trees. Portal Café is best known for their green chile cheeseburger, as they should be since they're close enough to reach across the New Mexico border and pick hatch chiles. It is a powerful combination. This is the kind of burger you hope to find when you're coming out of the woods. The pepper creates a smoky warmth that envelops the hand-formed burger, adding a depth to each bite with just enough spice to slap you across the taste buds.

Local hatch chiles also land in their burritos and enchiladas. They manage to create an intriguing menu while keeping it simple, focusing on sandwiches, pizza, fish, and a few Mexican options.

Vegetarian Options: The café will sub an Impossible burger, garden burger, or black bean patty. Pizzas, salads, and some Mexican dishes provide additional options.

Don't Forget: They offer an assortment of modest motel rooms for those wishing to extend their stay in this lovely canyon.

Details: 2358 S. Rock House Rd., (520) 558-2223, www.portallodge.com.

Cochise Trail, Sunsites

The Dragoons are a clutter of mountains northeast of Tombstone. They are a sudden idea of stone, a whim of granite rising abruptly from shaggy grasslands. Some mountains soar but the Dragoons seem to roll over the landscape. For 25 miles the Dragoons—surging, falling, cresting, and curling—appear as if a pounding surf had somehow turned to stone during high tide. Angled rock slabs and boulders are stacked in curious jumbles. A hem of woodlands adds accents of green. Pines, mesquites, and oaks with piously bowed limbs mingle with desert scrub.

Cochise Stronghold in the Dragoon Mountains once provided refuge to the legendary Apache leader Cochise. The Dragoons form both maze and natural fortress with clustered formations and angled cliffs. In the mountains, Cochise and his followers could find food, medicine, and year-round water. And from the high vantage point the Apache people had excellent views of valleys on either side. They could literally see the army coming a day before they arrived

Starting in the Cochise Stronghold Campground, the Cochise Trail branches off from an interpretive nature loop, which is a nice bonus as the signs introduce you to native plants and their uses to the Apache people. For the first mile the trail weaves through the woodsy canyon bottom, dotted with manzanita, beargrass, and yucca. Clumped boulders frequently interrupt the dense screen of vegetation. After a few moderate switchbacks, I arrived at Halfmoon Tank. This dammed stock pond supports a small riparian community ringed by granite pinnacles.

Three miles into the hike, I reached the saddle that marks Stronghold Divide. There is a piñon pine here that is an old friend of mine. Beneath those shady branches is one of my favorite trail snooze spots. And while I don't want to boast, I am a master of the trail snooze. A quick nap sprawled on boulders, across tree roots, on high rock ledges, it doesn't matter. I can doze anywhere outdoors and wake feeling refreshed. There's something about the combination of weariness and shade plus the joy sloshing around in my heart that proves conducive to a little shuteye. It feels like an angel sucker punched me as I tumbled suddenly but gently into dreamland.

Beyond the divide the trail drops steeply into Stronghold Canyon West. Most people use the divide as a turnaround point, but I pushed on because I love this next portion. There's a geological defiance to the western defile. The rock-crowned cliffs and bald domes become more pronounced. The Dragoons are peeled-skin mountains exposing an exotic knobby skeleton of granite.

The western half of the trail ends at a four-wheel-drive road in a woodland of oak and juniper. Of course, upon reaching this point, I had to turn around and make the steep climb back out. This is where the benefits of the trail snooze paid off in spades. I was over the saddle and back at the trailhead in no time flat.

Where: From Tucson, take I-10 east 72 miles to US 191. Turn south and drive 17.5 miles to Ironwood Rd. Turn right and drive 9.2 miles to Cochise Stronghold Campground. Portions of Ironwood are graded dirt but suitable for all vehicles. Trail begins on the east end of the campground, across a wooden bridge.
Cost: Free.
Difficulty: Moderate.
Length: 10 miles round-trip.
Dogs: Yes, on a leash.
Details: (520) 364-3468, www.fs.usda.gov/r03/coronado.

Hot Tip: Tucked away in Texas Canyon, Amerind is a renowned Native American museum, art gallery, and research center. It also includes a network of hiking trails amid the scenic formations similar to the Dragoons.

The Horseshoe, Benson

Open since 1936, The Horseshoe is a Benson icon. It's an institution passed from owner to owner, each acting as caretaker to preserve the ambiance and good food that makes it such an important part of the community.

The Horseshoe had undergone a recent change of ownership last time I visited. Someone was retiring and someone else stepped forward to continue the traditions. Inside, the place had been tidied up but still sported plenty of charm. I was happy they kept the tantalizing dessert case by the door filled with homemade pies and cheesecakes. Booths line the walls that are covered with historic photos. There's a small front room, a bar tucked around the corner, and counter seating. It's one of those great old-time counters, and I grab a stool where I can be close to the action.

Breakfast is important in small towns because that's when folks gather to socialize, connect, gossip, discuss deals, and make plans. That is better done on a full stomach, and Horseshoe has the breakfast menu to support it all.

Burgers are half-pound hand-pressed and served on a toasted bun. They have a half dozen or so specialty burgers including the namesake Horseshoe Burger, which comes with bacon, jalapeño, cream cheese, lettuce, tomato, onion, and pickle. My order arrives on a metal tray with fries spilling from a small bucket. The produce tasted quite fresh, with plenty to go around. Lots of onions, which I always like. There were pickles on my burger and a pickle spear lying beside it, like a green saber ready to be drawn if someone challenged my burger to a duel. I appreciated the abundance. The meat was tender and pliable, but a little under-seasoned. It was still an enjoyable burger. There's always growing pains with an ownership change, so by now it may be a great burger.

The outside of the building is still adorned with colorful murals and historic horseshoe-shaped neon signs. I wasn't socializing or cutting deals but was happy to be sitting at this historic counter in small-town Arizona. With my burger fast disappearing it was time to check out that pie case!

Vegetarian Options: Along with the many breakfast items, they make a veggie wrap, egg salad wrap, grilled cheese, and Caesar salad.

Don't Forget: The building housing The Horseshoe dates back to 1914 and was a post office, bus stop, and train depot.

Details: 154 E. Fourth St., (520) 586-2872, www.thehorseshoebenson.com.

Hot Tip: Kartchner Caverns lies hidden beneath the rough hills of the Whetstone Mountains just outside of Benson. This wet living cave features a bristling forest of stalactites, stalagmites, columns, and crystals filling the soaring rooms. Guided tours last about 90 minutes and are ADA accessible.

Juan Bautista de Anza National Historic Trail, Tubac

Water drastically changes the desert equation and nowhere is that more evident than the Santa Cruz River Valley. Driving south from Tucson, the desert doesn't turn spinier like you might expect, instead it softens, becomes downright pastoral. Cactus-dotted slopes give way to rolling grasslands shaggy with mesquite.

The Juan Anza Trail is not your typical desert hike, but that's what makes it special. The trail connects Tumacácori National Historical Park to Tubac Presidio State Historic Park via a riparian corridor rich with history. In 1775–1776, Juan Anza, captain of the Tubac Presidio, led 300 people and 1,000 head of livestock on an expedition to establish San Francisco, on the northwestern frontier of New Spain. He became the first European to create an overland route from Mexico through the unforgiving terrain of the Sonoran Desert to the Pacific Coast of California. This is part of the trail they took.

The pathway follows the Santa Cruz River, which flows north, unlike most rivers. It weaves its way through a shady mesquite bosque. The walking is easy across level terrain and on soft, sandy soil. Footbridges solve the river crossings and posts marked with the Anza Trail logo keep you properly aimed. Built by volunteers at the Anza Trail Coalition, this is another birding hot spot.

The trail ends at Tubac Presidio, which was designated as Arizona's first state park. It preserves the heritage and ruins of the first European settlement in what would become Arizona. Tubac was established as a Spanish presidio (fort) in 1752. Those early ruins are still visible in an underground exhibit. Visitors will also see an impressive museum that houses Arizona's first printing press with demonstrations, a furnished 1885 schoolhouse, and living history exhibits.

Scenery-wise, this trail is a simple woodland stroll along an intermittent river. But spending time at the weathered yet elegant Tumacácori church and Tubac Presidio to discover the area's rich history makes this a most memorable experience.

Where: From Tucson, go south on I-19 to exit 29. Drive north on East Frontage Rd., 0.7 miles to Tumacácori National Historical Park. The trailhead is located just north of the visitor center parking lot, directly across from the post office.
Cost: Free to hike the trail. There are admission fees for Tumacácori National Historical Park and Tubac Presidio State Historic Park.
Difficulty: Easy.
Length: 8 miles round-trip.
Dogs: Yes, on a leash.
Details: (520) 398-2341, www.nps.gov/tuma.

Hot Tip: Tubac is a picturesque village with more than 100 art galleries and gift shops packed into a few blocks. Winter is the busiest time, and they hold a popular festival every February. The Tubac Festival of the Arts is Southern Arizona's longest running art festival.

Wisdom's Café, Tumacácori

The Wisdom family has been welcoming neighbors and tourists alike since 1944. Wisdom's Café sits a half mile north of Tumacácori National Historical Park with giant fiberglass chickens standing guard. They're well known for hearty chimichangas, as well as their Mason jar margaritas. And that big half-pound burger isn't on the menu just for show; it's quite tasty.

Start with a giant cheese crisp, always a good appetizer choice. If you're not from Arizona you've probably never heard of a cheese crisp. I weep for all you have missed. No food is as simple yet so devastatingly delicious. A flour tortilla swabbed with a little butter, covered in shredded cheese, and baked until crisp. Fancy it up with onions or green chile strips if you want but really nothing else is needed. Served open-face, usually as an appetizer, they are a big plate of ooey, gooey, cheesy goodness.

The cheese crisp is a menu mainstay in Arizona but rarely found outside the state. Tortillas big as tire rims cloaked in cheese are meant to be shared. But if you plan on splitting one with me, better bring your Sunday teeth. I work fast. They should be eaten hot, and I refuse to sit idly by letting cheesy slices cool and congeal just because you're feeling blabby. All politeness ends at the edge of a cheese crisp.

No matter how you begin your meal, finish with a fruit burro. A hot flour tortilla stuffed with fruit filling, dusted with cinnamon and sugar is served a la mode and should not be missed.

Vegetarian Options: Like all great Mexican restaurants, vegetarians can eat their way through a large portion of the menu.
Don't Forget: Make reservations if you're planning to eat here during busy times, like February and March.
Details: 1931 E. Frontage Rd., (520) 398-2397, www.wisdomscafe.com.

First Love

I turned outlaw during the third grade, a pint-size desperado lured down a wicked path by a craving I couldn't control.

Twice a week I left elementary school to walk home for lunch, which was permitted as long as you went home. But I didn't. Instead, just a few doors down from school, I ducked into a dimly lit joint. I couldn't help myself; I was jonesing for the good stuff.

Soon as my tiny figure darkened the doorway, the man behind the counter knew what to do. He slapped a hamburger on the grill. Yes, I had a cow on my back. I was hooked on burgers. Let the other saps at school choke down a brick of prison-grade meatloaf, I was feasting on a juicy joy bomb, the most exquisite of foods, the coup de grease . . . the burger.

My school lunch cost 35 cents. A burger at Bill's Sandwich Shop—yes, I still remember the joint's name—cost a quarter, and a small bottle of Coke was a dime. What should I have done? I think that's when I first fell in love. Sitting at the counter, swinging my little legs, watching my burger sizzle on the flat-top, my bun turning crisp and golden next to it—this made adulthood seem full of promise.

The school finally busted me for violation of their pointless policy. They threatened to call my parents. But that still didn't stop me from ducking into Bill's as often as I could. I never got caught again.

Or so I thought.

During a conversation with my dad a few months before he passed away, the subject came up. I mentioned how often I snuck away for a burger but that I only got caught the one time. He just laughed. According to him, my parents received multiple phone calls from the school about my scofflaw ways. They just never did anything about it.

Mom was probably just thrilled that I was actually eating something for lunch since I was infuriatingly picky, and skinny as a shipwreck victim. And never in a million years would my father consider it a crime to go somewhere to eat a hamburger. Especially if it was a really good burger.

TUCSON

Tucson acts as Arizona's conscience. The town has sprawled in recent years yet they strive to preserve their multi-cultural heritage. Spanish, Mexican, and Native American influences are evident in the architecture, art, music, and cuisine of the community. That attitude of tolerance extends to the landscape. Ringed by mountain ranges and bookended by the two units of Saguaro National Park, Tucson doesn't battle the desert but embraces it. The Great Outdoors seems to always be just a block or two away and everyone takes advantage. My hiking boots wear nicely in the Old Pueblo, as Tucson is affectionately known.

In 2015, Tucson became the first place in the United States to be designated a UNESCO City of Gastronomy. The honor was bestowed for Tucson's rich culinary legacy represented by a variety of heritage food ingredients and traditional food preparation techniques creating a tapestry of unique flavors. Eating local here means you are part of something truly special.

Linda Vista Trail, Tucson

I envy folks in Oro Valley with this little escape hatch so close at hand. A minute after I parked, I was hoofing it along the lower slope of Pusch Ridge without a care in the world. The city faded away, leaving me with nothing but an army of cacti and tall cliffs forming the western edge of the Santa Catalina Mountains.

Linda Vista Trail makes a baggy loop through the desert landscape, with inner segments that allow hikers to customize their outing. I stuck to the longer outer segments, totaling 2.8 miles according to the trailhead sign. Since none of the junctions are marked, snap a photo of the trailhead map with your phone to consult if needed. But there's really no need to worry about getting lost with Pusch Ridge towering overhead and the city visible below.

To get most of the climbing out of the way at the beginning, take the trail clockwise. It's a twisting, rocky pathway through saguaros. While I rate this one as easy to moderate, there's enough elevation gain and uneven steps so you feel like you get a workout. And *feeling* like you got a workout burns just as many calories as an actual workout. Look it up if you don't believe me.

The best time to hike is an hour or so before sunset when rich light swabs the peaks overhead, turning the angular cliffs golden and pulling you close. During late spring the slopes bear bouquets of snowy white saguaro blooms. Views stretch back across the city all the way to the Tortolita Mountains. As I reached the high point of the loop near the edge of a shallow canyon an unmaintained trail points toward the top of Pusch Peak. This path makes a steep climb to the summit but should only be attempted by experienced hikers. It's

Fast Fact: Mount Lemmon, the highest peak in the Santa Catalina Mountains, is also the site of the southernmost ski resort in the United States.

At the western edge of the Santa Catalina Mountains, the Linda Vista Trail explores a lovely patch of desert. Photo by the author.

fine early on but gets sketchier as you climb. Also, steer clear of that trail from January 1 through April 30, when it is closed due to bighorn sheep lambing season.

Soon afterward the Linda Vista angles back downhill to the trailhead.

Where: From Tucson, take Oracle Rd. north to Oro Valley. Turn right on Linda Vista Dr. Trailhead is on the right.
Cost: Free.
Difficulty: Easy/moderate.
Length: 2.8 miles round-trip.
Dogs: No.
Details: (520) 749-8700, www.fs.usda.gov/r03/coronado.

Truland Burgers & Greens, Tucson

This place is a patio with a building attached. Open and airy, Truland sports vibrant colors and a modern but comfortable aesthetic. It makes a most inviting place to sit and enjoy a burger or a salad. Those are the twin pillars propping up this northside establishment.

While burgers and salads may seem to be the oddest of odd couples, there is a common thread here of healthy and sustainable ingredients. This is the same company that owns Graze Premium Burgers mentioned elsewhere in the book, and Choice Greens salad shops. At Truland they've combined those two concepts, expanded the menu, plus added a beer and wine bar and a selection of desserts. It's as if they never want me to leave.

Truland serves hormone- and antibiotic-free beef from Niman Ranch. Each burger includes two patties, smashed and seared on a hot grill to seal in the juices. They're cooked to medium-well and that's a considered decision from management. For those that want a thicker patty cooked to specs, they

Like all Truland burgers, the Early Riser is made with hormone- and antibiotic-free beef from Niman Ranch. Courtesy of Rick Mortensen, Phoenix.

can do that. But why not try it the Truland way first? The flavorful burgers aren't dripping juices but they're moist, tender, and nicely crisped at the edges. The double patties maximize the caramelized meat surface. Eight specialty burgers are available but all can be enhanced with extra add-ons. The Early Riser is a popular choice, covered with two slices of American cheese, a cage-free fried egg, all-natural nitrate- and nitrite-free bacon, and organic ketchup.

The side dishes are treated with the same respect. Kennebec potatoes are cut fresh and fried twice in non-GMO rice bran oil. Enjoy them straight up or tossed with garlic and rosemary. Then there's truffle fries—made with truffle oil, parmesan, pecorino, and parsley. Sweet potato tots, crispy brussels and potatoes, and a super food salad are other nonconventional sides.

Vegetarian Options: A whole slate of big, fresh, chopped salads as well as a fiesta grain bowl served warm give vegetarians plenty of choices. Of course, there's also a house-made vegan burger.

Don't Forget: If you're looking for an even more delicious way to get your vegetables, try the luscious four-layer carrot cake smeared with silky cream cheese icing and chopped walnuts.

Details: 7332 N. Oracle Rd., (520) 395-2975, www.trulandburgers.com.

"May your trails be crooked,
winding, lonesome,
dangerous, leading to
the most amazing view."
EDWARD ABBEY

Seven Falls, Sabino Canyon Recreation Area

The official trail name may be Bear Canyon, but nearly everyone calls it the Seven Falls hike because as improbable as it seems, that's your destination. Anytime you can find a seven-tiered waterfall in the desert, make the journey. Since this hike involves multiple stream crossings, it's always a good idea to check water levels before your adventure. Also, since this is a desert hike to a swimming hole, expect it to be crazy crowded on prime weekends.

The trail leaves from Sabino Canyon Visitor Center. The other option is to take a shuttle partway into Bear Canyon. That trims off 1.5 miles each way. Shuttles run hourly and there is a fee. If you set out from the visitor center, the trail points east, staying wide and flat as it parallels Bear Canyon Road with a few turns. Hikers should follow Bear Canyon Trail signs.

Once the pavement ends, the footpath begins a gentle climb beside a stream that can turn feisty on short notice. There are seven creek crossings on this section of trail entering the canyon.

One winter I was hiking here with the creek already running really high when it started raining. While the defile isn't narrow, it's never a good idea to be on a canyon floor with the potential for rising waters. I scrambled up a rocky wall and found an alcove to wait out the weather. Then an amazing thing happened. The rain vaporized and fog filled the canyon, wafting below me in tufted clouds. It was eerily quiet as I was engulfed in a glossy sheen of buttermilk and woodsmoke. For several minutes I couldn't see cactus, rock, or sky. Nothing existed beyond this swirling wispy wall of satin. It was not my typical desert hike.

The first six stream crossings are bunched together and pretty straightforward. Most of the time you can rock hop across. On other occasions, your feet are going to get wet. Be prepared for all possibilities. The final crossing can be confusing. Stay to the left along the streambank for a short distance

Terraced cliffs form a multi-tiered seasonal waterfall in Sabino Canyon. Photo by the author.

before making your way to the other side. From here, the trail clambers up the canyon wall in a few languid switchbacks. You round a corner and see the falls slicing a sharp passageway down the cliff. The trail branches here with the left fork leading to the base of the falls and the right fork continuing deeper into Bear Canyon.

Hang a left and scramble down to the rocky cleft. The waterfall is seasonal, tumbling in terraced cascades, creating juicy little swimming holes at every level. The torrent is most pronounced from snowmelt in late winter and early spring, and then often roars to life again after summer monsoons. But even when the falls are parched, you'll discover wide pools of clear water, a mirage-like oasis tucked away in the folds of the desert. It's like finding a sapphire in the couch cushions. Makes you wonder what other bits of magic lurk in the outback.

Where: From Tucson, travel east on Tanque Verde Rd. to Sabino Canyon Rd. Turn north on Sabino Canyon and follow it 4 miles to the Sabino Canyon Recreation Area Visitor Center.
Cost: Admission fee.
Difficulty: Moderate.
Length: 8.8 miles round-trip from the visitor center, or 5.8 miles with Bear Canyon Shuttle.
Dogs: No.
Details: (520) 749-8700, www.fs.usda.gov/r03/coronado.

Divine Bovine Burgers, Tucson

This may be the future of burger joints. It carries on a proud tradition while seeming completely modern. Divine Bovine is a new take on the classic lunch counter—casual, fast, and efficient. But it's also chef-driven, focusing on freshness and superior quality. And the burgers? Divine. As promised.

Order at the counter, which may chew up a chunk of time because the possibilities seem endless. There are more than a dozen specialty burgers, plus a full slate of ingredients if you want to build your own. You even choose the protein—beef, bison, a plant-based Impossible burger, or a seared or buttermilk-fried chicken breast.

But think long and hard before turning your back on the beef. At Divine Bovine, they use a custom blend of chuck, brisket, and short rib. That high-end combination forms a powerfully tender and rich patty to serve as a base. And a sturdy foundation is definitely needed because they're creating burger architecture, from traditional to avant-garde. The Funny Farm Hand, for example, comes with creamy peanut butter, jalapeno raspberry jam, candied bacon, sweet hot pickles, and white cheddar.

You can see it all made in the open kitchen (just like the old lunch counters) with patties hissing and

The Jalapeño Popper Burger is one of the brawny meat structures constructed at Divine Bovine. Courtesy of Rick Mortensen, Phoenix.

sputtering on the flattop, as the ingredients are assembled and collated. By the time orders hit the hot zone, they resemble beefy high-rises. Even though I tried to minimize my burger, it arrived as a skyscraper between buns.

The flavor came rolling off the monolith in waves. A little sweet, some savory, a crunch. But after a couple of bites I paused for some demolition, moving aside homemade pickles, roasted hot peppers, and the whole supporting cast. I craved a clean bite of the plump patty with its elegant pedigree. It sent my taste buds spinning and before I knew it half of it was gone and I was forking up the scattered toppings from my plate. Hey, there's no wrong way to eat a burger. But my way is more right.

Needless to say, everything is fresh, everything is made in-house. Fries are triple fried in peanut oil for a soft crunch of potato-richness and they also come loaded with sauces and add-ons to create shareable meals. Tater tots are little clouds of shredded potatoes mingled with cheddar cheese and green onions.

Vegetarian Options: Any burger can be made with an Impossible patty and paired with assorted side dishes.
Don't Forget: Wash it all down with a bucket of beers. They stock more than 50 cans and bottles.
Details: 1021 N. Wilmot Rd., (520) 203-8884, www.divinebovineburgers.com.

Hot Tip: Near downtown, Mission Garden interprets and celebrates the multicultural history of the Tucson region. Growing behind adobe walls at the foot of Sentinel Peak are heritage trees, heirloom crops, and native edible plants arrayed in unique timeline gardens. Programs, talks, and cooking demonstrations are offered through the year.

Hugh Norris Trail, Saguaro National Park West

Unlike some summit hikes that are head-bowed, foot-plodding slogs, the Hugh Norris Trail qualifies as a cheerful jaunt that keeps your noggin on a swivel while you gawk at one sweeping view after another. There are a few moderately steep pitches but that only sweetens the deal. It makes you feel like you earn the expansive vistas, among the best in Tucson in my opinion.

Set in Saguaro National Park, the trail carves a route through classic Sonoran landscape to the top of 4,687-foot-high Wasson Peak, highest point in the Tucson Mountains. Named for a Tohono O'odham police chief, the trail starts out on a cactus-studded bajada, then switchbacks upward to snag a rocky ridgeline. From there the trail angles toward Wasson, hugging first one side of the high shoulder and then the other, alternating the views.

A coffee klatch of saguaros crowds the slopes along with assorted barrels, chollas, and ocotillos. Clusters of casual boulders add more visual texture. You'll pass evidence of mining activity, including fenced-off shafts, and after about 2.7 miles you will reach the junction of the Sendero Esperanza Trail.

From here you're navigating a glut of panoramas that surround the ridge top. This stretch is often carpeted by wildflowers in the spring. The Hugh Norris was one of my very first Tucson hikes, an incredible introduction to the desert. I didn't realize then how life-changing it would be.

Near the end of the route, I passed King Canyon Trail entering from the right. Then there's one last twisted spiral of switchbacks and I was deposited atop Wasson Peak. Don't expect a shady forest greeting. The Tucson Mountains never gain enough elevation to shake off the heat and cacti. It remains a desert hike from bottom to top. I sat on the summit, a rocky knob with wrap-around views as the sun poked a spicy finger in my chest.

This is an elegant landscape, all stone and spine, lumbering mountains,

Hikers follow the winding ridgeline of the Hugh Norris Trail. Photo by the author.

and belligerent light. In the clear stillness I could hear the desert growling at me. Or maybe purring. Either way was fine by me.

Where: From Tucson, drive west on Speedway, which becomes Gates Pass Rd., until it dead ends at Kinney Rd. Turn right on Kinney and proceed 4.7 miles to the Red Hills Visitor Center. The trailhead begins off the Bajada Loop Drive, 2.5 miles north of the visitor center.
Cost: Admission fee is good for seven days in both national park districts.
Difficulty: Strenuous.
Length: 10 miles round-trip.
Dogs: No.
Details: (520) 733-5158, www.nps.gov/sagu.

Fast Fact: While saguaros send down a single tap root of 2 feet or more, most roots are only 4 to 6 inches below the surface and radiate out as far as the plant is tall.

El Guero Canelo, Tucson

I rue the day I ate my first Sonoran hot dog because it is one of those specific and persistent cravings that can't be satisfied by anything else. The Sonoran hot dog is the saguaro cactus of wieners. It is the closest thing Arizona has to an official hot dog. The messy concoction is a treasure trove of flavors but the essence is the bacon-wrapped hot dog. And for the record, "bacon-wrapped" may very well be the most wonderful hyphenate ever created.

Opened in 1993, El Guero Canelo was one of the first to introduce Sonorans to the Tucson market, selling them first from a food truck. The owner has since won a James Beard Award. For a freaking hot dog! Yeah, they're just that good.

The dog is a special kind of sin, swaddled in bacon and grilled, fusing the meats into a smoky flavor bomb. It is then tucked into a soft boat of a bun, fluffier than the traditional bolillo. Keeping the dog company are whole pinto beans, diced tomatoes, grilled and fresh onions, mustard, mayo, and jalapeño sauce.

As I previously wrote in my book *Awesome Arizona: 200 Amazing Facts about the Grand Canyon State*,

> This is what the borderlands taste like, that casual blending of cultures and flavors. The all-American hot dog gets a Mexican makeover. This is folk art. This is street music. Every bite unleashes a spicy, smoky, salty, creamy crescendo. The offhand elegance of the dish takes you by surprise and rocks you back on your heels as you ponder the years you've wasted shoving less complex wieners in your face. You begin craving another before you're halfway through the first one. It will cure a hangover, mend a broken heart, and raise your self-esteem.

The sinfully delicious Sonoran hot dog celebrates the best of the borderlands. Courtesy of Rick Mortensen, Phoenix.

El Guero Canelo has multiple Tucson locations but I usually visit the one on Oracle.

Vegetarian Options: The menu includes other dishes including cheese quesadillas.
Don't Forget: For an authentic across-the-border experience, wash your Sonoran dog down with a Coca-Cola bottled in Mexico and made with real cane sugar.
Details: 2480 N. Oracle Rd., (520) 882-8977, www.elguerocanelo.com.

Fast Fact: Held each February, the Tucson Gem and Mineral Show is the largest, oldest, and most prestigious gem and mineral show in the world. It began in 1955.

Painted Hills Trails Park, Tucson

Instead of just a single trail, let me throw a whole park full of them at you. Just imagine the powerful sense of accomplishment you'll experience when you hike every park trail in a single morning. Painted Hills gives you that chance.

This cozy 289-acre urban sanctuary is perfect for those with limited time or who don't want to venture too far out of town but still want a taste of wild country. It shelters remarkably dense groves of saguaros spread over low-shouldered hills on the city's west side. Just over 4 miles of trails circle the hills and snag a couple of bare summits while offering dazzling views.

Tucson created a few of these little hybrid trails parks in recent years, adding green space filling to the urban cake, and providing more desert access close to where folks live and work. Open dawn to dusk, Painted Hills Trails Park contains seven interconnected pathways. It sits just off the northeast corner of Tucson Mountain Park.

The trails are easy with only a few moderate stretches. From the parking area, I started on the wide, flat Mosaic Trail as it rambled through saguaros for 0.9 miles connecting to other singletracks to form short loops and climbs. I did them all. Peaceful Monsoon Loop is at the western end of the park and climbs to Recoil Peak and Bactrian Summit, where I enjoyed wide panoramas of the city spread along the base of the Catalina Mountains. Then I returned to the trailhead via Slingshot Trail. Around every curve an enticing new vista pulled me along. And unlike Tucson Mountain Park proper, dogs are allowed in Painted Hills, giving me a chance to pet several happy pooches.

Where: Painted Hills Trails Park is at 3590 W. Anklam Rd.
Cost: Free.
Difficulty: Moderate.
Length: 4 miles total.
Dogs: Yes, on a leash.
Details: (520) 724-5000, www.pima.gov/nrpr.

Pat's Drive-In, Tucson

There's a siren song to this little fry-hole I can't resist. The shambling white building is hidden away in historic Barrio Hollywood, a colorful working-class neighborhood, which happens to be right off the interstate. It's hard for me to drive past without stopping. I've pulled in even when I was on my way to dinner somewhere else, for crying out loud. These burgers are ridiculously addictive but small enough to justify as appetizers.

Most of Pat's patrons aren't there for burgers. They come for the sloppy chili dogs and fresh-cut fries served in paper sacks. A few picnic tables provide seating indoors and out, but it's mostly a drive-up, a grab-'em-and-go kind of place.

Burgers are slender patties topped with mustard, chopped onions, and lettuce. Decades fall away at each bite. These beauties taste like burgers grilled at long-ago five-and-dimes. How I miss those Woolworth and Kresge stores. These are burgers of a simpler time and place.

A longstanding tradition in Tucson, Pat's Drive-In has fed generations. Courtesy of Rick Mortensen, Phoenix.

Vegetarian Options: Try the grilled cheese sandwich. I've never had it, but Pat's looks like the kind of place that would make a good one.

Don't Forget: Pat's opened in 1961 and not much has changed over the decades. Nice to have joints like this still around.

Details: 1202 W. Niagara St., (520) 624-0891.

Hot Tip: The Presidio San Agustín del Tucson Museum is a reconstruction of the original Tucson Presidio built in 1775. See what life was like on the frontier of New Spain through exhibits and tours. Living History demonstrations, docent-led tours, and downtown walking tours are offered throughout the year.

Yetman–Rock Wren Loop, Tucson Mountain Park

Tucson Mountain Park is the sprawling backyard other cities dream about. The park protects 20,000 acres of pristine desert on the western edge of town. It shares the same mountain range, tall cactus forests, and lavish sunsets as neighboring Saguaro National Park. Between those two backcountry gems, it's almost impossible to stay indoors.

The Yetman Trail forms the long curving spine of Tucson Mountain Park as it stretches for 6.2 miles connecting two trailheads. Named for David Yetman, an author, environmentalist, and former Pima County supervisor, the lanky route delivers fantastic scenery with little elevation gain. It makes a wonderful hike as an out-and-back, although that's more than 12 miles on the trail. I like to combine trails to create other options. My favorite is a lollipop loop using Yetman and Rock Wren Trail.

I set out from the eastern trailhead off Camino de Oste. (The western trailhead is near Gates Pass Overlook.) Immediately the Yetman Trail dips in and out of a sandy wash. Thick groves of saguaros cover the surrounding hillsides.

At just over a mile, I came across the remains of an old stone house known as the Bowen Ranch. A newspaper editor built it during the 1930s. The big roofless ruin is anchored by two fireplaces and ringed by picture windows still filled with desert panoramas. This is my dream house. And if they'd sell, I'd take it as is. Forget the inspection, just let me unroll my sleeping bag in the corner. Who needs a roof when you've got a canopy of stars? Maybe put in a screen door to keep out the rattlesnakes, but that's about all the improvements it needs. And I'd bring a folding chair to sit in the shade of a palo verde tree so I could yell at all the hikers to get the hell out of my yard!

The trail climbs to a small saddle with impressive views. The Rock Wren

Trail comes in from the right at 2.2 miles, but I stayed on Yetman as it continues south then swings to the west. There are some up and downs through here but nothing tiring. Just past Cat Mountain I took the second junction for Rock Wren as it rises out of a wash and rambles across cactus-studded hills.

This is a beautiful segment, a twisty path, probably great fun for mountain bikers with its flows and curves. Craggy cliffs tower overhead and the path squeezes between tall saguaros. Rock Wren reconnects with Yetman after 1 mile and I returned to the trailhead, ready to call my realtor.

Where: Take Speedway Blvd. to Camino de Oste. Turn left and drive 0.6 miles to a parking area at the trailhead.
Cost: Free.
Difficulty: Easy.
Length: 6.4 miles round-trip.
Dogs: No.
Details: (520) 724-5000, www.pima.gov/nrpr.

"Burgers bring people together like no other food."
GUY FIERI

Red Garter Bar and Grill, Tucson

A persistent and longstanding rumor claims that the Red Garter is a strip joint. This notion dated back to a time when its logo was a shapely woman's leg sporting a bright red garter. The fact that there are no windows visible probably added to the speculation. The Red Garter is absolutely not a strip joint. But I stayed anyway.

It's just a comfortable neighborhood bar that carved out a niche as a dining spot. Coming in out of the blazing Tucson sun, the cool dark wraps around you. Let your eyes adjust as you take in the old-school vibe. Pool tables are in back and there's seating at a long bar that runs the length of the main room. Dining tables fill the space and booths line the back wall. It looks like lots of neighborhood bars. Then the food arrives.

This mom-and-pop establishment runs a serious kitchen. There's a surprisingly wide-ranging menu but half-pound burgers are obviously the stars. The menu lists 18 different burgers and they all sound tempting, but I stick with the basic Red Garter burger. I'm rewarded with an absolutely mouth-watering meal. The scrumptious package starts with 1855 Black Angus beef, a premium line prized for its marbling. It's hand-pressed and wonderfully seasoned with a house-made spice blend.

My medium burger was cooked perfectly and retained a tender juiciness with such vivid flavor it startled me. The springiness of the beef, the soft crumble spoke to its quality and the skill of the chef deftly wielding that spatula. Fresh tomato, lettuce, and onions meld into each bite. I expected a good burger, but this one turned out to be superb. The crunchy pickle spear proved a delightful finish. Each burger comes with a side, and I went with the shoestring fries, nicely browned.

The Mushroom Swiss burger is the most popular and I totally get it. Fresh sauteed mushrooms and melted Swiss—simple and direct. When you've got

Red Garter Bar and Grill is known for its lineup of tender, juicy, half-pound burgers cooked to perfection. Courtesy of Rick Mortensen, Phoenix.

meat this good, don't get fussy. Red Garter works with local vendors and that's apparent in every bite.

To sum up, Red Garter is not a strip club. I knew that beforehand. I was just there for the outstanding burger. The fact that I paid for it with a stack of singles doesn't mean a thing.

Vegetarian Options: In addition to a spicy black bean veggie burger, salads, soups, sandwiches, and finger food choices are found up and down the menu.

Don't Forget: Red Garter originally opened in 1969. It's also been named Tucson's "Best Pool Hall."

Details: 3143 E. Speedway Blvd., (520) 325-0483, www.redgartertucson.com.

Hot Tip: Take a stroll on 4th Avenue, Tucson's most eclectic shopping district. Bookstores rub shoulders with vintage clothing shops and art galleries. You'll find everything from recycled toys to unique jewelry, home décor, and gifts from Nepal tucked between ethnic eateries and bars. Located between University Blvd. and 9th Ave.

Loma Verde Loop, Saguaro National Park East

In the Rincon Mountain District of Saguaro National Park, I combined three trails—Loma Verde, Pink Hill, and Squeeze Pen—to make an easy loop. Loma Verde Trail points north through mesquite woodlands. It twice crosses a sandy wash and passes the remains of an old copper mine. Multiple trails connect with Loma Verde, but signs are posted at each junction. The Santa Catalina Mountains form a rugged skyline in the distance, dusted with snow in their highest reaches.

Saguaros, which are scarce on the first section of trail, begin to gather. But they are never quite as thick as the bristling forests of the park's western unit. Other cactus specimens take up the slack, with a number of chollas, barrels, prickly pears, and hedgehogs highlighting the diversity of the Arizona desert. Off to the left I spot a crested saguaro, always a treat. When the growing tip of a saguaro produces a fan-like shape instead of columnar arms, it's referred to as crested or cristate. Biologists aren't sure what causes the abnormal growth but it makes for intriguing specimens.

I turned right onto Pink Hill Trail bearing east. A quick scramble led to an overlook atop the low summit of Pink Hill for dramatic views of desert ringed by mountains. That's something Tucson has in abundance. I continued east through desert scrub until the junction with Squeeze Pen Trail, turning right as it swings back south rambling along the base of the

Hot Tip: Let kids blow off some steam at the Children's Museum Tucson. The downtown facility is filled with fun and educational hands-on exhibits and activities, everything from art studios to fire trucks to climbing walls.

Hikers can combine three trails for an easy introduction to the Rincon Mountain District of Saguaro National Park. Photo by the author.

foothills of the Rincons. From here I enjoyed good views of Tanque Verde Ridge as it climbs toward the timber in the higher elevations of the Rincon Mountains. The trail rejoins Loma Verde just a quarter mile from the trailhead.

Where: From Tucson, drive east on Broadway to Freeman Rd. Turn right on Freeman and drive south for 3 miles. Turn left onto Old Spanish Trail and proceed to the visitor center in a quarter mile. Loma Verde Trailhead is off the park's Cactus Forest Scenic Drive.
Cost: Admission fee is good for seven days in both national park districts.
Difficulty: Easy.
Length: 3.8 miles round-trip.
Dogs: No.
Details: (520) 733-5153, www.nps.gov/sagu.

Calle Tepa, Tucson

Tucson may be loaded with great burger joints, but if you can spend time in this soulful multi-cultural town without stuffing a few tacos in your face, then you and I are very different people. Calle Tepa captures the casual energy of a small-town plaza from south of the border. The brightly colored menu is painted on the wall, along with murals of street scenes, and doors and windows.

Lively music fills the space, and the salsa bar—stocked with a half dozen house-made blends—is actually the refrigerated tail-end of a Chevy pickup. The open kitchen is wrapped in stainless steel to resemble a food truck. This is where tortillas are made fresh, and where carne asada, barbacoa, chicken adobada, shrimp, and more sizzle on the grill.

Order at the counter and then load up at the lavish salsa bar with favorites like roasted garlic habanero and jalapeño mango. Tacos can be served Tepa-style with lettuce, pico, and queso fresco. But I prefer the lean, clean flavors of street tacos topped with just cilantro and onions that allow the grill-kissed meat to stand out. The spicy chorizo is especially devastating.

Burritos, tacos, tortas, quesadillas, tamales, mini-chimis and fajitas can be prepared with a variety of meats and also done in different styles. Start your meal with the Manchegos quesadilla, gooey slices of mildly sweet sheep cheese.

Calle Tepa has a bar side, a dining side, and a patio, plus they serve cold margaritas. You're sitting in a Mexican street grill eating tacos and drinking cold margaritas in a jar. Now this is how you go hiking in Tucson.

Vegetarian Options: There are plenty, but let's just focus on veggie tacos. Guaco taco with the fresh guacamole, fajita taco with bell peppers and onions, calabacitas with zucchini and corn, and taquito con papa with seasoned smashed potatoes.

Don't Forget: Happy hour (3 p.m. to 6 p.m. weekdays) means not just reduced drink prices but savings on quesadillas, tostaditas, and asada fries as well.

Details: 6151 E. Broadway Blvd., (520) 777-5962, www.calletepa.com.

Canyon Loop Trail, Catalina State Park

A sprawling desert, a wall of mountains, and a slender oasis—this hike has it all. Catalina State Park covers 5,500 acres spread across the foothills of the Santa Catalina Mountains. What once was an old ranch property was rescued from development by local residents who banded together. With a great mix of trails, the park has become a beloved destination for hikers, mountain bikers, and equestrians.

Canyon Loop dishes up some of the best the park has to offer in a short, easy-to-access package. Fun for hikers, it's also kid and pooch friendly. Most trails depart from a single trailhead. Located at the end of the main park road, the majority of pathways radiate outward from this designated starting point. You'll find a large parking area here, restrooms, picnic tables, and a small store operating during cooler months.

Across the road you enter a thin woodland of mesquite, then dip into a sandy wash, which often has water flowing. You'll encounter multiple stream crossings along the loop, so be prepared to rock hop or wade across. There's a short climb from the creek to a meadow lined with mesquite and saguaros, set against the dramatic backdrop of tall mountains. The wide, flat trail makes an easy stroll at the base of the Catalinas.

Reaching the end of the meadow the trail drops via a series of railroad tie-steps back to the wash. The second half of the trail follows the streambed lined by sycamore, oak, and hackberry, with big saguaros ambling down the slope, drawn by the water like all of us. This is an especially peaceful stretch, a bit of unexpected lushness. Even if the wash is dry downstream there are often pools sheltered here, connected by a trickling stream.

Water gurgles over the rocks. Clump grasses and boulders are sprinkled along the banks, beneath a mosaic of light and shadow. The damp sand

Saguaros stand watch along Canyon Loop Trail in Catalina State Park. Courtesy of Rick Mortensen, Phoenix.

crunched underfoot as I moved toward the cooling shade. Beneath the trees, a sudden onslaught of butterflies came whirling up from the water in a gossamer cloud. I stood still as they swarmed around my face for a moment, forming a halo of satin wings. How well the desert hides its secrets.

Finally, the trail drops down a few more stairs, crossing the creek. Here amid the channels of this watercourse, the Sutherland Trail branches off to the right, climbing a small hill. If it's spring, add this little detour. Wildflowers often erupt along the first mile or so of the Sutherland Trail.

Continue on Canyon Loop as it wraps up, following the big wash and curling back through the mesquite trees to your starting point.

Where: From Tucson, take Oracle Rd. north to Oro Valley. Turn right into Catalina State Park.
Cost: Admission fee.
Difficulty: Easy.
Length: 2.3 miles round-trip.
Dogs: Yes, on a leash.
Details: (520) 628-5798, www.azstateparks.com.

Fast Fact: National Hamburger Day is observed each year on May 28, honoring America's most popular sandwich.

Graze Premium Burgers, Tucson

Small, clean, and casual, Graze Premium Burgers offers the familiarity of a fast-food establishment but the flavor of an upscale eatery. They surprise in other ways too. For example, by putting a healthful spin on burgers. Patties are made with Niman Ranch all-natural antibiotic- and hormone-free premium beef. Kennebec potatoes are cut fresh and fried twice in non-GMO rice bran oil. Delicious on their own, they come with a variety of dipping sauces, everything from curry ketchup to sweet red chile. Naturally, the chicken is free-range and the veggie burger is locally sourced.

You can choose a single, double, or junior burger. They come with lettuce, red onion, tomato, and Graze sauce on a grilled brioche bun. But the fun doesn't have to stop there. Customize your burger from the expanded list of toppings. When I'm feeling like a walk on the wild side, I have them throw some grilled jalapeños or grilled mushrooms or both on there. Yeah. You can't pigeonhole me. Don't even try.

Of course, the healthy approach is great, but it only works if the final product delivers the goods. That's where Graze steps up. The slender patties are nicely seared. They come off the griddle firm but moist, like a toddler's fist. There's a beefy resonance to the juicy burger, enhanced by the fresh toppings.

Vegetarian Options: They offer a black bean and corn vegan patty, and also a tasty chopped salad.
Don't Forget: Belly up to the fountain machine for Maine Root sodas made with organic cane sugar.
Details: Two locations: 2721 E. Speedway Blvd., (520) 269-6888; and 5635 E. Broadway Blvd., (520) 347-2159, www.grazepremiumburgers.com.

Desert Seduction

When I first arrived in Arizona, I swooned over the high country clad in dense forests of ponderosa pine. I expected to be some kind of flannel-shirted mountain man breathing cool air, tromping through meadows drenched in summer wildflowers, and being serenaded by the symphonic flutter of aspen leaves. I never—*ever*—imagined I would fall in love with the desert. How does something like that even happen?

What tragic character flaw, what lack of common sense leads someone to become a desert rat baffles me to this day. No good can come of it. Loving the desert is a form of bad craziness. It's a daylight moon howl, a dance at the end of a pirate's plank, a slow walk to the O.K. Corral packing a squirt gun.

Desert rats develop a taste for danger because this is a weaponized landscape. Everything out there will stab, jab, sting, scratch, bite, or claw you. Every step leads you closer to ambush. Yet you always go back for more.

The swarm of perils keep me alert. I become intensely aware of my surroundings. The heat becomes a living thing, a sly stalking beast. The sun snarls while the sky nuzzles. The light startles with its clarity. And views stretch for miles across lean valleys crowded with cacti and pressed against mountains of stone and sinew. This is where a breeze is a blessing, shade is a triumph, and rain is a throw-your-hat-in-the-air, dance-in-the-sand miracle. Once you experience that—once the perfume of petrichor fills your nostrils—you are haunted by it forever.

I spend so much time alone in the desert I often think it's a place only I love. Then I round a bend in the trail and pass fellow hikers as grizzled as me. I'm not sure what brings others, but I'm drawn by the stillness. No one, not even the dawn, has a voice as quiet as the desert.

RIM COUNTRY AND THE WHITE MOUNTAINS

For the ultimate high-country escape, travel along the Mogollon Rim and climb to the splendid fortress of the White Mountains in eastern Arizona.

When I encounter someone who regards Arizona as nothing but desert, I steer them to the White Mountains. Mild climate, endless forests, and a wealth of recreational opportunities draw scads of summer visitors. Hundreds of miles of pristine rivers and streams carve up the highlands and 40 cold-water lakes sparkle like the jewelry of the nouveau riche, gaudy and glorious. Load up your tent, fishing gear, and mountain bikes. Pack a sweatshirt for the cool nights and binoculars for the wildlife you're likely to see. But whatever you do, don't forget the hiking boots.

Standing atop the Mogollon Rim is like being on Heaven's porch. Photo by the author.

Rim Lakes Vista Trail, Mogollon Rim (ADA Accessible)

I stepped out of the forest and reached the edge of the known world. A curtain of sky fell and everything suddenly vanished before me. Even though I knew it was coming, that first view still proved jarring. Standing atop the Mogollon Rim, the land dropped away far beneath my feet. Like a giant, I towered over the terrain. Power rushed to my head. For a moment, I was the King of Arizona.

The Rim Lakes Vista Trail may be the most inappropriately named hiking path I've ever trod. While lakes are nearby, I didn't see a single one from the trail. Instead, the views are of the cosmos. If I still possessed the eyesight of my youth, I'm convinced I could have seen the curvature of the earth. I stood on a vast shoreline of space and gazed toward horizons and heavens. I walked among clouds and wore birds as a boutonniere. They should put something like that into the trail name instead of just "lakes." Maybe that's why trail builders never consult me.

Meandering along the top of the rim, this easy path is mostly shaded as it dips in and out of pine forest and is paved part of the way. While it's no secret, the trail is never as crowded as I expect, which is great. More panoramas for me.

Start from the western end of Rim Lakes Vista Trail, which mostly parallels a stretch of Forest Road 300, also known as the Rim Road.

Fast Fact: The Mogollon Rim slashes for 200 miles across the midsection of the state, stretching from Sedona to the New Mexico border. It is a soaring escarpment that serves as a definitive boundary between desert lowlands and the lavish green of the high country.

The western terminus of the trail is at the Mogollon Campground. Day hikers should use the parking area just east of the campground. Follow a sign-marked path to connect to the sliver of pavement and turn left. The first quarter-mile is just a mild woodland stroll. Then the screen of trees breaks apart and those first epic views stir something deep within you.

And that's how it is for the bulk of the hike as the trail traces the edge of this high escarpment. Relentless vistas mingle with rock outcroppings and tenacious trees clinging to the edge. The paved portion of the trail can be managed by wheelchairs and strollers.

There are three pullouts along Rim Road where you may encounter drive-up gawkers. Don't sneer at them just because you're seeing more than they can even imagine. You're mastering one of Arizona's two defining geological features. Except this trek is much easier than hiking rim to rim at the Grand Canyon.

After about 2 miles, the pavement plays out and a rocky singletrack continues to Military Sinkhole Vista, the final viewpoint, and beyond to the Rim Lakes parking area, the trail's eastern terminus. Turn back sooner if you get the urge because you may want to save some time to visit nearby Woods Canyon Lake. After all, you were promised some watery views.

Where: From Payson, drive east on AZ 260 for 30 miles to Rim Road (FR 300), directly across the highway from the Mogollon Rim Visitor Information Center. Turn left on Rim Road and drive 7 miles. The parking area will be on your left near milepost 40, just before Mogollon Campground.
Cost: Free.
Difficulty: Easy.
Length: 7 miles round-trip.
Dogs: Yes, on a leash.
Details: (928) 535-7300, www.fs.usda.gov/r03/apache-sitgreaves.

Fast Fact: The Mogollon Rim is the second most lightning struck area in the world.

Macky's Grill, Payson

Hey, boots are boots. I'm in hiking boots but I'm surrounded by a décor of cowboy boots. Boots are used as planters, vases, and part of the fabric adorning the booths. Spurs are everywhere too, along with branding irons, horses, cowboy hats, and longhorns. The cowpoke theme serves as a reminder that the Payson area has a long tradition as ranch and cattle country.

Located in the Sawmill Crossing shopping plaza, Macky's Grill does brisk business with locals and travelers. On the big patio, dogs are not only welcomed but given the VIP (very important pooch) treatment. Opened in 1997, the restaurant is now run by the second generation of the same family. There's a wide-ranging menu and despite the cattle-heavy theme, many light and healthy options have been added in recent years.

Burgers are built on a foundation of 7 ounces of Gold Canyon Angus beef. Despite my tendency to keep things simple, I opted for the Pastrami Burger.

One of the most popular burgers at Macky's Grill comes stacked with thinly sliced pastrami and melted Swiss cheese. Photo by the author.

The beast arrived in a basket, crowding my fries to the side. Nearly a half pound of beef was layered with lettuce, tomatoes, spicy brown mustard, melted Swiss cheese, and a stack of thinly sliced pastrami. Per my request, the creamy sauce that usually comes along for the ride on this model remained in the kitchen.

This proved more than enough. It was like a sandwich piggy backing on top of a burger. The pastrami added a peppered smokiness balanced with a little tang from the mustard. Something about it made me think this full-bodied burger would be ideal for a rainy day. Fortunately, the booth looked quite comfortable in case I needed a nap after I finished.

Vegetarian Options: The menu includes not only a vegan garden burger but also a Beyond Burger.
Don't Forget: If you're still not full—and I'm not sure how that would be possible—Macky's offer's a good selection of desserts.
Details: 201 Main St., (928) 474-7411, www.mackysgrill.com.

"Between every two pine trees there is a door leading to a new way of life."
JOHN MUIR

Horton Creek Trail, Payson

Being a waterway in Arizona is often a seasonal job. They flow as feisty as an over-caffeinated terrier during rainy times and then the rest of the year lie around in sandy pajamas. Yet Horton Creek is no part-timer. Horton goes nonstop, rumbling in a furious rush through dense forest at the base of the Mogollon Rim.

The trail for Horton Creek starts from Upper Tonto Creek Campground, following an old wagon road. It parallels the stream yet stays slightly removed from it. While this is a fine shady ramble, the water beckons. A trace trail hugs the creekbank with filament pathways connecting the two routes. If a seductive cascade calls you down to the water you can follow the creekside path. When you want slightly easier walking—not scrambling among rocks and downed logs—just return to the wagon road.

When I lived on the other side of the country, my favorite getaway was the Great Smokey Mountains. Under a verdant forest canopy, clear streams tumbled down the slopes. Crystal-throated creeks, each with a distinctive voice, would hold me enchanted for hours. I hear the same music in Horton, the ever-shifting cascades and mini-falls, the flirty slap of current against the boulders, the wet sigh of widening pools, and the chorus of trills and ripples. I spent a long time on the creekbank, reacquainting myself with the language of splash.

The old wagon road and creekside path stay in close contact until the last half mile. The road turns steeper, crossing a rock-strewn segment, then launches into a few sharp switchbacks to reach a junction with Highline Trail. This is today's stopping point. But first follow the sign pointing to the right to check out Horton Spring, the source of this picturesque creek. Water gushes from the hillside, spilling over moss-covered boulders. I always take time to stop and say "Good hustle!" to the spring before heading back downstream. A spring that can create this kind of riparian beauty deserves respect.

Horton Creek drops through a lush forest in a series of cascades. Photo by the author.

Where: From Payson, drive east about 16.5 miles on AZ 260. Turn north on Tonto Creek Rd. (FR289) for 0.8 miles and park in the picnic area. The trailhead is on the north side of the campground.
Cost: Free.
Difficulty: Moderate.
Length: 8 miles round-trip.
Dogs: Yes, on a leash.
Details: (928) 474-7900, www.fs.usda.gov/r03/tonto.

Hot Tip: Discover a wealth of artifacts and exhibits reflecting the early history of the region including the bloody Pleasant Valley War at the Rim Country Museum in Payson. Visitors can also tour a replica of western writer Zane Grey's cabin. The original cabin burned down in the 1990 Dude Fire.

Buffalo Bar and Grill, Payson

Sitting on the main drag in Payson, Buffalo Bar and Grill is a long room with a small patio tacked on the end. The bar stretches practically the entire length of the building and walls are adorned with western memorabilia, bar signs, and John Wayne quotes. The menu includes soups, salads, shrimp, and steaks.

Signature burgers vary in size, and even in meats. There's a buffalo burger and a beef brisket burger. The Duke stacks up two one-third-pound patties then seals them together with a gooey blend of Swiss, American, and pepper-jack cheese served straight up—no garnish, pilgrim.

I went a different route, jumping on the sliders. Three mini-sirloin patties come topped with grilled onions and melted cheese. In most cases, I nix the cheese. Not because of any lactose issues but just because of the flavor profile. I love cheese in many scenarios, just not necessarily draped over my burger. But in this case, I didn't tamper, just let the concept run its course. And it all merged nicely, with the mildness of the cheese wrapping itself around the rich meat, stopping it from going too far—like one pal restraining another pal, pulling him back before he takes a swing at a burly biker in some honky-tonk. Each slider made a tasty, tender, chompable package.

Vegetarian Options: There's an Arizona Garden Burger on the menu, but you can also substitute a veggie patty on any of the other signature burgers.
Don't Forget: Don't miss their weekday happy hour appetizer specials, all kinds of fried goodies from 2 p.m. to 6 p.m.
Details: 311 S. Beeline Highway, (928) 474-3900, www.buffalopaysonaz.com.

Show Low Bluff Trail, Show Low (ADA Accessible)

I have a weakness for community trails. They may be crowded, seldom offer any kind of challenge, and are often more stroll than hike, but they serve a higher purpose. They lure people outdoors and give everybody a chance to reconnect with the natural world.

The Show Low Meadow Trail is like that. Here grandparents can walk with toddlers. Old friends gather for a morning chat. New friends are made over wildflower and bird sightings. Those in wheelchairs and strollers can be included for the paved portion across the meadow.

The lavish pasture catches your eye as you drive past, a piece of tall-grass prairie plopped down by the highway pushing back development. It's a place you have to stop, a place you want to explore. Rising above it is a high forehead of a pine-covered hill, Show Low Bluff. But I can't talk about that hike without including the Meadow Trail because they are part of a singular experience.

There's a large parking area with restrooms and picnic tables sheltered in a small barn right off AZ 260. A paved walking path leads to a bridge across Show Low Creek. The bluff trail actually begins in the pines on the side of the slope. But before you get there, you're soaking up the views across a sweep of grasslands. The city purchased this meadow where Native Americans and pioneer settlers once camped to preserve it. It features a wide paved path that was built with funding from Arizona State Parks. Show Low Meadow Trail is ADA accessible as it follows the creek for almost a mile. The stream is stocked with trout throughout the year.

I paused on the bridge taking it all in. Horses stood in belly deep grass at one end of the meadow and cows grazed at the other. A couple of teens fished from a small pier, while other anglers stood on the banks. A photographer crouched on the path snapping photos of wildflowers. I could see families with kids and dogs in tow enjoying a fine day in the mountains. One kid appeared to be skipping. Man, when was the last time I skipped? I think those muscles are atrophied.

Finally, I crossed the creek and entered the pines. Show Low Bluff is one of the meticulously crafted trails by the hard-working volunteers of TRACKS. They're responsible for the excellent network of trails in this region.

The lower segment of the short loop hugs the base of the bluff, shaded by trees but still connected to the meadow. It soon angles uphill, climbing gently to the midsection of the bluff where you find an interesting assortment of boulders, and then bends back toward your starting point.

After completing the loop, I wandered out across the meadow. It makes me happy seeing kids on the trail. This is how they fall in love with the outdoors. This is how they grow up to be the kind of people who want to protect our open spaces. This is how we all win.

Did I skip on my way back to the parking lot? Not with my feet, but my heart sure had a bouncy rhythm.

Where: The trailhead is at 769 S. White Mountain Blvd.

Cost: Free.

Difficulty: Easy.

Length: Bluff Trail is 1.5 miles round-trip.

Dogs: Yes, on a leash.

Details: (928) 368-6700, www.trackswhitemountains.org.

The House, Show Low

Dining here feels like you're at a friend's backyard barbecue. The House opened in 2015 and carved out a lane with good food and a family friendly space. Order at the small wood-paneled building, and then grab a table. There is seating inside for rainy days, but otherwise head outdoors. I'm not sure why they call it House when hardly anyone stays in it. Outside there's a huge patio with fire pits, and picnic tables are scattered about the big grassy lawn.

A small stage fills the back corner for live entertainment. Cornhole boards

It's called The House but most of the eating, drinking, and fun takes place in the yard. Photo by the author.

are lined up, and The House occasionally hosts tournaments. Then there's the Yard Bar, which is a cross between a saloon, a fort, and treehouse. The rustic shack serves a full slate of cocktails, but don't worry about things getting rowdy; the big patio is often filled with kids and dogs.

Despite the casual setting, they serve an elevated menu that includes chili, sandwiches, salads, and impressive burgers. Each are made with a half pound of fresh hand-formed beef patties. Try the House Burger, layered with a roasted poblano chile, pepper jack cheese, fried onion strings, and chipotle aioli—a nice combo of textures and flavors, a bit crunchy with a little spice on the back end. It's served with their homemade chips.

If your tastes run to the exotic, be sure to ask about their Burger of the Week. The staff collaborates on some genuinely original concoctions such as the Biscuits and Gravy Burger or Blackberry Ricotta Burger.

Vegetarian Options: Salads, sandwiches, wraps, and apps, plenty to choose from—just like at your house.

Don't Forget: Don't even think about leaving without dessert because the Red Barn Creamery and Sweet Shop is also part of the complex. They serve homemade ice cream, cookies, cupcakes, and an assortment of pastries.

Details: 1191 E. Hall, (928) 537-9273, www.thehouseshowlow.com.

Panorama Trail, Lakeside

I'm going to say it right up front: The name of this trail is a bit of a con. You absolutely do get big panoramas, some nice vistas. But they're only a part of the experience. What I remember are not the sweeping views but the stillness, the quiet moments in the patchwork of sun and shadows that fill these fragrant woods.

The trail cuts into the timber for a half mile, then splits. I took the loop counterclockwise and almost immediately spotted a shortcut. Seriously. There's an official trail sign that simply says "shortcut." I try to recall if I've ever seen a shortcut sign anywhere besides a Coyote-Roadrunner cartoon. Wile E. Coyote regularly used them as part of his foolproof plans. But I continued straight ahead. Of course, I would have made better time if I had worn my ACME jet-powered roller skates.

Panorama is one of the trails developed by TRACKS, a dedicated group of volunteers. Centered in the Show Low/Pinetop-Lakeside area, over 200 miles of trails were built in cooperation with the towns and the forest service. The pathways are mostly designed as loops and spoked with connectors allowing for a wide range of options. TRACKS attaches distinctive white diamond trail markers to trees to keep recreationists on the right path. About every quarter mile the diamonds are marked with a location code (letter and number). If a hiker needs to call for help, the locators prove invaluable.

I climbed the shoulder of Twin Knolls with

Hot Tip: The White Mountain Nature Center offers a free-flight raptor show several days a week in Pinetop-Lakeside that's as thrilling as it is educational. Kids love to watch and meet these remarkable birds.

impressive views stretching across a sea of pines. On clear days the San Francisco Peaks near Flagstaff are visible. The knolls are crowned with scrub oak, and slopes are swept bare from a long-ago fire. Soon the trail drops into a pleasant forest. For the next few miles, I meandered through mixed woodlands. Pines, junipers, and oaks with small meadows pooled around them create a peaceful setting.

The trail remains level until skirting Porter Tank and then ascends a low mesa. I love a good mesa. A mesa gives you some elevation, a lofty perch but treats your knees with a modicum of respect. Mountains are all up or all down but a mesa is not so adamant. A mesa is a mountain that's learned to relax. Sporadic views appeared through the screen of timber before I rejoined the cherry stem that led back to the parking area.

Where: From the Lakeside Ranger District office, travel 0.2 miles southeast on AZ 260. Turn left on Porter Mountain Rd. for 6 miles. The trailhead is on the left.
Cost: Free.
Difficulty: Moderate.
Length: 9.5 miles round-trip, about 7 miles if you take the signed shortcut.
Dogs: Yes, on a leash.
Details: (928) 368-6700, www.trackswhitemountains.org.

Moose Henri's Grille Corks & Taps, Lakeside

This funky little joint surprises in many ways. A low-ceilinged bar filled with simple tables, a bevy of televisions, and lots of personality, Moose Henri's features 30 craft beers on tap that change weekly, with an emphasis on Arizona microbrews. They offer beer flights so you can sample a half dozen at a time to pin down your favorites.

The menu is also slightly skewed for a sports bar, including selections like exotic quesadillas, overloaded mac, salads, and intriguing daily specials like smoked osso bucco. Their eight specialty burgers are a third of a pound, cradled on a soft rustic bun that felt good in my hands. My sense of hope was rewarded at first bite. They use a Black Angus and Wagyu beef blend that creates a lush, distinctive patty, full of rich flavor. I had the basic model but added diced green chile that brought a sly warmth, like the dawning of a mountain sunrise. Other options include a half-pound pasture-raised bison patty or their notable B.E.A.S.T. of the same size. This is a gamey-rich blend of bison, Wagyu beef, venison, and wild boar.

No deep fryer on premises means no French fries. All burgers come with sides such as coleslaw, green salad, hash browns, or a house dish that changes with the seasons. Better dig in, you've got a lot of brews to work through.

Vegetarian Options: A veggie patty can be substituted for any burger.
Don't Forget: If beer isn't your beverage, Moose Henri's offers 20 wines by the glass.
Details: 4207 W. White Mountain Blvd., (928) 368-5127, www.moosehenris.com.

Springs Trail, Pinetop

At the eastern edge of Pinetop, this rolling loop guides hikers, mountain bikers, and equestrians through a sun-dappled ponderosa pine forest and past lazy streams. With little change in elevation, it makes a great beginner hike or provides a quick outing to start or end a day while watching for wildlife.

Springs Trail is a straight-up loop with the trail splitting almost immediately. I swung to the right, taking it counterclockwise, which also follows the TRACKS sequential coded markers. It soon winds its way down to Thompson Creek. The slow-moving creek forms a marshy wetland thick with grasses and wildflowers.

For most of the next mile, the trail parallels the creek, crossing a couple of times on well-placed rocks. And banish any vision you might have of clear mountain streams spilling over smooth boulders. While Thompson Creek can fluctuate with the seasons it tends to remain a sluggish channel, forming pools of varying sizes before briefly disappearing as if swallowed by the matted grass. But lethargic or no, the power of water cannot be doubted. Just step back for a moment and watch the constant swarm of activity as creatures big and small make their way to this emerald bog.

The trail finally pulls away from the creek and pushes into the trees. The forest has been thinned returning it to a more natural state. Big ponderosa pines are spread apart in a

Fast Fact: Arizona contains the largest contiguous forest of ponderosa pine in the world, stretching from Flagstaff, across the Mogollon Rim, and through the White Mountains.

Thompson Creek meanders through a grassy channel along the Springs Trail. Photo by the author.

sunny park-like setting. Young oaks create an understory that turns colorful in autumn. During warm months carpets of fleabane sprinkled with yarrow soak up the extra sunlight, and thickets of wild roses line the trail.

Pinetop Springs forms another marshy area near the halfway point of the hike. Rustic little pastures are good spots to see elk or deer. While the trail presents no challenges, always check current conditions before setting out. During the rainy season it can turn quite muddy. It's best to avoid during those times so as not to damage the trail. That especially goes for horseback riders.

Near the end of the hike, I crossed over mostly dry Billy Creek on flat wooden bridges and returned to the trailhead. Last time I hiked Springs Trail, a small band of wild horses trotted past me just as I finished, a nice Arizona memory. The next time, things were tamer. Two horseback riders went through the gate in front of me discussing what a peaceful outing it had been. How right they were.

Where: From the Lakeside Ranger District office, travel 5.3 miles southeast on AZ 260. Turn left on Buck Springs Rd. Proceed to 0.5 mile to the junction of Sky Hi Rd. Turn left again and continue 1.1 miles to the trailhead.
Cost: Free.
Difficulty: Easy.
Length: 3.6 miles round-trip.
Dogs: Yes, on a leash.
Details: (928) 368-6700, www.trackswhitemountains.org.

Persnikkity's Café, Show Low

This place started as a tiny bakery and café and has continued to grow. Now the genial restaurant focuses on fresh, healthful dishes served in a cheerful atmosphere. Seriously. The staff at Persnikkity's are relentlessly friendly. It is a place loaded with charm from the music to the staff to the décor.

Order at the counter and someone hustles out the food. When my burger arrived, I asked for mustard. I was shown to the towering cabinet of condiments near the soda fountain. Shelves were lined with colorful bottles of anything you might desire to splash on a meal. There were hot sauces, hot honeys, and multiple ketchups. The mustards included wasabi, sriracha, sweet hot, bacon jalapeño, and dill. The gracious staffer was describing some of their characteristics like a mustard sommelier. When I grabbed the plain bright-yellow squeezy bottle of Heinz, I could sense a little part of her die inside.

Persnikkity's makes 6-ounce smash burgers out of Black Angus beef. They're hand pressed and served on a buttery potato bun. Now I like the structural integrity the potato bun provides but it also has a bit more chew. My single cheesy smash felt a little bread forward, just slightly out of balance. The meat was tender with a good depth of flavor, and I wanted to experience it in each bite. When I piled on my extra toppings the combination meshed nicely.

On my next visit, I'll double the patties for a better meat-to-bread ratio. Or maybe I'll try one of their signature creations like the Cowboy with sweet barbecue sauce, bacon, American cheese, and frazzles—bacon-flavored vegetarian corn crisps adding a yummy crunch. The tots were soft and wonderful.

The menu includes pitas, wraps, salads, burritos, and sandwiches. A "twisted brunch" is offered all day for those craving avocado toast, jalapeño

Plush tater tots surround a cheesy smashburger at Persnikkity's Café. Photo by the author.

bagel, and hot honey chicken pita. And please don't be afraid to dabble in their array of exotic mustards. Don't be so set in your ways like me.

Vegetarian Options: Nearly half the menu is vegetarian. I've also heard from more than one person that their Baja black bean burger is a delight.
Don't Forget: The baking hasn't stopped. Persnikkity's Sweet Confections (4461 S. White Mountain Blvd.) creates artful cookies, cupcakes, brownies, cakes, and more.
Details: 161 E. Deuce of Clubs, (928) 251-1965, www.persnikkityscafe.com.

Thompson Trail, Greer

If this isn't the greenest hike in Arizona, it has to be close. If this isn't the most peaceful hike in Arizona, it has to be close. If this isn't the prettiest hike in Arizona, well, you get the idea. The Thompson Trail traverses a narrow, forested canyon alongside the west fork of the Black River, where Apache trout still swim. It all makes for an enchanted day in the White Mountains.

From the small parking area, walk down the road about 100 yards to where it crosses over the Black River. The Thompson Trail starts as a wide two-track, which happens to be an old railroad grade. But it soon takes a more intimate turn. Before that happens, you'll pass the first of two human-made waterfalls. These are barriers designed to protect the habitat of the endangered Apache trout by preventing nonnative fish from encroaching. A second waterfall is built just downstream. The Apache trout, native to Arizona, is our official state fish.

As you approach a gate, the trail veers left toward the water and pinches down to a singletrack. It pulls you into the woods alongside the tumbling river. Now it feels like a trail. The Thompson flows like the water it chases, through the trees, crossing meadows and marshes through this lush canyon bottom.

On a late spring day, wild irises were sprinkled amid the grasses. Red columbines nodded gracefully in the breeze. Ferns were

Hot Tip: While there is no shortage of spots for anglers to choose from in the White Mountains, the Greer Lakes—Bunch Reservoir, Tunnel Reservoir, and River Reservoir—offer easily accessible serene fishing spots. Surrounded by shaggy forests, the three lakes support a population of rainbow, brown, and brook trout.

The Thompson Trail never strays far from the clear running west fork of the Black River. Photo by the author.

beginning to unfurl lacey fronds. Dandelions were everywhere. As someone who mowed a lot of suburban lawns where dandelions were reviled, it still strikes me as odd seeing them in wild country. Like maybe they're on vacation. Here they're cheerful and charming. Often weeds are just wildflowers growing where we wish they wouldn't.

The higher slopes bristle with the charred trunks of ghost trees consumed in the Wallow fire of 2011. Yet what gives me hope is the absolute mass of young aspens packed into that space. This is a new forest literally rising from the ashes, as aspens are the first trees to grow after a fire. They add a layer of fresh summer greenery that will turn golden in the fall. Aspens are trees full of promise for a better future, a reminder that beauty wins out in the end.

After almost 2.5 miles, the Thompson reaches the West Fork Black River Trail, which marks the turnaround point for this hike. I know loop trails are favored by many hikers, but with scenery this exquisite, no one should mind experiencing it all over again when retracing steps.

Where: From Show Low, drive 35 miles east on AZ 260. Turn right on AZ 273 and continue 14 miles to Forest Road 116. Turn right on this gravel road and proceed 4 miles to the small parking area at the trailhead. FR 116 is bumpy but manageable in a sedan.

Cost: Free.

Difficulty: Easy.

Length: 4.8 miles round-trip.

Dogs: Yes, on a leash.

Details: (928) 333-6200, www.fs.usda.gov/r03/apache-sitgreaves.

"I'm not a hero. I'm a man who sells burgers."

BOB BELCHER

Darbi's Café, Pinetop

When you travel the White Mountains, you always hope to find an eatery like Darbi's Café. Swaddled in wood from walls to ceiling, it feels like you've stepped into an oversized cabin complete with a stone fireplace. It's a homey place. But if you're meeting someone, you may have to search, because there are lots of rooms, lots of cozy corners.

This house was built on breakfast. Mountain air seems to amplify the need for the day's first meal and Darbi's delivers. They crack enough eggs every morning to make Foghorn Leghorn weep. Omelets and scrambles are made with three eggs stuffed with toppings and then paired with two more sides. Pancakes are fluffy and big enough to wear as a poncho if you bite a hole through the middle. Breakfast is served until noon.

So, here's the deal. By purchasing this book, you've entered into an implied contract with me, the author, indicating you intend to hike and then eat afterward, as laid out by the title—*Boots and Burgers*. But as I previously indicated, there's no need to worry. Unlike so many authors who are petty, rigid, and prone to litigation, I am benevolent and broad-minded. Live and let live, I say. Eat and let eat. Should you decide to dine before your hike, indulging in a Darbi's breakfast feast, you can do so secure in the knowledge that I will take no legal action against you. Just allow yourself plenty of time to digest the gargantuan meal. Because if you tackle the S.O.B. (Son of a Biscuit), which is a giant, open-face buttermilk biscuit smothered with sausage patties, hash browns, green chile sauce, sausage gravy, and two eggs, you'll need your trekking poles just to hoist yourself up from the table.

If you hike first and then come for the burger, your waistline still isn't off the hook. There are 10 burger variations, from plain to complex, all built on a big half-pound charbroiled patty. The Jalapeño Popper comes topped with cream cheese, jalapeños, and bacon. I enjoyed the burger with caramelized onions and garlic mushrooms. It's a simple but robust combo that almost always delivers the goods flavor-wise.

Vegetarian Options: Salads, veggie wrap, and many breakfast items.
Don't Forget: They offer half orders on some items and there is a lighter menu for the young and young at heart that leads off with a "dainty" quarter-pound cheeseburger.
Details: 235 E. White Mountain Blvd., (928) 367-6556, www.darbiscafe.com.

Hot Tip: Nothing I love better than a remote burger, and Show Low has a doozy. The Hole in One at 1554 Bourdon Ranch Road is likely Arizona's tiniest burger hut. A small shack, several miles from civilization and the nearest golf course, where a mom-and-pop team cook tender, tasty middle-of-nowhere burgers crowded together on a little flattop. Grab a seat at an outdoor table and enjoy this lonely gem.

West Baldy Trail, Greer

When you envision an idyllic mountain trail, you're dreaming of West Baldy. But plenty of others share that dream, so expect company on summer weekends. Best to play a little hooky; call in sick to work and then TGIT! (That's "Thank God it's Tuesday," for you hooky virgins.) You absolutely want some solitude as you amble across these sun-smooched meadows with the music of the river sweetening the morning.

From the parking lot the trail passes through a thin veneer of forest for the first mile and then voila! Suddenly I was walking across a picturesque meadow near the banks of a clear-running river. For the next 2 miles, that was my experience. I strolled through one grassy meadow after another, each bordered by forested slopes. Sunlight glinted off the west fork of the Little Colorado, a robust trout stream, as birds warbled among the branches.

The river loops right to the edge of the trail in places, at other times it pulls back under the shade of the trees. After about 3 miles I entered a radiant, reverent forest. There's something positively ancient here, lots of big downed logs, lichen-crusted boulders, and a loamy perfume that wafts through stands of pine, spruce, and fir. This is a forest left over from Middle Earth. I expected to see hobbits stroll past on their way to second breakfast.

The trail climbs at a steady pace, getting a bit steeper after a stream crossing. This is never a strenuous hike, but you do rack up a lot of miles at high elevation. Following the contours of the mountain, the trail keeps angling upwards. At one point, you pass through a large swath of trees killed by bark beetles. But after a couple of switchbacks, you climb above the ghostly grove and are back in green timber.

The West Baldy Trail crosses sloping meadows before climbing into heavy forest. Photo by the author.

From the ridge a few vistas are visible and you also get a first glimpse of the top. The actual summit is on the White Mountain Apache Reservation and access is restricted to tribal members only. Please respect their laws and don't trespass. The West Baldy Trail merges with East Baldy Trail in a saddle near the reservation border below Mount Baldy.

From here you've got a couple of options. You can return the way you came or hike down East Baldy (another mountain beauty) and use the Connector Trail, which you passed in the meadows below. That makes for a 17.5-mile hike. With a car shuttle you can climb one trail and descend the other side on East Baldy. All you need to make that work is to line up a hooky-playing sidekick.

Where: From Show Low, drive 35 miles east on AZ 260. Turn right on AZ 273 and continue 8.6 miles to the trailhead which will be on the right.

Cost: Free.

Difficulty: Moderate.

Length: 14 miles round-trip.

Dogs: Yes, on a leash.

Details: (928) 333-6200, www.fs.usda.gov/r03/apache-sitgreaves.

Fast Fact: On January 7, 1971, the temperature at Hawley Lake plunged to 40 degrees below zero. It was the coldest temperature ever recorded in Arizona. Three years earlier, Hawley set the record for snowfall, with 91 inches on the ground following a weeklong storm. Hawley Lake is located about 30 miles southeast of Pinetop on the land of the White Mountain Apache Tribe. During the summer months it is a fishing and recreation site.

The Lion's Den Bar & Grill, Pinetop

This saloon sits on the edge of town and has gone through many incarnations. The original owner opened a small café in 1939. A few years later he moved into the current location. Several name changes followed before The Lion's Den finally stuck. For much of that time it was a rowdy joint that survived two fires, countless fights, basement poker games, and a horse falling through the floor. You have to figure there's quite a story attached to the horse incident.

The Den, as it's known today, stays calmer. Still a bar, yet one fostering a more family-friendly vibe. The inside is wrapped in wood paneling and flickering television screens, but multiple patios and a large backyard lure patrons outside to enjoy the fresh mountain air. Live music is a mainstay attraction with bands keeping things jumping. You'll find a selection of bar food like sandwiches, wings, and deep-fried mini-tacos. They also make their own potato chips.

Yet it's the burgers that have earned a reputation far and wide. Sometime in the long-ago past, they started making wine burgers, and customers flocked to the mountain hamlet to try them. The half-pound patties are cooked on a flattop. The hot surface is sloshed with a big gulp of red wine that sends up a boozy cloud of white steam as if winos had just chosen a new pope. It also adds a sweet smoky taste. Specialty burgers are offered, or you can customize your own from assorted toppings. Served on a toasted bun the burgers are so tender you wonder how they ever kept a cow upright.

Vegetarian Options: The grilled cheese special combines a gooey blend of Swiss and American, along with green chile and tomato on sourdough.
Don't Forget: Along with the live music, line dancing, karaoke, trivia, and plenty more activities are part of the summer lineup.
Details: 2408 E. White Mountain Blvd., (928) 367-6050, www.thelionsdenpinetop.com.

The Power of Hooky

I call myself a travel writer but that's sugarcoating the truth. What I am in reality is a professional bad influence. Everything I write is to encourage you to play hooky.

Call in sick and go for a hike. Skip out of that afternoon meeting and go for a bike ride. Ignore those weekend chores and take a road trip. Arizona is the most gorgeous state in the country, get out and see all of it that you can.

Any day spent hurling yourself at beauty is a day well spent. Chase delights. Seek out joy in all its incarnations. Stalk mystery and magic. Because why else are we here?

I am a firm believer in the beneficial rejuvenation that hooky provides. The small rebellion of hooky keeps us from being overwhelmed and maintains balance in our lives. When responsibility locks down our spirit, occasional forays of hooky keep the door ajar. Slipping beyond the clawing grasp of minor obligations to seize a bite-sized morsel of freedom once in a while reconnects us to that rakish, devil-may-care person we always planned to become. Make judicious use of hooky as a shortcut to happiness. It has worked for me ever since I started sneaking out of elementary school to snag a forbidden burger.

I call myself a travel writer, but what I am in realty is the Hooky King of Arizona.

ARIZONA'S WEST COAST

Of all the unexpected sights in Arizona—and the state is lousy with them—the West Coast may be the most startling. Who expects something like this? Long stretches of white sand end at the edge of shimmering water. Palm trees sway in the breeze. Seagull wings flash in the sun as boats drift past and kids swim, splash, and laugh at the beaches. It is not a scene most people associate with the Grand Canyon State.

The Colorado River defines the western edge of Arizona and creates a slender albeit authentic coastline. But push back from the water and you run smack into serious desert. Instead of the familiar and relatively verdant Sonoran Desert, a sliver of the Mojave muscles in. The majestic saguaros grow scarcer. Vegetation dissipates here with spindly creosote bushes fanning out across rocky knife-edged slopes. Amid this sun-chewed terrain, you'll find an abundance of places to explore.

Smooth rock walls squeeze together forming the slot canyon known as Crack in the Mountain. Photo by the author.

Crack in the Mountain Trail, Lake Havasu City

Lake Havasu City serves as the central hub of a splashy playground. And while nearly everyone goes for the water, landlubbers like me dig their unsung network of trails. Crack in the Mountain for example, sends you slithering through a twisting slot canyon near the banks of the Colorado. Located in SARA (Special Activities and Recreation Area) Park, the trail is known locally as SARA's Crack.

Start out on a wide path from the parking area following yellow trail markers. You soon drop into a sandy wash. Around the 1.2-mile mark, the wash bends left and stone cliffs rise, forming the edge of the defile. And this should go without saying but I'll say it anyway. Never enter a slot canyon if there is even a slight chance of rain. If it has rained recently, water may block your passage through the crack. Okay. Now you're ready to go in.

After you make your way through an initial corridor, walls of pinkish-hued rock close around you like a lung collapsing. Banded layers are preserved like swirls in marbled ice cream. The pearl-smooth walls remain just a few feet apart in the heart of the narrows as you wind your way through this stone-wrapped tunnel. There's a 7-foot dry waterfall perfect for sliding down. There's usually a rope anchored to the rock providing assistance to non-sliders. Expect to use your hands scrambling over other obstacles as well. That's part of the fun.

Each time I'm here, I'm reminded that everyone should spend time in a slot canyon. I always feel relaxed in this sliver of space. With boots on the ground and a hand on each wall, you connect to the landscape in a way you never do elsewhere. It is restorative. Slot canyons impart long forgotten life lessons, stuff we knew when we were kids but forgot. Tight spaces are meant to be squeezed through. If walls weren't meant to be touched, they wouldn't be so smooth. Focus on small things. Slide at every opportunity. The world can be big and overwhelming, so you should always have a good hideout.

The canyon widens at 1.4 miles. You can stop here and return through the Crack or climb a short (but slightly steep) pathway up the right bank to the Blue Trail following the ridgeline back. Or continue down the wash (angling to the right when vegetation blocks the path) to the banks of the Colorado River. You reach a quiet cove near Balanced Rock. From here, climb the ridge and return via the Blue Trail.

Where: Trailhead is in SARA Park, 6 miles south of London Bridge. From downtown Lake Havasu City, drive south on US 95 to S. McCulloch Blvd. at Milepost 177. Turn right and travel 0.7 miles to the parking lot on the right.
Cost: Free.
Difficulty: Moderate.
Length: 2.8 miles round-trip through the Crack and back; 5 miles round-trip if you go to the Colorado River.
Dogs: Yes, on a leash. A harness might be needed as well.
Details: (928) 453-3444, www.golakehavasu.com.

Hot Tip: Winter Blast is a fireworks extravaganza that takes place every February in SARA Park. It's the Western Pyrotechnic Association showing off their wares for four consecutive nights, and it's the best fireworks show I have ever seen.

Tavern 95, Lake Havasu City

Located on Lake Havasu City's south side, Tavern 95 provides post-workout nourishment for anyone hiking or biking in nearby SARA Park. Something about squeezing through a slot canyon just seems to whet an appetite. And that is something Tavern 95 knows how to handle.

There's a small bar area, dining room, and patio. Somehow it pairs the comfortable feel of a neighborhood tavern with the expansive and nuanced menu of a white tablecloth establishment. While the selections range from New York strip steaks to shrimp carbonara to loaded flatbreads, the common theme is the vibrancy of the flavors. This is a chef-driven place with lots of little twists.

They bring that same creative energy to their burgers. Each is made with 100 percent premium Gold Canyon Angus chuck, brisket, and short rib blend, then grilled to order. They're served on a homemade brioche bun, with a few exceptions. The All-Nighter, for example, comes heaped with a fried egg, American cheese, orange marmalade ham, French fries, and hollandaise sauce with an oversized English muffin holding it together.

If you yearn for spicy, try the Jalapeño Burger with ghost pepper cheese, flash-fried jalapeños, and smoky chipotle mayo, with lettuce, tomato, onion, and pickle on the side, to mitigate some of the sneaky heat.

But as always, I'm a simple man. One of the very best meals I've had at Tavern 95 was after a long hot day tromping on the trails; I ordered the Tavern sliders—three mini burgers topped only with sauteed onions. I sat there with my cold drink, munching my small burgers that were rich, vibrant, and complicated, like beef orchids. The depth of flavor shocked me, and I savored every bite. There is a simple devastation to a well-executed slider. They are

A slate of well-crafted gourmet burgers awaits diners in the casual comfort of Tavern 95. Courtesy of Rick Mortensen, Phoenix.

the haikus of the burger world, tiny but poignant and memorable. They make me happy to be a hungry hiker.

Vegetarian Options: Veggie patties can be substituted for any burger. They also offer some large salads and a couple of delicious flatbreads.
Don't Forget: Happy Hour runs from 2 p.m. to 5 p.m. Monday–Friday. It's a good opportunity to sample their impressive selection of discounted appetizers.
Details: 3453 Maricopa Ave., (928) 566-4869, www.tavern95lhc.com.

Shoreline Trail, Lake Havasu City (ADA Accessible)

Okay, I'm cheating with this one because it's not a hike at all, just a stroll. But it's one of the most exquisite strolls in Arizona and a big tropical welcome mat for all visitors—a reminder that the wonders of the state are numerous. Taking a leisurely saunter on the Shoreline is one of the first things I do when I hit town. It reconnects me to this place, makes me feel like an extra in *Beach Blanket Bingo* with Frankie Avalon and Annette Funicello, and reminds me that even in Arizona, surf's up. You just have to know where to look, but surf's up, daddy-o.

The Shoreline Trail offers a paved concrete sidewalk the whole way and is ADA accessible. It travels south from London Bridge along Bridgewater Channel and through Rotary Park while never leaving that wide expanse of water. Eventually, the city would like to expand it in both directions. For now, it delivers an easy-breezy West Coast sampler. It's also known as the Channel Walk.

In a couple of short miles, I was immersed in all the sights and sounds that make Lake Havasu City special. I walked beneath the iconic London Bridge, passed lighthouses, sandy beaches, palm trees, and volleyball games. Boats glide through the channel and music seems to always be wafting over from the

Fast Fact: The largest antique ever purchased stretches across a channel in Lake Havasu City. London Bridge, built in 1831, was purchased by town founder Robert McCulloch, shipped across the pond, and reassembled on the shore of Lake Havasu. Like many retirees, the bridge now luxuriates in Arizona sunshine.

parks. Just like that, I knew I was on vacation. This town knows how to put me into relaxation mode.

Just be aware that walking can be highly addictive. You start with a gentle stroll amid soothing beauty and the next thing you know, you're hiking deep into the desert admiring vistas that poke your heart while you dream about a tender burger waiting at the end of the day.

Where: London Bridge is always a good starting point.
Cost: Free.
Difficulty: Easy.
Length: 2 miles round-trip.
Dogs: Yes, on a leash.
Details: (928) 453-3444, www.golakehavasu.com.

Burgers by the Bridge, Lake Havasu City

This is one of the few places with the word "burger" in their name where I occasionally order something else. I have been known to grab their famous fish and chips here; fresh, crisp, and full of flavor—the best in town. Something about sitting in the shadow of London Bridge makes me yearn for a right proper old chippy.

Of course, when you're named Burgers by the Bridge you better deliver on both counts. With the high arched curves of London Bridge rising just overhead, so close you can almost touch the bricks, they've got that part covered. The burgers too. They're half-pound Angus patties, hot and juicy, a good beach burger that comes with a side of vacation vibes.

A selection of seafood highlights the menu, along with pizza, sandwiches, salads, and wraps. They offer a half dozen specialty burgers, as well as extra topping choices. Order at the counter then grab a seat outside beneath one of the little thatched roofs. Each table is like its own tiki hut.

Burgers by the Bridge is Lake Havasu City's unofficial patio. Courtesy of Rick Mortensen, Phoenix.

Sitting by the water on a shady patio with a flotilla of boats navigating Bridgewater Channel makes a good introduction to the Lake Havasu experience. This is just a great hang spot, a place where you want to sit and eat, or sit and drink, and let the day drift past. These are moments that go beyond just what's on the plate in front of you.

Vegetarian Options: Enjoy a large house salad or a veggie pizza.
Don't Forget: A full bar means great happy hour specials. They also do a nice assortment of alcohol and ice cream blends to take the edge off that Havasu heat.
Details: 410 English Village, (928) 302-6780, www.burgersbythebridge.com.

Hot Tip: Even if you don't gamble, it's worth taking a ferry ride to the Havasu Landing Resort and Casino on the California side of the lake. It's a beautiful, inexpensive boat ride across the water that lasts about 17 minutes. Enjoy more great views when you get there.

Whytes Retreat–Ripley's Run Loop, Cattail Cove State Park

Cattail Cove State Park hugs the south end of Lake Havasu before it squeezes back down into the Colorado River again. The park with campsites and beaches also offers a web of fun hiking trails that combine stunning water views and gaunt hills. Grab a map from the ranger station before setting out. With a big shimmering lake as landmark, you're not going to get lost, but the trails form lumpy concentric loops so you may end up hiking farther than you originally planned.

The easy trek to Whytes Retreat starts from the south side of the boat ramp on McKinney Loop. The sandy path traces a shoreline ridge that never strays far from the water. From the elevated perch, views across the lake to the Whipple Mountains in California are unceasingly gorgeous.

It's about a mile to Whytes Retreat, a campsite and beach along a curving spit of land. The beach consists of fine gravel, spiced with small white shells. On the backside of the spit is another hidden cove. I like to climb down the hill along a spine of rock poking into the water. It's easy to sit there on a sliver of bank, in that sheltered place, completely out of sight and off the grid. How nice to be temporarily marooned, away from computers, cell phones, and deadlines. One of these days, I promise myself, I'll build a bamboo hut here with a recliner of coconuts like they had on *Gilligan's Island* and live out my days happily stranded.

Until then, I returned via Ripley's Run. A couple of other trails shave off some mileage, but I like this big bite of colorful terrain as it curves inland, deeper into the hills, creating the perfect juxtaposition of water and desert. It's like the sweet and salty pairing that chefs utilize to enhance both flavors.

Ripley's swings a wide arc through the desert as it drops into a narrow wash squeezing between stone walls. It's sort of a mini slot canyon, an intimate defile. You have to navigate three dry waterfalls in the gorge, but they're fairly simple.

Hikers, castaways, and beach bums will all enjoy the sandy path leading to Whytes Retreat. Photo by the author.

If you can manage slightly uneven stairs, these should be no problem. Once the trail emerges from the wash, it climbs a rocky slope. I followed the crest of the hills back toward the developed portion of the park. Along the way, I enjoyed big panoramas of the lake, which seems even more vibrantly blue when set against these mountains of chocolate and beige. Ripley's Run ends at the Wayne's Way loop. Turn right and follow this back to Cattail Cove.

Where: From Lake Havasu City, travel 15 miles south on AZ 95 to the park. The trail begins on the south side of the boat launch.
Cost: Admission fee.
Difficulty: Moderate.
Length: 3.2 miles round-trip.
Dogs: Yes, on a leash.
Details: (928) 855-1223, www.azstateparks.com.

Jersey's American Grill, Lake Havasu City

Burgers aren't even the specialty at this downtown establishment. With a name like Jersey's it's no surprise there's a back-East feel to the place. They take pride in their Philly cheesesteaks—big torpedoes of meat, cheese, and spicy toppings. You can even build your own Philly, starting with shaved seasoned ribeye on an Italian roll, then piling on everything from caramelized onion to cherry peppers to Cheez Whiz. Hey, fuhgeddaboudit!

If you want to go Philly at Jersey's American Grill, you'll catch no flak from me. Never bet against the house. They also have regular steak, pasta dishes, pizza, and white truffle mac and cheese. That's a lot to process. You'll just be cheating yourself out of a big, juicy, messy burger is all I'm saying.

The Bad Ass Burger at Jersey's American Grill lives up to its name. Courtesy of Rick Mortensen, Phoenix.

They use hand-formed certified Angus beef; settle it on a brioche bun and build from there. The Bad Ass Burger comes fully dressed with lettuce, tomato, onion, provolone, a thick cut of meaty bacon, avocado, and roasted pepper aioli. With so much going on, you're getting different flavors and textures in every bite.

Vegetarian Options: They do a black bean burger with lettuce, tomato, onion, and the house red pepper aioli. Salads, appetizers, and the creamy indulgence of white truffle mac and cheese are also yours for the asking.

Don't Forget: Jersey's also does a mean Sunday brunch.

Details: 2049 McCulloch Blvd. N., (928) 680-3663, www.eatjerseys.com.

"Not all those
who wander are lost."
J. R. R. TOLKIEN

Badger Trail, Kingman

Make a steady slog up the southern end of the Cerbat Mountains, where you'll gain impressive views of Kingman and the surrounding countryside. The trail navigates assorted rock outcroppings and the lean vegetation common to the Mohave Desert as it wraps around the contours of the mountain. The views expand outward the higher you climb. The Badger offers a nice workout and interesting rock textures.

It's not overly steep but steady. The trail gains about 1,100 feet in just over 3 miles. The Badger is also entirely exposed, so it can turn scorching. At one point, climbing a high shoulder, I spotted a mantle of snow. Great, I thought. I'm having a heat stroke. But no, as I got closer, I recognized a field of white quartz scattered across the ridge.

Despite its stark appearance, wildflowers can paint the slopes following a wet winter. I've seen some of the most vivid blooms of beavertail cacti on the Badger. Bright, jangly blossoms of pinks and purples tucked among the yuccas and ocotillos.

The trail climbs to a saddle where you'll intersect the Castle Rock Trail and Camp Beale Loop. I usually push on to Castle Rock, a huge jumble of boulders remarkable for their lack of resemblance to a castle. But vistas of Kingman and the surrounding basin help me to overlook this minor inconsistency, and it makes for a nice definitive end point. This adds 0.6 miles each way to the hike.

Hot Tip: The Route 66 Museum is a treasure trove of artifacts and exhibits focusing on the cultural significance of the Mother Road. The Museum is located in the Historic Powerhouse in downtown Kingman, along with the visitor center.

Where: Trailhead can only be accessed from northbound lanes of US 93. Travel 4.2 miles north from Kingman and turn right into the parking area immediately past the AZ 68 interchange.

Cost: Free.

Difficulty: Moderate.

Length: 6.4 miles round-trip, 7.6 miles round-trip to Castle Rock.

Dogs: Yes, on a leash.

Details: (928) 718-3700, www.blm.gov/visit/badger-trail.

"I'll gladly pay you Tuesday for a hamburger today."

J. WELLINGTON WIMPY

Stuff It Burgers, Kingman

Nobody comes to Stuff It Burgers for the ambiance. But come they do, lured by the promise of gourmet burgers. The small café occupies the far corner of a long, low building. Walk in to find a front counter with the daily special penned on a whiteboard and a cooler full of canned drinks. Tables are tucked into the nooks and crannies of the space. Sound seems to bang around off the walls in the tiny eatery, so it can be loud at times. If you're planning a romantic anniversary dinner, look elsewhere. If you're in the mood for a delicious burger, you hit the jackpot.

Several signature burgers adorn the menu ranging from the simple to surprisingly complex, and custom builds and add-ons are available. When mine first arrived, I felt a moment of trepidation. The patty was too thin, toppings too tall. The burger was off-kilter. Yet all it took was one bite to realize my fears were groundless. The freshness of the meat was immediately evident.

Smashed patties are nicely seared to a crusty exterior at Stuff It Burgers. Courtesy of Rick Mortensen, Phoenix.

The smashburger had a nice char and more than held its own among the cacophony of other flavors. It's exactly what you want in a smashburger, crusty on the outside but tender inside just like a next-door neighbor in every television sitcom. Very tasty indeed. I love it when a burger comes together.

The onion rings were big and crispy. They also make a signature fry sauce in-house that looked too creamy for me but that others seemed to enjoy immensely. Stuff It Burgers is a good reminder that you should never judge a book by its cover—except my books because they always look great on the outside. Burgers can be small, big, tidy, sloppy, surprising, and confusing. All that matters is how they taste.

Vegetarian Options: There's a grilled cheese on the kid's menu.
Don't Forget: Stuff It Burgers is a two-pronged business. They started with a food truck and that wheeled burger machine still sets up around town on certain days and at big events. It's never a bad idea to confirm hours before heading to the restaurant.
Details: 2170 Northern Ave., (928) 377-7550.

Fast Fact: Americans consume more than 50 billion burgers annually. If you don't include me, that number drops significantly.

Monolith Garden Trail, Kingman

It doesn't hurt to have a map or trail app because Monolith Garden Trail goes round and round and round again. And then around a couple more times. The trail is actually a series of multiple connected loops as it makes a tangled route through dramatic boulder fields and crumbling ramparts of volcanic ash. But with three different trailheads and multiple forks, it turns Monolith Garden into a bit of a maze.

The trails slash across the Cerbat Foothills Recreation Area, same as Badger Trail, and several others. They're all linked, which is great for mountain bikers and hikers who like to explore. Far as I'm concerned, Monolith Garden is the creamy nougat center of the recreation area—just a really fun outing.

I started from the Metwell Drive trailhead and cut across rocky hills dotted with ocotillo and crucifixion thorn. Soon after passing through a gate, I reached the loop portion, which I took clockwise. I passed two signed junctions branching off to the right. These can be utilized if you prefer making a shorter loop. But unless I'm limping, I don't believe in shorter loops. I continued straight ahead, skirting the edge of a small canyon with scalloped rock walls. The Mojave is a more languid desert than the Sonoran. It lacks the vertical notes of the saguaro and vegetation is more haphazard. But that just means the geological texture of the terrain is exposed. The Mohave's rowdy past is laid bare for everyone to see.

One thing I love about this trail is how quickly it cuts you free. I wasn't far from the highway to Las Vegas, so a stream of high-rollers rushed past, all anxious to be hand-fed shrimp cocktails by Elvis impersonators while soaking in hot tubs filled with tequila and gummy worms, or whatever the popular trend is in Sin City. Meanwhile, I'm winding through open country detached from the madness. Although, if I'm being honest, I could go for some tequila-soaked gummy worms.

The trail continues through a rolling landscape of low slanted hills, past

Unexpected formations loom along the Monolith Garden Trail. Photo by the author.

rock towers, and hunched ridgelines toothy with columns. As I swung back around, I ignored a couple of trails entering from the left. These are the tentacles of the Foothills Rim Trails, trying to coax me deeper into the desert. Tempting, but not practical today.

Then I started passing junctions coming in from the right. These are more of Monolith Garden's inner loops allowing hikers to wrap things up quicker in case you are anxious to get on the road to Vegas. At the third trail junction, I hung a right and worked my way back to my original trailhead.

Hot Tip: Every July 4, the former mining town of Oatman hosts the Sidewalk Egg Fry, to have some fun and highlight sizzling summer temperatures. Oatman perches in the Black Hills, southwest of Kingman on Historic Route 66.

As a postscript, for the first few years I hiked the Monolith Garden basin, signs were non-existent. They've since added a trailhead map and signs at trail junctions, so it's easier to navigate. I've also explored the inner loops and they're all enticing. I especially liked the formations along the Igneous Connector.

Where: The easiest trailhead is on Metwell Dr. From I-40, turn north on US 93. Turn left on Metwell, approximately a half mile from the interstate. Bear left on the dirt road and in 0.2 miles turn right into the signed trailhead.
Cost: Free.
Difficulty: Moderate.
Length: 8.5 miles round-trip.
Dogs: Yes, on a leash.
Details: (928) 718-3700, www.blm.gov/visit/monolith-garden-trail.

Floyd & Co. Real Pit BBQ, Kingman

This hospitable spot has fed me for years and I've yet to try a burger. I'm a hardcore burger guy, but here's my theory: If you arrive in a strange town and know nothing about local restaurants, eat at a barbecue place. You'll almost never go wrong. People don't open a barbecue joint as part of some well-researched business plan. They do it because they've been barbecuing all their lives. They have a passion for making food "low and slow." It's in their marrow. People learn to cook for others, but they barbecue for themselves.

That's certainly the story here. For years, the Floyd family served their down-home pulled pork, slow-cooked ribs, and hearty side dishes at Mohave County events from a food truck. Along the way they built up a huge, hungry clientele clamoring for more. When they opened a cozy eatery in 2009, crowds poured in. Appropriately enough for someone dishing up Memphis-style barbecue, they landed on Beale Street and were in the forefront of the revitalization of downtown Kingman.

Floyd & Co. Real Pit BBQ specializes in meaty racks of St. Louis–style ribs that are tender but not helpless. They offer just a hint of resistance, refusing to surrender without a bite. These are ribs with character. That texture makes them all the more delicious. The meats are cooked to perfection over hickory wood fires.

Then in 2016, they expanded the business. With the next generation of Floyds leading the way. They purchased the former coffee shop next door and began making artisan wood-fired pizzas with hand-pulled mozzarella and Arizona ingredients perched on a light, chewy crust with a crunch. They use oak wood for a cleaner, hotter burn of the pies, and offer an assortment of wood-fired sandwiches, calzones, and creamy gelato.

The Real Pit BBQ side retains its rustic charm with booths, mismatched tables, vintage Pepsi machines, and old signs making you feel like you've

Floyd & Co. houses both a down-home barbecue restaurant on one side and a wood-fired pizza parlor on the other. Courtesy of Rick Mortensen, Phoenix.

stumbled onto an old-time barbecue shack. The pizza side is sleeker and more modern. Sit wherever you want and let your stomach be your guide about which side to order from. Don't worry, there are no wrong answers.

Vegetarian Options: Several of the signature pizzas are vegetarian and, of course, you can build your own.
Don't Forget: They always have great lunch specials, perfect for a hungry hiker.
Details: 420 E. Beale St., (928) 757-8227 for BBQ, (928) 753-3626 for Pizza, www.floydandcompany.com.

Painted Desert Trail, Imperial National Wildlife Refuge

North of Yuma, the Imperial National Wildlife Refuge harbors an intriguing mix of river, marshy wetlands, and backwater lakes bracketed by stark desert. The refuge was established to protect migratory birds and other wildlife along 30 miles of lower Colorado River, including the last unchannelized section before the river enters Mexico. It's a lively place in winter when feathered visitors like the cinnamon teal and northern pintail show up.

Yet away from the water, desert crowds around. One corner of the landscape is especially colorful, making for a great surprise hike. Grab a trail brochure at the visitor center that details some of the things you'll see on this trek.

The Painted Desert Trail makes a 1.3-mile loop into the outback. Unlike the more famous Painted Desert in Northern Arizona formed by layers of sedimentary rock, this riverside landscape resulted from volcanic fury some 20 to 30 million years ago. A variety of minerals tinted the cooling ash and created an intriguing palette of hues. Then long-term erosion shaped the hills and hoodoos.

The trail first follows a wash, crosses a ridge, and then traces another sandy wash back to the trailhead. It's a lavishly fractured terrain, weaving among colorful mounds. The walking is easy, with only a short climb to the ridgeline for some fine views, a mosaic of desert patterns and the wet knife of the river carving a verdant slice in the distance.

The brochure refers to this as Sonoran Desert and I'm sure it is. But while the Sonoran is known for its diversity, this particular corner possesses a stark moonscape quality, although more colorful. This trail could double as a set for a Martian film shoot.

Although as a counterpoint to the harsh terrain, I was serenaded on my hike by a cheerful chorus of birds. With the trail being so close to the river, lots of birds were flitting among a few scattered ironwood and palo verde trees. It's rare to experience so much avian activity in such a seemingly barren land.

Gaunt but vivid terrain can be found along the Painted Desert Trail north of Yuma. Photo by the author.

During the milder seasons, Imperial National Wildlife Refuge offers birding tours, guided hikes, and stargazing events.

Where: From Yuma, travel north on US 95 for 24 miles to Martinez Lake Rd. Turn left and continue 10 miles to Red Cloud Mine Rd. Turn right and follow signs 3.5 miles to the visitor center.
Cost: Free.
Difficulty: Easy.
Length: 1.3 miles round-trip.
Dogs: Yes, on a leash.
Details: (928) 783-3371, www.fws.gov/refuge/imperial.

Fast Fact: The largest populations of waterfowl and neotropical birds can be found at the refuge during the spring and fall migrations.

Chile Pepper, Yuma

Burritos mean all things to all people. Anything that can be swaddled in a tortilla ends up on trendy menus. At Chile Pepper, they practice good burrito fundamentals and remind us just how delicious simplicity can be. Burritos from Chile Pepper are familiar, comforting, and hauntingly addictive. You have a choice of meats, but it's the bean and cheese burrito that flies out the door by the sack full. The beans are plump and rich, blended with the right proportion of gooey cheese.

However, my personal favorite is the bean and rice. Not just my favorite burrito at this particular restaurant but my favorite burrito of all. I look forward to these little handhelds any time I come to Yuma. And they're wrapped in a tortilla that is close to perfect. Made fresh daily, the tortillas are fluffy as a pillow, lightly singed, and they absolutely melt in your mouth. If I ever write a sequel titled *Boots and Burritos*, these will be most prominent.

If you're accustomed to mega-burritos the size of dachshunds, these will seem small. But they're just right for dipping into the plastic cups of the thin but intensely flavorful salsa that comes with them. At these prices, you can afford more than one. Or add a few crunchy rolled tacos to the meal. The Gutierrez family started Chile Pepper in 1954, so generations of Yumans have grown up on their food.

Vegetarian Options: As mentioned, the bean and rice burritos, or the bean and cheese burritos are signature items.
Don't Forget: The sister restaurant, Mr. G's Drive-In, opened in 1963 and serves the same great menu.
Details: 2401 S. Fourth Ave., (928) 783-4213, www.mrgschilepepper.toast.site.

Telegraph Pass, Yuma

This is Yuma's stair-climber trail, popular with hikers, families, and cardio-fiends alike. Great views and a good workout draw plenty of folks to this steep ascent on the eastern edge of town. Of course, Yuma's not exactly a metropolis, so even a popular trail doesn't feel overrun. I enjoyed plenty of solitude on a weekday hike.

There is no official trailhead. Just follow one of the multiple-use trails across rolling foothills to the base of the mountain. The landscape is an interesting confluence of deserts, rocky and barren. It's punctuated by creosote like much of the Mojave Desert, but there's also ocotillo, some barrel cacti, and even a few saguaros tucked among the cliffs, refugees of the more verdant Sonoran.

The mile-long hike to the base of the mountain is a nice warm-up for the main course. Once you reach the gate, the trail makes a seriously steep climb, gaining 1,200 feet in the mile to the top. At least this portion is paved, making footing easier and more certain.

Huffing and puffing up to Telegraph Pass, I pondered the evolution of how we communicate. Maybe it was the cluster of radio antennas crowning the summit. Or maybe because it seemed each of the few people I passed was gabbing on cell phones or making little videos. That's baffling behavior to me. I don't want to deny anyone their shiny gadgets, but for me part of the joy of hiking is being temporarily off the grid. Are we that fearful of being disconnected? I long for the days of the telegram. If we still sent wires, think how much needless chatter would be eliminated.

Consider turning off your phone during a hike and listening to what quiet sounds like. Listen to the sound of your ragged breathing, the soft crunch of footsteps on the trail, and the rustle of dried leaves as a lizard scurries past. You won't get that in a text.

Views from the summit are spectacular, with all of Yuma laid out below. There are endless farm fields laser-leveled and shimmering green as if

Telegraph Pass provides a high fine perch for sunset viewing. Courtesy of Rick Mortensen, Phoenix.

someone had ironed Ireland. Beyond them, the dusky curve of sand dunes and craggy mountains spill across the desert.

Where: Follow Interstate-8 to the eastern side of Yuma. Take exit 14, Foothills Blvd. Turn north, then turn right on North Frontage Rd. Continue until it dead ends.
Cost: Free.
Difficulty: Strenuous.
Length: 4.6 miles round-trip.
Dogs: Yes, on a leash.
Details: (928) 783-0071, www.visityuma.com.

Fast Fact: Although Yuma Territorial Prison was known for harsh conditions, it also led the way for innovations in the town. The first electricity in Yuma, first hospital, and first library were all at the prison, which is now operated as a state park and museum.

Lutes Casino, Yuma

If you feel like the décor at TGI Fridays is too minimalist, visit Lutes Casino, an anchor of downtown Yuma. Assorted collectibles gobble every spare inch of space in the barn-like hall. Paintings and posters cover the walls. Neon signs, bicycles, kayaks, and mannequins dangle from above. A foot sticks through the ceiling. There's a piano in the middle of the room. It looks like a swap meet exploded. Yet people flock here for the grub, not the bric-a-brac.

Originally built as a general store in 1901, Lutes was turned into a pool hall around 1920. A few pool tables in back keep the tradition alive, but the rowdy days when gambling and fights were commonplace are long gone. The place is now packed with families and tourists. If you want to teach your arteries a lesson, just order the Lutes Special—an unholy but completely delectable union of cheeseburger and hot dog, preferably loaded with salsa. Shape-wise, the two icons don't really match up, with the split dog poking out from under the bun like a meat missile set at DEFCON 1. The Special has been the flagship burger since 1951.

Over the years, additional burgers and south-of-the-border specialties have been added. Their popular salsa is made fresh daily. The veggies are so crunchy you'd swear they have a garden out back—and they sort of do. Yuma is a hotbed of agricultural activity, growing more than 90 percent of all leafy vegetables consumed in the United States in the winter.

Sitting at Lutes surrounded by the eclectic shrapnel of Americana, Lutes always leaves me with hard questions. Burgers or tacos? Beer or milkshake? Solids or stripes? And will they let me have that barber pole if I ask nicely?

Vegetarian Options: Despite a menu built on the carnivorous concoction known as the Special, Lutes offers a Beyond burger, garden burger, and quinoa burger, along with their classic potato tacos.

Don't Forget: While there's never been gambling at Lutes Casino—at least no legal gambling—it is likely the oldest pool hall in the state.

Details: 221 S. Main St., (928) 782-2192, www.lutescasino.com.

Top 10 Reasons to Take Up Hiking

10. It sounds like the kind of crazy thing someone would do in a Hallmark Christmas movie to meet their worst enemy who eventually becomes their soulmate.
9. Every bag of peanut M&M'S you buy suddenly qualifies as trail mix.
8. There's probably some kind of YouTube challenge involved and you don't want to be left out.
7. It's the chauffer's day off and how else can you get to the polo match and/or cockfight.
6. Helps fund the massive multinational hiking sock conglomerates.
5. It's the only way you can stop and smell the roses since all the stupid roses are outside.
4. Everyone should spend some quiet reflective time alone with just their thoughts and venomous snakes.
3. Shedding unwanted pounds will help you look good in a wedding gown/mall cop uniform/prison jumpsuit, depending on your future plans.
2. There's a strong possibility you might run into me on the trail.
1. They don't call it the Great Indoors.

Top 10 Reasons Not to Hike

10. It's quiet. Maybe too quiet.
9. Don't want to muss up nature by leaving a bunch of footprints.
8. Lost hiking boots in a game of strip poker.
7. Will hurt chances of getting into *Guinness World Records* as most sedentary person.
6. Electronic ankle monitor alerts authorities whenever you leave the yard.
5. Two words: dung beetles.
4. Then what's the point of even having a hammock?
3. If God had wanted us to hike, He wouldn't have given us cars.
2. There's a strong possibility you might run into me on the trail.
1. Uneven terrain could cause you to spill your margarita.

PHOENIX AND THE VALLEY OF THE SUN

WEST VALLEY

I don't believe there's an urban area like metro Phoenix anywhere else in the country. With its sea of rooftops, web of freeways, and legion of Circle Ks, it resembles plenty of other cityscapes. But look closer. The skyline here is not defined by skyscrapers but by mountains.

Rough desert slopes rise in every corner of the Valley. They are often surrounded by vast tracts of intact desert. Tens of thousands of acres of green-space has been set aside as city parks and preserves. And the entire Valley is ringed by more than a dozen large county parks. National forest land pushes up against the city edge, and a collection of enticing lakes beckon from the outskirts.

What this all means is that you'll find lots of great hiking opportunities here despite the urban density. And thanks to that urban density, incredible burger joints are plentiful.

At least 22 incorporated cities cover more than 14,000 square miles in Maricopa County and Pinal County, comprising the area known as the Valley of the Sun, or simply the Valley. It's called the Valley of the Sun because, well, you know.

It also means use extreme caution when hiking here during warmer months. Stay hydrated, and hike only in the cooler morning and evening hours.

Views from Yavapai Point Trail showcase a mix of desert and water. Photo by the author.

Yavapai Point Trail, Lake Pleasant Regional Park

A big chunk of desert north of Phoenix lies submerged beneath cool blue water. Lake Pleasant Regional Park presents eye-popping contrast, its rough hills whiskered with saguaros surround a middle-of-nowhere oasis. It is a paradise for kayaking, boating, fishing, swimming, camping, even scuba diving. But since this book is called *Boots and Burgers*, not *Flippers and Fries*, I'll focus on the hiking.

A variety of trails fan out across the park. Some follow the shoreline or ramble across open desert. Watch for wild burros on any hike since the area supports a population of them. There's even a Wild Burro Trail where sightings are common.

Yavapai Point Trail, which climbs to an overlook above the water, dishes up the best views. Quickest access starts from Cottonwood Day Use Area. Set out on Pipeline Canyon Trail for 0.2 miles to the signed Yavapai Point junction. You'll aim toward the lake and enjoy a few teasing flashes of blue. There's plenty more to come.

After passing a second junction with Pipeline Canyon Trail, Yavapai Point snakes into the hills. No mountain bikes or horses are allowed past this point. The angle of ascent steepens a bit and switchbacks begin. Views extend down narrow Pipeline Canyon as that trail continues toward its southern terminus. During spring wildflower season, consider starting from the southern end of Pipeline Canyon Trail (off North Park Road). It's a longer hike to Yavapai Point but brings you through a corridor of poppies, lupines, and brittlebush lining that end of the gorge.

Over the final switchbacks, Yavapai Point turns rockier as saguaros and chollas bunch together. A window of vividly blue water appears through a notch in the hills and widens. Finally, the trail swings around from the backside slope and crosses the crest of the hill.

Lake Pleasant spreads out below, dotted with islands, as waves of mountains recede toward the horizon. The lake profile changes through the year as water levels fluctuate. Pleasant catches runoff from the Agua Fria River but also serves as a storage reservoir for the Central Arizona Project. More water from the Colorado River is pumped into Lake Pleasant during fall and winter and then water is released in spring and summer to meet higher demands.

The water rises and falls with the seasons, but there is always more than enough to bring joy to this arid terrain. I plopped down on a hilltop bench and watched a skier carve designs across the lake's surface. Kayakers hugged the shoreline and campers relaxed in the sand along Fireman's Cove. We had all come to the middle of the desert to celebrate a pool of water.

Where: Lake Pleasant Regional Park is located 15 miles west of Interstate-17. Take the Carefree Highway and turn north on Castle Hot Springs Rd. Continue past the main gate and enter through the north gate. Turn right on Cottonwood Ln. The trailhead is at the end of the road.

Cost: Admission fee.

Difficulty: Moderate.

Length: 3.4 miles round-trip.

Dogs: Yes, on a leash.

Details: (602) 506-2930 ext. 2, www.maricopacountyparks.net.

Hot Tip: The Discovery Center at Lake Pleasant offers visitors a good introduction to the lake with exhibits on history, wildlife, plant communities, and information on upcoming events. Spotting scopes and signage on the balcony help identify points of interest that range from features of the dam to the distant ridge of Four Peaks. Kids will love the adjacent playground filled with animal-themed slides and swings.

Peoria Artisan Brewery, Peoria

Filling a corner of a big shopping plaza, Peoria Artisan Brewery looks like a typical craft brewery. A small bar and tables fill the main room swaddled in dark paneling except for a wall of windows displaying the brewing operation. More tables are out back on a shady patio. When the meal arrives, you know you came to the right place.

They serve serious food here, featuring a rotating seasonal menu. Highlighting the choices are a strong lineup of burgers made using Arizona Angus beef. The most popular is the PAB burger, smeared with bacon jam, then rounded off with lettuce, tomato, onion, muenster cheese, and aioli. But I ventured further afield and tried the PAB&J topped with smoked bacon, cherry jam, and chipotle peanut butter on a brioche bun.

Peanut butter-laden burgers have been around for years, but I always steered clear. Not sure why. Two lifelong favorites of mine—you'd think they belonged in each other's arms. Yet I always pictured it as a relationship doomed from the start like Tony and Maria from *West Side Story* or Pepé Le Pew and the

With a dozen house brews on tap and burgers made with Arizona Angus beef, there's plenty to like at Peoria Artisan Brewery. Courtesy of Rick Mortensen, Phoenix.

paint-streaked cats he always mistook for skunks. But the PAB&J proved to be a revelation. Good earthy flavors offset by the sweetness of the jam. The thin layer of peanut butter never intruded but danced around the edges. It paired beautifully with the crisp notes of their Precocious Pilsner, one of a dozen house brews and six guest beers on tap that day.

Another tough decision was choosing a side dish. I narrowed it down to dirty fries or fried pickled vegetables. The fries are seasoned with house-made spices, and the veg medley is lightly breaded and fried to a delicate crunch. I had both and still can't decide which was better.

Vegetarian Options: Any burger can be made with a black bean patty. They also have salads, buffalo cauliflower, a veggie sandwich, and skillet-baked mac and cheese with a three-cheese crust.
Don't Forget: Along with a flight of beers you can enjoy the dirty fry bar; house-cut Kennebec potatoes, seasoned or not, along with any four scratch-made dipping sauces.
Details: 10144 W. Lake Pleasant Pkwy., (623) 572-2816, www.peoriaartisanbrewing.com.

Hot Tip: The Pioneer Living History Museum features 20 historic buildings spread across 90 acres. Learn what life was like in Territorial Arizona, aided by costumed volunteers. Some buildings have been reconstructed, but many are original like the "Flying V" cabin with rifle ports built by John Tewksbury, who was killed in the bloody Pleasant Valley War. Located just off I-17 north of the Carefree Highway, the museum closes for part of the summer.

Circumference–Palisade Loop, Deem Hills Recreation Area

Covering 1,000 acres in northwest Phoenix, the Deem Hills Recreation Area provides an unexpected little escape. Two hills are crisscrossed by a web of trails and include a large community park at the main west trailhead. That's where visitors will find a playground, soccer field, and dog park. Since I was only here for the hiking, I pulled up at the smaller, quieter east-side trailhead.

This section of the park also features slopes shrouded in basalt. According to trailhead signage, the basalt is the remnants of ancient lava flows from volcanoes in the Flagstaff area that broke through the earth's surface here in the desert. For the rest of the hike, I was obsessed with the fact that there's an underground lava tube, an old molten subway, beneath I-17, stretching all the way to Flag. How did I never know this?

I showed up in the fall and realized the Deem Hills should be on everybody's Halloween hiking list. With slopes as black as a witch's hat, they make a slightly haunting, apocalypse-flavored getaway—just right for the season. All sorts of options are available via the network of interconnected trails. The Circumference Trail wraps a winding loop around the entire recreation area. The Ridgeline Trail climbs to the highest points in the park.

Since this was my second hike of the day, I wanted something quick and quiet. Combining Circumference Trail with Palisade made a stealthy loop under 3 miles while showcasing city views and rough backcountry.

I started on Circumference, then immediately turned uphill on paved Water Tower Road. After just a quarter mile the Palisade Trail branches to the left and I took it, climbing through a field of dark basalt boulders adding that seasonal touch of menace. But this is also a peaceful outing. Despite modest temperatures and lovely vistas, the trail was practically deserted.

Atop the hill, Palisade intersects and joins Basalt Trail for a short jog through desert scrub before separating. Soon afterward, Palisade bends sharply east following a ridge. Views stretch to different corners of the Valley highlighting suburbs, mountains, and the thin line of the canal that cuts north of Deem Hills. This is part of the Central Arizona Project, the 336-mile system providing water to the central and southern portions of the state.

I passed a couple of connector paths to Circumferencc Trail, one right after another. Handy in case you need to shave off a little time. But I followed Palisade until it dead-ends at Circumference after 1.5 miles. A left on Circumference and I made my way back down the slope that's covered with the well-traveled blood of prehistoric volcanoes.

Where: Trailhead is at 27428 N. 39th Ave. From Phoenix, travel north on I-17 to Happy Valley Rd. exit. Turn west and continue 1 mile, turning right on 35th Ave. The road twists and turns for 1.5 miles, becoming Pocono Way, then 33rd Ave. Turn left on Pinnacle Vista for 0.7 miles to 39th Ave. Turn right and trailhead is on the left.

Cost: Free.

Difficulty: Moderate.

Length: 2.7 miles round-trip.

Dogs: Yes, on a leash.

Details: (602) 495-6939, www.phoenix.gov/parks.

Hot Tip: The Deer Valley Petroglyph Preserve is a museum and easily accessed archaeological site near the Deem Hills. A short interpretive trail leads to an amazing concentration of ancient figures and symbols etched into the rocks by the people who once lived in this desert. The preserve is operated by Arizona State University.

Original Hamburger Works, Phoenix

I'm glad this place serves great burgers because I would show up just for the signs. I have a weakness for vintage signs, and a terrific collection adorns the walls here. Amid classic Coke and Pepsi signs are others championing Barq's and even Double Cola. Man, that one takes me back. Sinclair Gas, Clabber Girl Baking Powder, and Phoenix favorite Mary Coyle Ice Cream are represented. It relaxes me being surrounded by so much nostalgia, and I'm grateful the joint is not the Original Haggis Works because I'd probably choke down an occasional sheep stomach just for the privilege.

Fortunately, Original Hamburger Works provides an even more

Vintage signs adorn the walls and burgers fly off the grill at Original Hamburger Works. Courtesy of Rick Mortensen, Phoenix.

compelling reason to visit: mesquite-broiled burgers cooked over an open flame, along with chicken and hot dogs. Standing in line to order gave me an up-close look at the process. From behind a window, the cook spatulas rows of patties from the broiler amid sudden eruptions of orange flame. It's like watching a magic show as the grill man disappears in a cloud of smoke and then reappears again.

The menu includes five specialty burgers. Six, if you count the Retirement Burger, which will set you back $1,050,060 but includes the restaurant and company car. If you want cheese with that, you have to shell out 50 cents more.

Better still, choose your burger dimensions (they range from 3 ounces all the way up to a pound) and then drag it through the wagon loaded with toppings and condiments. Create your ideal burger. The tomatoes and leaf lettuce seemed quite fresh, and they stock those old-school neon green pickle slices that are becoming harder to find. I pile on enough of everything to create my own side salad from the spillage. Now I can imagine I'm eating healthy.

I sat beside a sign that encouraged me to "Drink Coca-Cola in Bottles," and dug into my mesquite-kissed burger that was smoky and tender. The chargrilled flavor swept me back to summer cookouts. This beats sheep stomach any day.

Vegetarian Options: A garden burger and several salad options are available.
Don't Forget: Besides the dining area swaddled in vintage signs, there's a full bar and televisions in the other room.
Details: 2801 N. 15th Ave., (602) 263-8693, www.greatburgeraz.com.

Fast Fact: Phoenix is the only state capital with a population of more than one million residents.

Dixie Mountain Loop, Phoenix Sonoran Preserve

This trail has an urban address, but it beats with a wild country heart. It quickly pulls you away from civilization in the Phoenix Sonoran Preserve. The preserve comprises more than 9,600 acres broken into two units, south and north. The Dixie Mountain Loop spins a circle through the southern portion.

From Desert Vista Trailhead, start out on Hawks Nest Trail. It makes a short (0.4 mile) climb to a small saddle. Near the top of the trail look to the left for a saguaro holding a big branchy nest that in recent years has been occupied by owls.

The trail ends at Dixie Mountain Loop, fanning out in both directions. According to the website, going counterclockwise softens the ascents so that's what I did. But I seemed to be the only one. Several hikers passed me heading in the opposite direction, so maybe locals have a different opinion. Either way, it's a pretty gentle ramble.

The city vanishes behind a ring of hills and I was left with unbroken desert. Following recent storms, the slopes were pleasingly green. Rain-swollen barrel cacti were plump as baby walruses. Teddy bear chollas seem to be everywhere. They are the Ewoks of the desert, small and cuddly, yet they'll stab you in a heartbeat. These fuzzy assassins are not to be trifled with. Yet something wonderful happens at certain times of the day. The right slant of sunlight splinters on those spines in small silver bursts. For a few moments it seems as if each little cactus is lit from within, emitting a warm glow meant just for me. They are mesmerizing—from a safe distance. Watch for stray cholla segments in the trail eager to hitch a ride on any passing boot.

Glimpses of the city reemerge only sporadically before vanishing again. The trail narrows in spots and is almost entirely exposed, so be prepared for relentless sunshine. To spice up your workout, two spur trails offer short but

Morning light illuminates groves of teddy bear cholla along the Dixie Mountain Loop. Photo by the author.

mildly steep summit climbs reaching the highest peaks in the southern section of the preserve. And how often do you get a chance to bag two peaks on one hike? The Dixie Mountain Summit Trail makes a rocky twisting ascent for 0.2 miles to a high perch with impressive views. Farther along, the Western Vista Trail makes a slightly longer but less demanding climb.

Near the end of my hike, I passed the rusted skeleton of an old SUV, nose down in an arroyo. I pondered the lengths desert dwellers will go to find a shady parking spot. One last moderate climb and I was back at Hawk's Nest. With a healthy population of brittlebush and other assorted wildflowers, Dixie Mountain often blazes with color in spring.

Where: Trailhead is at 1900 W. Desert Vista Trail. From Phoenix, travel north on I-17 to Jomax Rd. exit. Take Jomax 0.9 miles to North Valley Pkwy., turn left (north) and continue 0.9 miles to Copperhead Tr. Turn right and then take the second left on Melvern Tr., followed by a quick right on W. Desert Vista.

Cost: Free.

Difficulty: Moderate.

Length: 4.6 miles round-trip, or 5.6 miles including both summit climbs.

Dogs: Yes, on a leash.

Details: (602) 495-6939, www.phoenix.gov/parks.

"If I couldn't walk fast and far, I think I should just explode and perish."

CHARLES DICKENS

The Stand Arcadia Burger Shoppe, Arcadia

Feel free to hike the hottest, hardest, dustiest trail you can manage before rolling up to this little joint. Go ahead, bring the sweat-stains, a layer of trail dirt, even funky body odor. It doesn't matter because you're not going inside anyway.

The Stand is drive-thru only. Two lanes wrap around the building adorned in bright colors and eye-catching murals. They need twin lanes to keep up with demand from their devoted fan base. That stems from the fresh beef that's ground every morning, carefully selected fresh produce, house-made sauces, and old-timey hand-scooped, hand-spun milkshakes.

They only offer five burgers. The Standard is piled high with veggies and homemade sauce. The Big Kahuna starts with The Standard and then throws on pineapple, thick-cut bacon, and honey lava sauce. When it comes to side dishes, hand-cut fries are the only option. Why tamper with the classics?

It's the shakes that force the tough decisions. They advertise several: chocolate, vanilla, salted dulce de leche, chocolate chile, banana stand, cookies n' cream, cold brew coffee, and strawberry. But if you're looking for more of a secret-menu vibe, they also whip up other flavors at times. And if that's not agonizing enough, you can order combination milkshakes. Chocolate dulce de leche, strawberry banana . . . the mind reels.

Just don't confuse this with fast food because you snagged it from a drive-thru. You're not going to eat while driving. This carefully crafted feast deserves your full attention. They double-bag orders, wrapping it nice and tight. It will stay hot and fresh for several minutes. If you don't live in the vicinity, no worries. Just drive your sweaty grimy self to a nearby park. There are a couple, so you can sink your teeth into something wonderful without distractions.

Vegetarian Options: It's worth a trip just for the milkshakes.

Don't Forget: If you need a nearby park to relax and enjoy your burger, there's Los Olivos Park Place Plaza (2802 E. Devonshire Ave.) and little Kachina Park at 4304 E. Campbell Ave.

Details: 3538 E. Indian School Rd., (602) 314-5259, www.thestandphx.com.

Waterfall Trail, White Tank Mountain Regional Park (ADA Accessible)

Forget I mentioned this one. Better just skip this trail altogether. I don't know what I was thinking. It's often crowded and partially paved. And lastly, there's not even a waterfall most of the time.

On the other hand . . .

It's easy and accessible. It will lead you to some amazing petroglyphs, offers lovely scenery, and occasionally showcases a cascade of water tumbling down a cliff in the middle of the desert. Water. Falling. In the desert.

Whatever you do, don't miss this trail!

The Waterfall Trail is tucked away in White Tank Mountain Regional Park anchoring the far western edge of the Valley of the Sun. The White Tanks are a freestanding range of rough-cut mountains. A large natural basin, known as a tank, once held water all year round. Surrounded by white granite cliffs, the waterhole became an important stop for prospectors and travelers. It also provided the name for the mountains.

Containing nearly 30,000 acres, White Tank is the largest of the Maricopa County parks. It includes a nature center, branch library, amphitheater, picnic areas, campgrounds, and 33 miles of trails. Some of the longer trails are considered extremely difficult. At just under a mile, the Waterfall Trail is not one of those.

For the first 0.5 miles the Waterfall Trail is flat, paved, and barrier-free. This section can be managed by wheelchairs and strollers, but keep in mind it is often crowded. One of the reasons that many people flock to this trail is simple. While the waterfall itself may be ephemeral, another attraction stays put.

Fast Fact: Despite being the hottest North American desert, the Sonoran Desert is the most biologically diverse thanks to two annual rainy seasons.

Just before the pavement ends, you reach Petroglyph Plaza. Here dozens of symbols are etched into the desert varnish, which is the dark coating on the rocks. Most were made by the Ancestral Sonoran Desert people, and date back more than 800 years. Some were made by the Archaic people, hunters and gatherers who traveled these lands, and are much older. Do not touch or deface the rocks in any way.

As I left pavement and petroglyphs behind, the trail narrowed and became a little more rugged following a rocky ravine up the slope. The wash is usually dry but if there are pools or even—be still my heart—flowing water, then that bodes well for a potential cascade at the end of the line. Rock walls rose up around me, enclosing the path. A light veil of coolness fell as I approached the cliffs. Moisture-kissed shade spilled down from the high ramparts.

There's a short climb at the end as I entered the stone-wrapped cul-de-sac. At the base of the cliff sat a pool of water. The waterfall only runs after heavy rain, usually in winter and spring or immediately following a monsoon storm. I've seen photos and it can be a torrent, however fleeting. That's not the case on my visit. Yet the back wall is caressed by a trickle. The faint echo of a splash sounds like a hummingbird gargling. But I am content. All seems right with the world. Water falls in the desert.

Where: From Phoenix, take I-10 west to the 303. Go north on the 303 to the exit for Northern Ave. (110A). Turn west on Northern, and then turn right on Cotton Ln. to Olive Ave. Turn left on Olive, driving west 5 miles to the park entrance. Continue 2 miles to Waterfall Canyon Rd.
Cost: Admission fee.
Difficulty: Easy.
Length: 1.9 miles round-trip.
Dogs: Yes, on a leash.
Details: (602) 506-2930 ext. 5, www.maricopacountyparks.net.

Hot Tip: If your sweet tooth throbs like mine, pay a visit to Cerreta Candy Company in Glendale. The family-owned factory has been producing candy, nuts, barks, brittles, toffees, and popcorn for decades. They offer short factory tours on weekdays. Watching it being made is almost as much fun as trying a few samples. Almost.

Benny's Burgers & BBQ, Sun City

This cheery counter-serve eatery sits near a busy corner in a shopping plaza yet still manages to feel like a neighborhood burger joint. On a Saturday afternoon the place hosts just about every demographic imaginable. A table of teens were chowing down on tasty looking wings. A senior couple sampled each other's milkshakes. And a young family laughed with the counter person while waiting for a to-go order.

I'm not sure what demographic group I fall into—grizzled, grumpy, burger-chasing hikers, I guess. But there I was tucking into one of Benny's classics. The thin flame-grilled patty is piled with toppings and smeared with a mustard-ketchup blend. I like that they offer mustard-ketchup pairing as one of their sauces. That's totally an old-school move. This burger comes with a side of memories. Combining mustard and ketchup was the aioli of the 1960s.

The Spicy Mango Bacon Burger from Benny's offers a medley of flavors and textures. Courtesy of Rick Mortensen, Phoenix.

Yet Benny's serves up more than nostalgia. They create an assortment of specialty burgers you're unlikely to find elsewhere, like the sweet and spicy Korean Burger that comes with sauteed mushrooms, crispy bacon, and a zesty Asian slaw. Or the popular Spicy Mango Burger that combines pico de gallo, bacon, freshly diced mango, and their house-made chipotle sauce. Those kinds of options, along with barbecued spare ribs, hot dogs, sandwiches, wings, and Korean tacos, appeal to the less grizzled among us. This neighborhood joint welcomes everyone.

And don't think for a minute I'm hopelessly mired in the past. On my next visit, I'm totally snagging a Korean Burger.

Vegetarian Options: A veggie burger is on the menu, along with a couple of side salads and fried vegetables.

Don't Forget: If you're a fan of spicy food, ask for an extra kick of heat on your dish. They'll gladly oblige.

Details: 10001 W. Bell Rd., (623) 815-2156, www.bennysburgershop.com.

Freedom Trail, Piestewa Peak

I can't imagine a more appropriate name for this trail that throws a lasso around Piestewa Peak. Right in the heart of town, it hustles you away from civilization and into lonesome desert in no time flat.

Rising to 2,608 feet, Piestewa Peak towers above the Phoenix Mountains Preserve. The trail to the summit is one of the Valley's busiest trails, a teeming thoroughfare of sweaty humanity. The Freedom Trail circles the base of the mountain and, other than the short segment it shares with the Summit Trail, is sparsely traveled, a secret hiding in plain sight.

Once you enter Phoenix Mountains Preserve, you can access the Freedom Trail from several points. Often parking areas near the Summit Trail will be crowded. Just continue a little farther to one of the other lots.

Cross the wash that runs like an out-of-service moat at the base of the mountain and scramble up the other side where you'll find the Freedom Trail #302. Hang a right. The Freedom shares its route with other trails, so you'll see them joining and departing at various junctions. Just follow the 302 markers and remember you're circling Piestewa Peak, so keep the mountain over your left shoulder.

Fast Fact: Piestewa Peak is named in honor of Arizona soldier, Lori Piestewa, who was killed in action in Iraq in 2003. A member of the Hopi tribe, Piestewa was the first Native American woman killed in combat in a foreign war.

The trail begins climbing, passing informational signage and a memorial bench as it points toward a prominent saddle. The saddle is the high point of the trail, where more benches give you a chance to pause and enjoy long views.

Descending from the notch, the trail cuts across the slope through a cluster of jagged rock formations. This is my favorite section. I dawdled through here enjoying the angular eye candy thrusting in all directions. Even in the middle of the city this trail gives you a taste of desert mystery. I never tire of that feeling. In Arizona, you don't have to go far to get your heart squeezed.

It's a long traverse for the next mile overlooking residential neighborhoods. Then another climb to a saddle as it swings back around the mountain. At the crest you join the bustling Summit Trail, which is more open-air gym than hiking route. Among the crowd you'll likely see lots of toned, fit people in carefully selected outfits. They even sweat in a sultry manner. Scramble down the rocky ledges to the bottom of the hill and head back to your car.

Where: In Phoenix, take AZ 51 (Piestewa Freeway) to the Lincoln Dr. exit. Head east for 0.5 miles on Lincoln and turn left on Piestwa Peak Dr. Proceed into the preserve.
Cost: Free.
Difficulty: Moderate.
Length: 3.7-miles round-trip.
Dogs: Leashed dogs are allowed with one large caveat. Dogs are not permitted on the section shared with the Summit Trail. If you want to complete the loop, leave the pups at home.
Details: (602) 261-8318, www.phoenix.gov/parks.

Hot Tip: S'edav Va'aki Museum is a 1,500-year-old archaeological site once inhabited by the Ancestral Sonoran Desert people, known to archaeologists as Hohokam. Visitors can walk a loop trail exploring a platform mound, ball court, replica houses, demonstration garden, and ancient irrigation canals. The canal system built by the Ancestral Sonoran Desert people would become the basis for the founding of Phoenix centuries later. Exhibits inside the museum provide additional insight into how these resourceful people lived.

Harvey's Wineburger, Phoenix

This is the Arizona burger that haunts me. This is the burger I dream about. No matter how dark it is inside Harvey's, those glorious, stellar burgers shine like a beacon that always guides me back.

Harvey's Wineburger is a dive bar dating back to the late 1950s. It is dark inside. Day-drinking dark. Moe's Tavern dark. When the door opens to briefly reveal a sliver of sunlight, I always expect the other patrons to turn and hiss, revealing vampire fangs. It is a cavern of liquor and darts. Harvey's also just happens to be a cathedral of flavorful, juicy hamburgers—quite possibly the best in the state.

There's something about a dive bar burger. Something in the attitude. They just come off the flattop with a swagger. But Harvey's offers more than that. The quality of the meat, the careful prep and cooking process, and the complex seasoning held within that historic griddle all combine to create an Arizona sunset of a burger, brilliant and unforgettable.

They start with just a shade under a half pound of fresh certified Angus chuck. It's prepped into balls of rich premium meat, then hand pressed at order. The burger is seared with a light crust, then splashed with a generous gulp of red wine and immediately covered with a lid sealing in the juices. The result is a beefy masterpiece. A Mona Lisa smile of a burger. Plump as baby legs, ripe as a summer peach, a juicier burger does not exist in this world. It goes beyond juicy. Harvey's Wineburger is sumptuous. Like biting into a rain cloud. It is plush and silken, a resplendent caramelized structure with just enough charred crust to hold the package together. Each bite absolutely melts in my mouth. I break off pieces and gobble them like beef candy.

There are a few specialty burgers and add-ons, but honestly, I don't want the distractions. On my last visit I had gobbled my entire burger plain before I realized I hadn't added a smear of mustard. Harvey's always served an

Luscious, plump, and impossibly juicy, the wineburgers at Harvey's may be the best bar meal to be had in Arizona. Photo by the author.

excellent burger, but they upgraded their meat a few years ago under a new owner. Now the burgers occupy a whole new level. Yes, they're on the beef candy level.

Vegetarian Options: A grilled cheese and a few appetizers are on the limited menu, but there's no meatless version of the wineburger.
Don't Forget: Even though Harvey's is a dive bar, you can also drink in style. They carry a selection of hard-to-find specialty bourbons.
Details: 4812 N. 16th St., (602) 248-9950, www.harveyswineburger.com.

Kiwanis Trail, South Mountain Park & Preserve

I rated this South Mountain trail as easy because, frankly, the book needed a few more easy trails. But if you want to call it moderate, I won't bust your chops. Hey, I get it. When I'm swapping trail stories with my buddies, you'd think every hike I take is a grueling death march almost beyond the realm of human endurance.

The Kiwanis Trail does gain 500 feet, so it's a bit of a climb. On the other hand, it's short, only a mile long, footing is good, and there are lots of interesting details, which also makes this a great kid-friendly hike. Go ahead and call it moderate, just don't mention any 8-year-olds that scurry past you.

Despite the name, South Mountain isn't some towering standalone peak. The park protects three mountain ranges—the Gila, Guadalupe, and Ma Ha Tauk—and spreads across 16,000 acres. With more than 50 miles of trails crisscrossing the landscape, there's plenty to explore. Kiwanis makes a great introduction.

The trail starts out level as it threads its way through a shallow, cupped canyon. Knowledgeable hikers will quickly recognize the skilled hand of the Civilian Conservation Corps (CCC) that left behind such a remarkable legacy

Fast Fact: The fourth Sunday of each month is Silent Sunday at South Mountain Park & Preserve. The park's main roadway is closed to motor vehicle traffic. During this time the park roads may be used for walking, jogging, and cycling. Shorter road closures take place on all other Sundays in the mornings and evenings. Check the website for hours.

Brittlebush bloom along the Kiwanis Trail in South Mountain Park & Preserve. Photo by the author.

with their 1930s construction projects. The trail is mostly hard-packed gravel and stone steps contoured to drain quickly.

The slender gorge showcases a lush mix of desert vegetation. The canyon creates a natural channel funneling through rain runoff. Hills rise up the deeper you go, along with clusters of boulders. Watch for petroglyphs etched into rock faces dating back to Hohokam culture. Several panels can be spotted that include human, animal, and geometric designs. But use only your eyes. Never touch ancient rock art, as the oils from your skin can damage them. And don't clamber off-trail for a closer look, which degrades the habitat and puts you in all sorts of danger. (It's a well-known fact that rattlesnakes always guard petroglyphs.) Bring binoculars and keep your boots firmly rooted on the trail.

The going turns steeper halfway up. Glance back occasionally as slivers of city views continue to widen the higher you climb. Yet wrapped within the confines of this little canyon, it all feels far removed. A couple of check dams can still be seen in the drainages, compliments of the CCC.

A nice stand of saguaros lines the upper reaches of the trail, which ends abruptly at curvy Telegraph Pass Road. You can turn around here. Or cross the road and climb to Telegraph Pass lookout, an open-air stone hut with arched windows that resembles a gnome temple. It's a short but steep climb—absolutely securing your moderate trail rating—for a little cool shade within the stone walls, one last gift from the CCC. This path also pushes onto the 15-mile National Trail delving deeper into the backcountry of South Mountain.

One final note about Kiwanis Trail. If you plan your outing, this is one of those rare desert hikes that can be enjoyed during summer. It's short and the canyon walls provide shade in early morning and near sunset.

Where: From Phoenix, drive south on Central Ave., to the park's main entrance (10919 S. Central Ave.). The road curves west and passes a ranger station. Continue past the service road and turn left at the next junction. Turn left again on Piedras Dr. and follow it to Kiwanis Trailhead.
Cost: Free.
Difficulty: Easy/moderate.
Length: 2 miles round-trip, or 2.6 to the lookout tower.
Dogs: Yes, on a leash.
Details: (602) 262-7393, www.phoenix.gov/parks.

Hot Tip: The Heard Museum houses a renowned collection of Native American artifacts and artwork. This Smithsonian affiliate gives a contemporary voice to Native cultures. In addition to the high-quality collections, the Heard hosts educational programming and vibrant festivals.

Lucky Boy, Phoenix

If you cruised the streets of Phoenix in the 1950s and 1960s as a teenager, Lucky Boy was part of your route. It was a place where you could grab burgers, fries, and shakes with the gang. And according to every movie and television show ever made, that's what all teens did back then. A local chain, there were once nine Lucky Boys scattered around Phoenix absorbing much of the Brylcreem-fueled energy of the time. Only one survived. I like to support survivors.

Opened in 1951, the Lucky Boy on 16th Street and Osborn Road is a geometric sliver of a building tucked beside a Circle K. There's a drive-thru and a tiny parking lot. Inside it retains the vintage décor and menu that will stir a wave of nostalgia. Burger joints can do that. I lived in an entirely different part of the country in the 1960s, but the first time I walked through the door of Lucky Boy, I recognized it. First time I bit into one of their quarter-pound burgers, my taste buds took a stroll down memory lane. It was a comforting feeling. This was the flavor of mid-century Americana.

You can double, triple, or even quadruple the charbroiled patties. They come with a choice of sauces—tangy ranch, Thousand Island, barbecue sauce, or my choice, mustard and ketchup. All burgers include lettuce, tomato, onion, and pickle. Additional add-ons are available.

I always wonder if these old-fashioned burgers will resonate with people who didn't grow up with them. But my question was answered while I sat at the window counter happily munching. Everybody in the drive-thru was younger than me, several with kids in the back seat. Here they were, making memories of their own. Nice to know that grabbing burgers, fries, and shakes with the gang never goes out of style.

Vegetarian Options: Hey, they've got shakes and malts! Plus, a grilled cheese.
Don't Forget: Did I mention the shakes and malts? Very tasty.
Details: 3430 N. 16th St., (602) 274-6440.

Lookout Mountain Summit Trail, Phoenix Mountains Preserve

It's no secret that most hikers harbor peak-bagger tendencies. Within each beats the heart of a mountain climber. On long uphill stretches we like to imagine we're in the Death Zone, slogging to the top of Everest.

Every winter weekend, half the residents of Phoenix push for the summit of Camelback Mountain while the other half scramble to the top of Piestwa Peak. That's their backyard Everest and K2. As an alternative, consider the hike to the top of Lookout Mountain. It provides a fast workout, fewer crowds, plus excellent views. And I am all about easy access and fewer crowds. Bonus: You won't need supplemental oxygen.

Lookout is part of the Phoenix Mountains Preserve. There's a small lot with overflow parking on 16th Street. Both Circumference Trail (#308) and Summit Trail (#150) start together but quickly separate with 150 breaking to the left.

You'll angle up the north face of the slope, pointed toward a saddle. The short path zigzags up the hill but never gets excessively steep. Once you reach the saddle, the trail turns east and loses definition as it crosses a ridgeline of tilted rocks. It may require some scrambling as you make your way over it. At the end it levels off, and there are plenty of nice sitting rocks where you can soak in the surprisingly lavish vistas at the end of a 0.6-mile hike. The sea of rooftops is interrupted by assorted urban mountains. Enjoy this lovely perch then return the way you came.

Or consider another option. Lookout Mountain offers a twofer. Scale the summit and then circle around the base. Remember the Circumference Trail (#308) you briefly trod? It makes a 2.6-mile circle around Lookout. When you get back to the bottom, consider finishing that out.

The Circumference Trail starts off wide, then pinches down to a single-track. It never loses sight of neighborhoods but makes a nice rolling loop. Vegetation is thin on Lookout with only a smattering of saguaros. It's mostly palo verde trees and creosote, with a healthy population of barrel cacti as you

A hiker enjoys a well-earned panorama from the summit of Lookout Mountain. Photo by the author.

swing around from the backside, some of them tall and lanky, like saguaros going through puberty.

Where: The trailhead is at 15600 N. 16th St., south of Greenway Pkwy.
Cost: Free.
Difficulty: Moderate.
Length: 1.2 miles round-trip, 3.8 miles if combined with Circumference Trail
Dogs: Yes, on a leash. Dogs are prohibited when temperatures reach 100 degrees.
Details: (602) 262-7901, www.phoenix.gov/parks.

"Anybody who doesn't think that the best hamburger place in the world is in his hometown is a sissy."
CALVIN TRILLIN

Chicago Hamburger Company, Phoenix

If there's a restaurant with a more loyal fan base than Chicago Hamburger Company, I don't know it. During a lunch rush, I sat at a small corner table windmilling sliders into my burger-hole while a steady stream of customers came through the doors. Construction workers, road workers, medical personnel in scrubs, a baby-toting mom, retired guys in ballcaps, a cowboy—and just about everybody was greeted by name by the staff. Or vice versa. Soon as they walked in, they started ribbing the crew behind the counter. You don't find that much anymore. And the world is poorer for it.

This is a true neighborhood joint, right down to its marrow. The skinny room is a shrine to the Windy City. Walls are covered with Chicago memorabilia including sports posters, political signs, license plates, blues albums, transit maps, and framed newspaper articles dating back to Dillinger and Capone. The place may be skinny, but it has big shoulders.

The menu has that same distinctive voice. Vienna beef hot dogs steamed for plumpness, Italian beef sandwiches, Italian sausage mixed with sweet and hot peppers, and full-size burgers, one-third and two-thirds of a pound of fresh ground chuck cooked over an open flame. The Guacamole Burger comes heaped with melted provolone, sauteed onions, tomato, and a special house-made guac.

And let's not forget the legendary sliders. Nothing fancy or upscale about them. They are straightforward and direct, and bigger than you'd expect. That's the Chicago way. Topped with chopped onions, streaked with mustard and ketchup, the meat nestles on a fresh, supple dinner roll and arrives piping hot.

Those dinner rolls come from a local bakery. The sausage is local too. In fact, most of what they serve at Chicago Hamburger Company is sourced

Beloved by locals, Chicago Hamburger Co. is a longtime anchor of their Phoenix neighborhood. Courtesy of Rick Mortensen, Phoenix.

from small businesses, both in Phoenix and on the shores of Lake Michigan. How about that? A neighborhood joint looking out for its neighbors. You don't find that much anymore either.

Vegetarian Options: They make a veggie burger, plus a triple cheese sub with plenty of fixings on warm Italian bread, and also a garden salad.

Don't Forget: They grill bratwurst on Wednesday and Saturday.

Details: 3749 E. Indian School Rd., (602) 955-4137, www.chicagohamburger.com.

Hot Tip: The Desert Botanical Garden is a spectacular landscape, veined by nature trails and bristling with over 20,000 desert plants from around the world. Set amid the red rock buttes of Papago Park, the garden introduces visitors to the native plants and people of the desert regions. Indoor and outdoor exhibits, and plenty of hands-on activities, make this an excellent family outing.

North Mountain National Trail, Phoenix Mountains Preserve

Consider North Mountain a hill with benefits. It's not necessarily the hike you dream about, the hike you want to do the rest of your life. But it is always available. It's quick, uncomplicated, and you get a fast, calorie-burning workout right in the heart of Phoenix.

Designated as a National Recreation Trail, North Mountain throws just about everything at you. A portion is paved but the rest is steep, narrow, and rocky. Expect plenty of other hikers, and more communications towers and antennas than at NORAD. But you'll also be treated to some big panoramas and impressive sunsets.

Start from the Maricopa picnic area, which sits at the north end of the loop road into the North Mountain Recreation Area. Your workout starts right away as you climb a steep rocky slope to a saddle at 0.15 miles with a brown marker post bearing the number 44. These are the ones you'll follow. Turn left, going up a collection of steps until you reach a paved road.

Follow this service road to the summit. The pavement makes for easier walking but the grade remains steep. What I like about the road is that it's wide, so hikers tend to spread out. Even during busy times, it never feels too crowded. City views expanded as I climbed. This trail highlights how this urban area is choked with mountains. There's Piestewa Peak, Four Peaks, South Mountain, and a cluster of other summits I can't name but I'm sure the locals recognize.

There's a bench at the top where you can catch your breath. This makes a good turnaround point if you prefer to stick to the pavement, because climbing down the other side to complete the loop becomes a very different experience. Look for another brown post marking where the trail leaves the road and follows the ridgeline south for a few hundred feet.

Once the trail drops from the ridge, it doesn't fool around. You plunge downhill in a steep, rocky descent. Watch your footing. Keep to the left as the trail leads down the eastern side of the mountain. You'll pass another couple of trail markers, the final one at a three-way junction. Take a left and descend to the Quechan picnic area, the end of the trail. Walk north on the one-way road back to your vehicle.

Where: The trailhead is at 10600 N. 7th St., south of Thunderbird Rd.
Cost: Free.
Difficulty: Moderate.
Length: 1.6 miles round-trip.
Dogs: Yes, on a leash.
Details: (602) 262-7901, www.phoenix.gov/parks.

Aioli Gourmet Burgers, Phoenix

It took me years before I could try this place—just because of their name. As someone who avoids creamy mayo-based concoctions, I felt like this establishment and I had a philosophical disparity. Finally, I decided to focus not on our differences but on our shared interests, gourmet burgers.

When I walked through the doors at last, I discovered a bright and cheery space in the back corner of a shopping plaza. Clean lines, red accents, and a cute patio. I was instantly relieved when I spotted an old friend across the

Along with a brick-and-mortar restaurant, Aioli Gourmet Burgers also runs food trucks around town. Photo by the author.

room. Bottles of yellow mustard were lined up at the condiment and drink station. Whew!

Even though they are quite serious about the possibilities of aioli and offer all sorts of varieties with their burgers, it is not mandatory. When I told the kid at the counter not to let it anywhere near my burger, he never batted an eye. Better still, they really are grilling some gourmet burgers here.

Eight specialty burgers top the menu including the award-winning White Truffle Swiss Burger that comes with roasted mushrooms, caramelized onions, Swiss cheese, and white truffle aioli. They have an aioli for every burger including roasted garlic, black pepper, and barbecue. But my burger—smeared instead with mustard—still sang with flavor. It was utterly juicy and released a soft burst of beefiness at each bite. Perfectly made, it paired well with the slender fries that are golden and crispy.

I'm glad Aioli Gourmet Burgers and I arrived at this understanding. They follow their vision, I adhere to my stubborn ways, and we both benefit. While I dined at their brick-and-mortar location at 32nd St. and Shea, watch for their colorful food trucks across the Valley.

Vegetarian Options: Caesar salad and caprese salad are available, along with some interesting appetizers. You can also sub a plant-based Beyond patty for any burger.

Don't Forget: If you're ravenous but pressed for time, participate in the Triple Threat Challenge. Finish any three-patty burger, loaded fries, and a shake in under 15 minutes and everlasting fame is yours. Plus, a free T-shirt. Your face will be plastered on the Wall of Fame. Losers also receive a free shirt but their sad mug lands on the adjacent Wall of Shame.

Details: 10652 N. 32nd St., (602) 971-5555, www.aioliburger.com.

15 Signs You Live in Arizona

1. Seeing a river that contains actual water is cause for celebration.
2. You sneer at Daylight Saving Time.
3. You can name five great swimming holes without even trying.
4. Either you own horses or friends of yours do.
5. You actually have a favorite ghost town.
6. If you're ever a contestant on a game show that requires the correct pronunciation of words like "Mogollon," "Gila," and "Prescott," you're going home with big money.
7. You've driven to wine country without leaving the state.
8. You think Sedona has gotten too big but still cherish some amazing red rock memories.
9. Some of the greatest meals you've ever eaten have come from food trucks and taco stands.
10. You've replaced more windshields than windshield wiper blades.
11. It just doesn't feel like Christmas until luminarias are lit.
12. If a parking space is slightly shaded, you'll grab it, even if it is so far from your destination you have to Uber to the door.
13. Even though you pretend you're pulling off the interstate for a bathroom break, it's just an excuse to grab a slice of Jack Daniels pecan pie at Rock Springs Café.
14. Watching winter weather reports from other parts of the country is a secret guilty pleasure. Sometimes you make popcorn.
15. You've seen sunsets so rich with color they would make Van Gogh break his paintbrushes across his knee in frustration.

PHOENIX AND THE VALLEY OF THE SUN

EAST VALLEY

Scottsdale occupies a large portion of the East Valley and is best known for luxury resorts, art galleries, and ultra-trendy nightclubs. But that only tells one side of the story. They also have an unforgettable backyard.

It began with a few passionate activists. They formed the McDowell Sonoran Conservancy and fought to protect the mountains and desert of North Scottsdale, most of which was private land ripe for development. The grassroots effort continued to expand despite overwhelming odds. Political leaders got on board and Scottsdale residents voted in favor of sales tax increases to raise money to purchase land. The result is the largest urban preserve in the United States, a crown jewel of outdoor recreation, and a reminder that just a few determined people can make a difference.

Established in 1995, the McDowell Sonoran Preserve encompasses more than 30,000 acres and includes more than 225 miles of trails. Thanks to the community effort, a full one-third of Scottsdale remains pristine, public open space.

Hikers in the East Valley have room to ramble. This is also where you'll find the Tonto National Forest, Superstition Mountains, sparkling lakes, and other impressive parks and mountain ranges. It's a good place to work up an appetite.

Multiple boulder fields are scattered along the winding Gooseneck Trail. Photo by the author.

Gooseneck Trail, McDowell Sonoran Preserve

For me it was love at first sight.

I studied the long wiggly squiggly line on the map and thought, that's a trail I need to hike. There were twists and turns aplenty but all with a clear aim. For nearly 7 miles the Gooseneck Trail flows in long sinuous curves carving a direct route through the central region of Scottsdale's McDowell Sonoran Preserve. Most of the preserve's 30,000 acres are spread across the broad northern and southern regions with scenic blends of rugged mountains and desert plains. But the slender pipeline of the central section knits them together.

Starting from the Fraesfield Trailhead, Gooseneck ambles west before crossing the road and turning south. Soon as traffic noise fades, things get interesting. The trail begins to weave through creosote flats sprinkled with clusters of oddly configured boulders.

The hunks of granite first caught my attention, lots of angles and textures, but I also studied the greenery. The creosote is one of the desert's hardiest plants, sinking roots where even cacti fear to grow. The shrubs are an explosion of spindly branches sporting small waxy leaves and a spray of yellow flowers. There always seems to be an unruly madness about them. Yet they have a special gift. They turn water into perfume.

It's creosote that releases the sweetly pungent fragrance whenever it rains in the desert, the scent known as petrichor. No aroma is as haunting or evocative to a desert dweller. A thousand memories come wafting back when we smell creosote holding handfuls of rain. Along this portion of the Gooseneck Trail are some of the most robust creosote plants I've ever seen, like a thin forest. All I could think was that I desperately needed to hike this trail again on a drizzly dreamy day.

I even stumbled onto some middle-of-nowhere water from a recent storm.

A pond filled a shallow basin, no doubt a stock tank from ranching days lapping against a berm lined with mesquite trees. I studied the muddy edge of the tank trying to read the hieroglyphics formed by countless animal tracks as a flock of swifts performed aerial acrobatics. We were all pretty happy about this water situation.

Soon after leaving the mini-lake behind, the trail crosses low hills that push against the wall of the McDowell Mountains. Saguaros gather and clumps of boulders return, except now they're bigger, more belligerent somehow. Gooseneck ends at its junction with Rock Knob Trail near the base of the mountains. The granite spire of Tom's Thumb is visible along the ridgeline. It's just over a half mile to reach Tom's Thumb Trailhead if you're doing a two-car shuttle.

Even though you'll be tempted, don't save this trail for a rainy day. You'll find plenty of desert magic along Gooseneck no matter what the weather.

Where: Fraesfield Trailhead is at 13400 E. Rio Verde Dr.
Cost: Free.
Difficulty: Easy.
Length: 13 miles round-trip.
Dogs: Yes, on a leash.
Details: (480) 998-7971, www.mcdowellsonoran.org.

Hot Tip: Famed architect Frank Lloyd Wright was one of the Valley of the Sun's earliest snowbirds. He built a winter home called Taliesin West in the foothills of the McDowell Mountains in the 1930s. Today it is the headquarters of the Frank Lloyd Wright Foundation and UNESCO World Heritage Site. It is open for tours and programs.

Happy's Hamburgers, Scottsdale

By swanky Scottsdale standards, Happy's Hamburgers is a hole-in-the-wall. And I mean that in the most affectionate way possible. Happy's is everything I want in a burger joint—simple, unpretentious, and delicious—tucked away amid a hodgepodge of shops. Cozy and welcoming, Happy's leans toward a 50s-style diner/malt shop vibe with tables scattered across the black-and-white checkerboard floor.

The burger is old-fashioned as well; fresh Angus patties wrapped in caramelized onions nestled on a soft steamed bun. It's all about the preparation starting with burgers rolled into plump meatballs. Thin-sliced onions are tossed on the grill and smashed into the beef, creating a divine synergy.

You can trace onion-smashed burgers back a century to El Reno,

Scrumptious sliders are always a popular choice at Happy's Hamburgers. Courtesy of Rick Mortensen, Phoenix.

Oklahoma. Trying to survive hard times in the 1920s when beef was costly and onions were cheap, restaurant owners decided to add onions to stretch their meat supply. Since it also creates a fantastic burger, it quickly caught on. The onions fry and caramelize in the burger juices, melding flavors and raising the moisture content. Burgers are absolutely luscious wrapped in the sweetness of onions. The fresh steamed bun is still warm, creating a soft, succulent pillow of pure deliciousness.

They cover all sizes of appetite at Happy's, starting with their sliders. Signature burgers come as double patties. And those with a serious appetite can dig into one of their handcrafted half-pounders, like the Pizza Burger draped with pepperoni, mozzarella, parmesan cheese, and house-made marinara sauce. And for those that might need their beefy fix in the morning, try the Breakfast Burger, a signature onion-infused ground beef patty stacked with American cheese, fried egg, and hash brown patty. What a way to start your day! Happy isn't just the name of the place. It's how you feel walking out.

Vegetarian Options: Veggie burger and breakfast muffin are on the menu.
Don't Forget: Happy's offers frosty shakes and homemade cheesecake.
Details: 10435 N. Scottsdale Rd., (480) 630-2330, www.happyshamburgers.com.

Granite Mountain Loop, McDowell Sonoran Preserve

I've often said that despite sharp and spiny fingers, the Arizona desert has an uncanny ability to steal your heart. This trail proves it. Immerse yourself in a land of texture and drama. Granite Mountain Loop is a boulder-strewn peak, one of five prominent mountains in the northern half of the McDowell Sonoran Preserve.

From the Granite Mountain Trailhead I set out on the Bootlegger Trail, angling northwest toward a rocky skyline. For 0.7 miles Bootlegger curls through a corridor of big stone slabs and quiet pools of desert. I turned onto Saddlehorn for a short jog before connecting with the 4.2-mile Granite Mountain Loop.

The trail stays along the lower slope of the mountain as it makes a languid circle around it. This is a peaceful stretch of scenic desert, and I have to remind myself that I'm still in luxurious Scottsdale. The combination of weathered boulders blended with a cactus forest proves intriguing. There's always some new shape to see, a fresh detail to focus on. The rocks here have character and personality.

Granite Mountain changes tone from the western flank. It seems steeper, more rugged. I can't resist making a short detour, turning onto the Balanced Rock Trail. It's only 0.3 miles to the namesake formation, a weird multi-ton mushroom of stone that has no business still being upright. But then neither do I. Feels like we're kindred spirits. Battered by sun and heat, wind and rain, we haven't toppled yet.

Finishing my loop around Granite Mountain, I reached the junction with Saddlehorn Trail and for the first time noticed the distinctive formation that

Fast Fact: Free guided hikes of the McDowell Sonoran Preserve are offered by volunteer stewards from mid-October through April.

Saguaros grow among the scattered boulders on the flanks of Granite Mountain in Scottsdale. Photo by the author.

inspired the name. So I understand how Granite Mountain, Balanced Rock, and Saddlehorn Trails got their monikers. I'm still hazy on Bootlegger. Hiking back to my ride, I peered intently into rocky alcoves looking for a stash of old-time hooch, but no luck. Guess I'll settle for a burger.

Where: Granite Mountain Trailhead is at 31402 N. 136th St.
Cost: Free.
Difficulty: Moderate.
Length: 6.1 miles round-trip, or 6.7 miles to Balanced Rock.
Dogs: Yes, on a leash.
Details: (480) 998-7971, www.mcdowellsonoran.org.

Blu Burger Grille, Scottsdale

This North Scottsdale eatery allows guests to put their unique spin on a burger. Choose the types of meat, bun, toppings, and sauces. Patty options include fresh free-range Black Angus, grass-fed American Kobe beef, organic bison, turkey, salmon, veggie, or portobello mushroom.

You can even dip into the kitchen's stash of special ingredients for add-ons. It's like you're whispering in the chef's ear. The possibilities are mouthwateringly endless. Or keep it simple and slide into one of their signature classics like a Truffle Brie Burger or Caprese Burger.

High ceilings with plenty of windows gives Blu Burger Grille a bright, casual feel. A wall covered in awards testifies to their ongoing success. It all starts with a foundation of quality ingredients, especially the meats. Everything follows from that. While I don't like to brag, the burger I concocted could spawn its own franchise. It started with a perfectly grilled Angus patty. Cradled on a puffy onion bun, it wore a crown of hearty gorgonzola cheese, caramelized onions, and center cut applewood-smoked bacon. The ingredients blended beautifully with every bite of the silky soft burger.

Other entrees include grilled salmon, penne pasta, and spicy shrimp. Sandwiches and salads round out the menu. But can you really walk into a place so well-versed in the art of burger making without sampling the wares?

Vegetarian Options: In addition to the previously mentioned veggie burger choices, they also do a Caesar salad, an egg salad sandwich, and several appetizers.

Don't Forget: Save room for their velvety homemade gelato.

Details: 32409 N. Scottsdale Rd., (480) 575-8040, www.bluburgergrille.com.

Cholla Trail, Camelback Mountain

Of all the mountains scattered throughout the Valley, none present such a distinctive profile as Camelback. Looming over tony neighborhoods on the borders of Phoenix and Scottsdale, Camelback Mountain offers an enticing summit to residents and visitors alike.

Two hiking trails reach the top of Camelback. The Cholla is slightly less steep and less crowded than the Echo Canyon route, although that's a relative comparison. As an urban trail, Cholla often feels like a conga line of people snaking their way up the spine of the kneeling dromedary. And the last quarter mile is cruelly steep, requiring scrambling, climbing, and prayer.

Even finding a parking spot can prove challenging. The trailhead is tucked away in a residential neighborhood off Invergordon Road. An improved trailhead (moved from Cholla Lane in 2022) includes restrooms and drinking water.

You'll wend your way up the long eastern ridge of Camelback, first on stone steps and then climbing steep switchbacks before leveling off. The occasional saguaro guards the path along with clumped boulders, foreshadowing the rocky conclusion ahead. In just under a mile you reach a high saddle, a good place to catch your second wind. I don't recall needing a second wind as much in my youth. Now sometimes I need a third, fourth, sometimes eighth wind. I don't know how many winds we have altogether but as I age, I'm grateful for each of them.

There's more climbing to another saddle.

Fast Fact: On days when the National Weather Service issues an Excessive Heat Warning, all trails on Camelback Mountain and Piestwa Peak close from 9 a.m. to 5 p.m. This is an effort to reduce heat-related injuries and deaths. During warm-weather months, hike only in the early morning or evening hours.

The popular Cholla Trail makes a steep ascent up Camelback Mountain. Photo by the author.

Gorgeous views keep getting better. Enjoy them here because once you make for the top you need to focus. The final pitch to the summit is a precipitous scramble across granite vertebrae. The trail is mostly theory at this point as you thread your way up and over boulders. Painted blue dots and reflectors help keep you on the easiest route. No technical skills are required, just short climbs up rock faces. Fortunately, the rough texture of the stone provides good foot traction and sturdy handholds.

Your efforts are rewarded when you reach the 2,704-foot summit to find gorgeous head-spinning views. You see what a furious clutter of mountains exists beyond the sprawling metropolitan area. Take a well-earned breather, pick out landmarks, and snap some photos.

When you're ready to return, use caution. Climbing down can be trickier than climbing up. And remember, uphill hikers have the right of way. With gravity now on your side, you'll be tempted to cannonball through the poor saps still slogging up the mountain. Show benevolence lest the forces of the universe conspire to twist your ankle in karmic retribution.

Where: From Loop 101 in Phoenix, exit onto Chaparral Rd. and drive west for 3.2 miles until it dead-ends at Invergordon Rd. Turn north. Parking is on Invergordon in designated spaces only. There are also dedicated spots for ride-share services to pick up and drop off hikers, probably the best option.
Cost: Free.
Difficulty: Strenuous.
Length: 3.6 miles round-trip.
Dogs: No.
Details: (602) 261-8318, www.phoenix.gov/parks.

Paradise Valley Burger Company, Scottsdale

Most food delivered in a plastic basket—and I speak with some authority here—isn't noted for its presentation. Thus, I was pleasantly surprised during my first visit to Paradise Valley Burger Company when my Beachhouse burger arrived looking like it belonged on fine china. A house-roasted poblano pepper draped the patty. A perfectly centered mound of smoked mozzarella balanced a pyramid of fresh pico de gallo that stood as tall as a dalmatian. I admired the artistry for about two seconds then smooshed on the lid of the brioche bun and dove in.

The philosophy at Paradise Valley is to keep things all about the food. Tucked in a shopping plaza, the eatery is totally nondescript. It's a no-frills business that allows them to put everything in the basket.

All burgers are pressed in-house daily. They're served as thin

The elaborate Brulee Burger headlines the menu at Paradise Valley Burger Co. Courtesy of Rick Mortensen, Phoenix.

smashburgers, double patty–style to maximize the char surface. Besides the Beachhouse, the signature dish is Burger Brulee. Sugar burnt on the bun adds a sweet note and holds the egg, bacon, cheese, and pickled onions together in a crunchy yummy package. Fries have a delicate crispness that melts into a warm cloud of potato softness. Creamy milkshakes are made with hand-scooped ice cream.

With innovative and tasty options, Paradise Valley Burger Company has been a regular on multiple Food Network programs through the years. Yet long before Guy Fieri ever showed up, it was me. There I was, sitting at a table chomping beef and scribbling in a notebook. For some people, *Diners, Drive-Ins and Dives* is an entertaining and informative show. But for a few of us, it's just a longtime way of life.

Vegetarian Options: Substitute a grilled portobello mushroom or Impossible burger for any beef patty on the menu. There's also a garden salad and grilled cheese.

Don't Forget: They've got a second location in Tempe.

Details: 15689 Hayden Rd., (602) 535-4930, www.pvburgercompany.com.

Fast Fact: It was an Englishman that named Phoenix. Phillip Darrell Duppa was one of the original pioneers who suggested the name because this new town was rising from the ruins of the former Hohokam civilization like the mythical Phoenix bird of Greek mythology.

Kovach Family Nature Trail, McDowell Sonoran Preserve (ADA Accessible)

Family is not just a name but also a theme of this trail at the edge of Lost Dog Wash. Interpretive signs along the route explore family relationships of the plants and animals that compose this desert community. Everything in nature is connected and this trail offers a firsthand lesson in those links.

Only 0.5 miles long, the Kovach Family Nature Trail is a double loop laid out like a scraggly figure eight at the Lost Dog Wash Trailhead. Named for a family that championed Scottsdale's McDowell Sonoran Preserve since its earliest days, the trail meanders among a fine assortment of cacti. Stately saguaros, burly barrels, and adorable but ruthless teddy bear chollas rub spiny elbows with ocotillo, brittlebush, and triangle-leaf bursage—all identified by helpful signs. More than 30 plants are labeled along the route. The trail makes a sly and scenic classroom.

Best of all, everyone is welcome. With a level grade and firm surface, the Kovach Trail is ADA accessible, suitable for wheelchairs, walkers, and strollers. For those with mobility issues it's a chance to get back into nature. It also can be an introduction to desert hiking for kids. Shaded stone benches are positioned along the trail if anyone needs a rest or just wants to pause for the views. Everyone can

Fast Fact: The McDowell Sonoran Preserve contains four accessible trails. Besides Kovach Family Nature Trail, they are the Bajada Nature Trail at the Gateway Trailhead, the Jane Rau Trail at Brown's Ranch Trailhead, and the Camino Campana at Fraesfield Trailhead.

enjoy the picturesque desert setting beneath a broad sky, making this trail perfect for you and your family.

Where: Lost Dog Wash Trailhead is at 12601 N. 124th St.
Cost: Free.
Difficulty: Easy.
Length: 0.5 miles round-trip.
Dogs: Yes, on a leash.
Details: (480) 998-7971, www.mcdowellsonoran.org.

"A man on foot, on horseback or on a bicycle, will see more, feel more, enjoy more in one mile than the motorized tourists can in a hundred miles."
EDWARD ABBEY

Pizzeria Bianco, Phoenix

Far as I'm concerned, this is pizza nirvana. I love pizza almost as much as burgers. Naturally I've sampled them all across the state, discovering some amazing pies along the way. But this is the one I crave. It is the gold standard of pizzas.

And I'm far from the only one who thinks so. Pizzeria Bianco has been rated as the best pizza in the country by the *New York Times*, *Bon Appetit*, *Vogue*, Rachel Ray, and many others. Chris Bianco was the first pizza chef to win a James Beard Award (he later won a second) and was in the forefront of the artisanal pizza movement. And he continues to rack up acclaim and

The artfully crafted Sonny Boy is just one of many culinary masterpieces created at Pizzeria Bianco. Courtesy of Rick Mortensen, Phoenix.

television appearances. He's the reason we have so many fabulous pizza parlors around Arizona.

The downtown restaurant opened in 1996, where waiting in line for hours became part of the ritual. A second location in Town & Country Mall, which was also the site of his original restaurant in 1988, is more convenient for my wife and I, and it offers quicker access to these exquisitely balanced pies. The creamy homemade mozzarella, the garden-freshness of the sauce sits atop a thin but puffy crust, charred, chewy, and rich as dinner rolls.

A half dozen specialty combinations grace the menu. The Rosa is a remarkable blending of flavors using Parmigiano Reggiano, ribbons of red onion, partially-crushed Arizona pistachios, and rosemary needles. The end product is nutty, fatty, woodsy, crunchy, chewy perfection. But I'm devoted to the Sonny Boy, a smoky crispy delight that's packed with thin slices of salami curled at the edges and Gaeta olives like dark, earthy jewels.

Vegetarian Options: My vegetarian wife loves the classic simplicity of the Margherita. There's also the Rosa and the Biancoverde, a white pizza with arugula. And of course, the yummy balanced salads.

Don't Forget: They serve pastas too. I'm sure they're wonderful and I doubt that I will ever try one. I'm here for the pizza.

Details: 4743 N. 20th St., (602) 368-3273, www.pizzeriabianco.com.

Axle Grease–Hawknest Loop, McDowell Sonoran Preserve

The Pima–Dynamite Trailhead opened in the McDowell Sonoran Preserve in 2021. It was the last of the major trailheads planned for the preserve and unlocked a lot of new territory. Yet some people are dissuaded by the big power lines crossing near the parking area. That's their loss, because shortly after you walk away from the trailhead you enter a piece of inviting desert.

In my opinion, Axle Grease is the primo trail at Pima–Dynamite. It should serve as the backbone for much of your exploration in this corner of the preserve. From the trailhead it tracks almost due north, breaking away from the power lines with swooping curves through impressive saguaro groves. Groupings of the lean giants tower over the trail. It feels like a real Arizona day when you spend it communing with saguaros.

Axle Grease stretches for 4.5 miles tracing the edge of the preserve so it's a good out-and-back or a way to probe deeper into the backcountry. The long sinewy curves of the trail make this a popular ride for mountain bikers. Several interconnected trails also allow for customized loops.

One of my favorites is to follow Axle Grease for a couple of miles and turn right on Rock Tank Trail. Even though I only use a short piece of Rock Tank (0.4 miles) it delivers a lot of visual interest as it crosses a shallow basin amid rough boulder clumps. After zooming along on Axle Grease, it was nice to slow down and admire the texture and details of Rock Tank. At least until I reached Hawknest Trail. Hang another right on Hawknest and it leads back to the trailhead in a straight shot for a dandy 3.7-mile loop.

Where: Pima–Dynamite Trailhead is at 28777 N. Pima Rd.

Cost: Free.

Difficulty: Easy/moderate.

Length: 3.7 miles round-trip.

Dogs: Yes, on a leash.

Details: (480) 998-7971, www.mcdowellsonoran.org.

Fast Fact: National Cheeseburger Day is celebrated in the United States on September 18.

Detroit Coney Grill, Scottsdale

What a surprise to find a piece of Motor City plopped down in a Scottsdale strip mall. Detroit Coney Grill is a restaurant and sports bar with a dog-friendly patio. As you might guess from the name, coneys rule here. For the uninitiated, a coney is a hot dog stuffed into a steamed bun and loaded with chili, onions, and mustard. In Detroit, they're practically a religion. Coneys are also revered in Cincinnati, where I grew up. Although ours were covered with that special Cincinnati chili, a thin Mediterranean-style sauce slightly sweeter than what's ladled up in Motown. Which one is better? That's a debate for a different day. I came for a burger.

A huge menu covers the wall behind the counter. There are plenty of specialty burgers, but I opted to build my own. Detroit Coney Grill grinds their own beef into slender 2-ounce patties. A coarse grind allows them to create the best ratio of meat to fat for optimal flavor. Then you decide how many crusted beef patties to throw on your sandwich.

Detroit Coney Grill is known for their splendid hot dogs as well as their burgers. Courtesy of Rick Mortensen, Phoenix.

Don't be surprised if your burger comes out as tall as a cathedral spire. The Detroit Coney crew does not skimp with the toppings. My burger looked like it had just robbed a farmers market, escaping with everything it could carry on its back. Big leaf lettuce, thick-cut tomato slices, a pile of onions, and enough pickle slices to rebuild a full cucumber. I was wowed by the freshness of everything. It's a delicious combo all paired nicely with their fries, made from Idaho russet potatoes and hand cut throughout the day.

You can also snag a bottle of Faygo pop from the cooler, still bottled and beloved in Detroit. A sign on the wall says if you ask for a soda, you'll get a pop. It's not a thinly veiled threat, they're just planting their Midwestern flag in the great "soda or pop" debate. And they'll get no argument from me.

Vegetarian Options: Plenty to choose from including salads, wraps, and a complete line of vegan and veggie sandwiches.

Don't Forget: They serve Detroit-style pizza on weekends.

Details: 6953 N. Hayden Rd., (480) 597-4300, www.detroitconeygrill.com.

Marcus Landslide Trail, McDowell Sonoran Preserve

The Marcus Landslide Trail forced me to say something I never thought I would admit: I wish I had stayed awake more often in science class.

A half million years ago a nuclear bomb went off in the McDowell Mountains. At least that's the amount of energy expended when a great slab of mountain suddenly sheared off, plunged earthward, and roared across the valley floor. The triggering event for the landslide could have been anything from a hard rain to an earthquake.

Nearly 26 billion pounds of rock, soil, and vegetation flowed about a mile in a furious torrent, reaching speeds of 44 miles per hour, before finally coming to rest. The noise from the landslide must have been deafening. The wall of dust and dirt thrown skyward blotted out the sun. This tale of long-ago cataclysm and violence unfolds through interpretive signage along the wide smooth path.

The Marcus Landslide Trail is located in the southern portion of Scottsdale's McDowell Sonoran Preserve, leaving from the Tom's Thumb Trailhead. It ambles along the base of the mountains for 1.5 miles, cutting through a virtual forest of cholla cacti. The smaller spine-intensive teddy bear cholla is savagely fuzzy. The taller chain-fruit cholla takes on a Dr. Seussian quality with its weirdly drooping branches and haphazard attitude. Intriguing to look at, both will happily stab any part of you that gets too close, so stay on the trail.

Rising above is a collection of boulders as big as cars and cottages. The ridgeline bristles with them, making this a popular destination for rock climbers. Despite all the eye candy, I paused to read every sign. The narrative puts meat on the bones of all I see. I learn about the erosion and subsurface weathering that causes some rocks to take the form of giant mushrooms and why some boulders are covered with lichen.

As the trail curves closer to the mountains the signage identifies the breakaway scar, a concave scoop along the second highest ridgeline in the

The Marcus Landslide Trail explores some of the geological history of the McDowell Sonoran Preserve. Photo by the author.

McDowell Mountains, known locally as East End. Just then, the level trail tilts sharply uphill. I realized I was climbing the slide mass. This long hump of land stretching across the desert floor had once been part of the mountain. It's a levee in search of a river. The slide mass is roughly 4,000 feet long, 1,650 feet wide and rises more than 100 feet above the original land surface.

Hot Tip: At Scottsdale's Museum of the West, visitors will find six centuries of rare Hopi pottery, pristine Navajo chiefs' blankets, a collection of working cowboy gear, and saloon memorabilia. If you weren't in love with the mystique of the Old West before, you will be before you walk out.

The final segment of trail makes a loop of 0.7 miles at the end as it picks its way through the boulders that took such an abrupt journey eons ago. Today they seem perfectly content where they are. I wondered if any great wooly mammoths had been overtaken by the landslide and stopped frequently to scan the ground, searching for giant tusks poking up through the brittlebush.

At least, I'm pretty sure mammoths roamed this landscape back then. Man, I wish I hadn't slept through so many classes. But that science book was the softest pillow I've ever known.

Where: Tom's Thumb Trailhead is at 23015 N. 128th St.
Cost: Free.
Difficulty: Moderate.
Length: 4 miles round-trip.
Dogs: Yes, on a leash.
Details: (480) 998-7971, www.mcdowellsonoran.org.

Rehab Burger Therapy, Scottsdale

For years, Rehab Burger Therapy has thrived in Old Town Scottsdale. The eatery sports a funky beach theme inside built around a well-stocked bar and knowledgeable bartenders fast-pouring the hooch. Happy revelers spread out onto the patio. But the kitchen maintains a distinctive, creative vision, concocting 20 different burgers in an array of surprising combinations. Burgers are made from a blend of chuck, brisket, and sirloin. They come in two sizes, the 10-ounce "rehab" and the 5-ounce "relapse." Some monstrous rehab burgers are piled so high with toppings they require building permits.

The PBJ & Bacon Burger seems like the sort of thing that Vegas-era Elvis would order. Tempting, but I'm not sure I could fit into my bejeweled jumpsuit afterward. The Spicy Mac-N-Cheese Burger requires two men and a stout boy to dig it out from beneath the crush of cheesy pasta shells spiked with jalapenos, poblanos, and green chiles.

I opted for the Backyard BBQ Burger. It came layered with onion rings, colby jack, and a spicy pineapple barbecue sauce, which brings a nice zing of sweet heat. At Rehab the tinkering never stops, with a different specialty burger trotted out every weekend. If the burgers aren't wild enough for you, a selection of house-made sauces lets you add your own twist to the saga.

Vegetarian Options: Besides their signature panko-crusted black and white bean burger, you can sub any rehab-size burger with a veggie patty. Salads and pastas are also available.
Don't Forget: Choose your type of bun: traditional, pretzel, wheat kaiser, gluten-free, or a lettuce wrap.
Details: 7210 E. 2nd St., (480) 621-5358, www.rehabburgertherapy.com.

Butcher Jones Trail, Saguaro Lake

I've always steered clear of this spectacular shoreline hike during peak times. On a warm late-spring Saturday with temperatures tickling the century mark, most desert trails are deserted. Solitude is mine for the taking almost anywhere else I go.

Instead, I drove to Butcher Jones Beach at Saguaro Lake. Water proves irresistible to desert denizens so I knew I would be one of many. I wisely arrived early enough to secure a parking space, but already the beach was filling up. Families staked out their turf, coolers were unpacked, and kayaks carried to the water. But I followed the Butcher Jones Trail sign into a thicket of mesquite trees and lost sight of everyone.

The trail sees only moderate usage because most people are here for the water and beach. After emerging from the mesquite, the path traces the shoreline squeezing among the desert plants on its way to Peregrine Point. Several spur trails angle down to the water's edge. From here, the trail bends northeast following the contour of a marshy finger cove, lined with both cacti and cattails. You don't find those two palling around every day.

Even though I only encountered the occasional hiker, this is by no means a quiet hike. Boat motors, music, and conversation came wafting off the lake. There was a festive air to the day. Would I want all my hikes to be this lively? Not a chance. But even a card-carrying curmudgeon can take a weekend off from his antisocial crustiness.

Views along the Butcher Jones are relentlessly stunning. The curving shoreline, rising cliffs, and sparkling lake create a devastating combination. Many of the saguaros wore a halo of large white blooms, Arizona's official state flower. Even the ironwood trees were blooming, their cascading branches cloaked in small orchid-like flowers. That was an unexpected bonus.

About 2 miles in, you'll turn away from the water and head inland across a

An ironwood tree in bloom adds a pop of color to the Butcher Jones Trail. Photo by the author.

patch of open desert. With saguaros, chollas, and palo verde trees surrounding you, it's easy to forget the lake is so close by. The trail reaches a signed fork with one branch heading to Burro Cove and the other to Shoreline Access. Both reach the end of the trail in about a quarter mile at overlooks that stay above the water. Here you'll enjoy views of the lake and Four Peaks in the distance.

While Butcher Jones is never difficult, it is slender. A skinny path knifing through desert scrub with lots of spiny plants leaning in. Stay alert and try to be compact. Don't wear your beach towel as a superhero cape. Don't wear anything flowing or billowy because you'll be constantly snagged. I'm not sure what billowy hiking apparel is even available, but this is not the trail to make a fashion statement.

Where: From Phoenix, take Loop 202 east and exit at Country Club Dr., which is also the Beeline Highway (State Route 87). Drive 22 miles north on 87 and then turn right onto the Bush Highway, heading toward Saguaro Lake. At just under 3 miles, turn left on Butcher Jones Beach Rd. and follow it until it ends at the Butcher Jones Recreation Site. A Tonto Pass is required and there is an automated kiosk near the beach.
Cost: Admission fee.
Difficulty: Easy/moderate.
Length: 5 miles round-trip.
Dogs: Yes, on a leash.
Details: (480) 610-3300, www.fs.usda.gov/r03/tonto.

Hot Tip: Experience more of the rugged beauty of Saguaro Lake on a tour boat cruise filled with desert vistas and Arizona wildlife. The double-decker Desert Belle offers narrated cruises as well as live music, wine, and craft beer cruises.

Giant Hamburgers, Mesa

Soon as I walked in, it felt like I had come home. Just when I thought there were no genuine lunch counters left, I showed up at Giant Hamburgers. There I found an old-school joint with booths lining the wall, two-tops on the floor, and bar stools at the end of the counter with a perfect view of the double griddle, one side for breakfast and the other graced with burgers.

While I stood in line, the counter man was busy helping a couple at the pie case. I must have looked famished because the grill man took pity. He bent over, pulled out a big fresh patty of meat from the cooler and held it up at me. I nodded and he slapped it on the flattop. I was still waiting in line to order but already had a burger going.

It arrived wrapped tight in plain paper like a gift. It really is giant, or at least substantial. There's an entire garden packed beneath the wide slender patty. Must be half a head of lettuce, three big ripe tomato slices, and a thick round of white onion so crisp it cracked like a rifle shot at each bite. The whole concoction was a tasty mouthful. All through the meal I kept thinking that my dad would have absolutely loved this place. This was his kind of burger, hot off the flattop and piled with fresh produce. Great. There I sat at a lunch counter, the haven and hideout of my childhood, tearing up a little. Well, it was a good burger.

The fries were impressive too. A batter coating provides extra crunch. They're cooked in canola oil and are the only things that go in the fryer so they retain a pure potato flavor.

I sat at the counter watching the grill man spatula patties and cook bacon and green chiles while toasting buns. It was an almost forgotten ballet. It was lunch *and* a show. For me, it brought back lots of great memories.

Just a hundred yards away from Giant Hamburgers on a prime corner of the shopping plaza was a Whataburger that had a line of cars at the drive-thru. Now in no way am I disparaging Whataburger, or any other fast-food

Walking into Giant Hamburgers feels like a return to simpler, more carefree times. Photo by the author.

establishment. Those places have fed me for years and are absolutely necessary. All I'm saying is, just sometimes, consider parking your car. Walk around the corner and find the little mom-and-pop. Slide into a booth or sit at the counter. Don't just have a fast meal. Make some memories of your own.

Vegetarian Options: They do a garden burger, a grilled cheese, and several breakfast items.
Don't Forget: They could just as easily call the place Giant Pies. There's a case full of them by the register and if you order a slice, they serve a full quarter pie! You can request a small slice, a mere one-sixth of a pie. And if you have that kind of willpower, I salute you.
Details: 2753 E. Broadway Rd., (480) 733-6542, www.gianthamburgers.com.

Go John Trail, Cave Creek Regional Park

If you set out to create the classic desert hike, you'd concoct something like Go John. It's a loop through cactus-covered hills with enough climbing for a workout while never turning harsh. Just under 6 miles, it keeps you outdoors most of the morning but finishes before your stomach starts growling. The scenery changes constantly, panoramas of distant mountains mixed with intriguing rock formations close by. And in spring it's absolutely swimming in wildflowers.

The Go John Trail is a centerpiece of Cave Creek Regional Park, which protects nearly 3,000 acres north of Phoenix and west of Cave Creek. The park contains a nature center with exhibits and educational materials, a picnic area, campground, horse staging area, and 14 miles of interconnected trails.

You can take Go John in either direction. Most folks head north from the parking lot, hiking the loop clockwise. That sends you almost immediately uphill on an old jeep road to get a lot of climbing done early. Normally I favor that approach, but not here. I'll explain why later.

Heading east, Go John pulls you into rolling hills. You get a few glimpses of subdivisions but they soon fade away. Cave Creek Regional Park is surrounded by other small preserves and sits near the border of Tonto National Forest, so the backcountry swallows you. The hike retains a refreshingly remote feel. As the trail angles northeast, it makes a steady but gradual climb.

Fast Fact: You might think you're circling Go John Mountain on the Go John Trail. Logical assumption but incorrect. Go John actually rises to the east, just outside the park.

I traversed hills doused in the bright yellow blooms of brittlebush, just waking up with the

The Go John Trail aims for Gunsight Pass. Photo by the author.

spring warmth. A variety of wildflowers are sprinkled among the cacti along the entire route. The trail turns west and drops into a brushy little drainage. And this is why I hike Go John in this direction. Emerging from the ravine, Gunsight Pass loomed overhead.

I followed saguaros up a rocky slope through Gunsight Pass. And that may be the most Arizona sentence I've ever written. Halfway up, I stopped to study my backtrail to make sure a posse wasn't chasing me.

Panoramas widen beyond the notch, exposing an expanse of distant mountains. Lying to the north is the distinctive profile of Elephant Mountain. I rambled for another mile or so until reaching the final leg of the loop. This piece of Go John is one small portion of the mighty Maricopa Trail that circles the Valley of the Sun connecting the county parks. There's a gate and bench here as well as ample signage. The Go John winds its way south. The Overton Trail enters from the right, but just keep bearing left.

Soon afterward you'll pass a fenced-off mineshaft. Although prospecting was done in the area, nothing of significance was ever discovered. I finally crossed a rocky saddle and below me, still a half mile away, sat my little SUV, waiting patiently to hustle me to a well-deserved burger.

Where: From Phoenix, drive north on I-17 to Carefree Highway, eastbound. Drive east for 6 miles on Carefree Highway to 32nd St. Turn north and continue 1.5 miles to the park entry gate. Pay the admission fee and follow the main park road to the Go John Trailhead.
Cost: Admission fee.
Difficulty: Moderate.
Length: 5.8 miles round-trip.
Dogs: Yes, on a leash.
Details: (602) 506-2930 ext. 8, www.maricopacountyparks.net.

Hot Tip: The Cave Creek Museum is filled with intriguing exhibits. Their most popular events are the Arizona Gold Mining Experience that highlights the complete hard rock ore extraction process, including firing up the big ten-stamp mill, which pulverizes ore into a fine gravel. The events take place the second Saturday of each month and tickets must be purchased in advance. Cave Creek Museum is open October through May.

Big Earl's Greasy Eats, Cave Creek

The sign yanked me off the road for my initial visit. Big Earl's Greasy Eats occupies an old service station wrapped in patios. Lot of history here. The 1936 gas station had been built in the Sunnyslope neighborhood of Phoenix, then moved to the dusty outpost of Cave Creek in 1952, where it offered fill-ups into the 1980s. But I knew none of that when I first wheeled into the lot.

I only had eyes for that swooped and angled sign, a masterpiece of retro advertising. Crowned by a fully dressed burger, a big red arrow emblazoned with the words "Big Earl's" pierced my heart as if it had been shot from Cupid's bow. At the bottom of the sign was the simple but bold proclamation "The Last Honest Hamburger!"

It is my quest, I realized. I search always for an honest burger, an authentic burger. The perfect burger. I seek a burger that connects me to the past while keeping my taste buds rooted in the present.

Big Earl's delivers on its promise. They serve scramblers and big burritos in the morning and then switch to sandwiches, salads, and burgers made with Black Angus beef the rest of the day. Every dish comes with a side of Streamline Moderne design. Big Earl's is thought to be the only example of the old-school Standard Oil station left in the Valley, with its eye-pleasing aesthetic of curved edges and long horizontal lines. Twin gas pumps anchor the big comfortable patio lined with tables beneath shade awnings.

Order at the counter beneath chalkboard menus. One-third-pound patties can be doubled or tripled beneath an onslaught of fresh ingredients. Several specialty burgers are on the menu, but the Big Earl remains the flagship. It comes with lettuce, tomatoes, pickles, onions, and their house-made seasoned mayo, which I replaced with mustard. I sat in the shadow of one of Arizona's all-time great signs on a warm spring day. I had my desert,

A stylish retro sign lures hungry travelers to the sanctuary that is Big Earl's in Cave Creek. Courtesy of Rick Mortensen, Phoenix.

my juicy burger, and the open road before me. What else could I possibly need?

Vegetarian Options: You can try a veggie or vegan burger, a couple of salads, and plenty of breakfast items.
Don't Forget: They also operate a vintage candy shop right next door and on Saturdays show free drive-in movies on the back of the building.
Details: 6135 E. Cave Creek Rd., (480) 575-7889, www.bigearlsgreasyeats.com.

Goldmine–Dynamite Loop, San Tan Mountain Regional Park

Turn your back on this trail and it will take a swing at you. It's a sucker punch of a trail.

Don't panic. It's not malicious or even strenuous. It just comes at you sudden-like. Hike the route I suggest and you don't have much time to warm up. Soon as you step out of the car you're heading uphill. But it's definitely worth it.

San Tan Mountain Regional Park harbors more than 10,000 acres of sweet desert pinned between mountains in the southeast corner of the Valley. Although San Tan is managed by Maricopa County Parks, it actually lies in Pinal County. Nine trails can be accessed from three trailheads. For this hike, start from Goldmine Trailhead at the northern edge of the park.

You'll pass the junction with Dynamite Trail, but continue bearing left on Goldmine. You'll soon see a spur path to the graves of Marion Kennedy

A mountain biker rides the Dynamite Trail into the San Tan Mountains. Photo by the author.

and Mansel Carter. These two friends prospected this area looking for gold but found a different kind of treasure. They fell under the spell of the Arizona desert, as so many of us have. Pay your respects and return to the main trail.

From here you begin climbing the shoulder of Goldmine Mountain. This rocky section is short but steep, gaining 600 feet of abrupt elevation. By tackling it this way you get the hard work out of the way while you've still got fresh legs, and that burger will feel well-earned.

You finally reach the saddle where a sitting bench makes a welcome sight. Or be an idiot like me and take the spur trail to the left for even more climbing as it scrambles to the summit. Gaze back across the cityscape, which in a word is sprawling. The rest of the hike is pretty easy-breezy. Just kick back and enjoy the desert quiet and broad views.

The Goldmine angles downhill, sharply at times, to the valley floor before it junctions with San Tan Trail at 1.5 miles. If you were to continue on Goldmine (another 1.4 miles), you would reach the park's main entrance with a visitor center, picnic area, restrooms, and other trails. A good staging area for future visits.

But I turned right on San Tan and enjoyed a desert saunter, dipping in and out of washes. The city vanished behind the mountains and I was alone in this lovely basin. Saguaros grow sparsely here, but I noticed plenty of their cactus comrades like chollas, hedgehogs, and a robust assortment of barrels. After just 0.4 miles on San Tan, turn right again on Dynamite and begin closing the loop.

Dynamite winds north for 2.4 miles and is a pretty pathway with long, swooping curves. The trail starts up the backside of the slope on a gentle grade. When it cuts through a notch in the hills revealing the concrete glint of civilization, it's jarring. I had conveniently forgotten all that existed. Now that's my kind of hike! Dynamite rejoins Goldmine near the trailhead, and all too soon the hike is over.

Where: From Mesa, take US 60 east to the Higley Rd. exit. Turn south on Higley Rd. and travel 12.5 miles until it ends at Hunt Highway. Head east on Hunt Highway for 3.8 miles to Wagon Wheel Rd. Turn south on Wagon Wheel and proceed 1 mile to the signed trailhead at the corner of Skyline Dr.

Cost: Admission fee.

Difficulty: Moderate/with a strenuous climb.

Length: 4.5 miles round-trip.

Dogs: Yes, on a leash.

Details: (602) 506-2930 ext. 7, www.maricopacountyparks.net.

Hot Tip: The Riparian Preserve at Water Ranch is a 110-acre wetland and wildlife sanctuary in Gilbert with ponds, walking paths, and a floating boardwalk. It's a popular spot for birders and includes a children's play area.

Joe's Farm Grill, Gilbert

Here they have mastered the art of the burger. Amid green and peaceful surroundings, they cut through the noise and distractions and simply execute, with an eye for detail.

Joe's Farm Grill is housed in the former Johnson family residence, now an airy, hip cafeteria with walls of windows and big shaded backyard. It's surrounded by Agritopia, a 12-acre urban organic farm. I ordered at the counter then planted myself on a picnic table outside, happy to be surrounded by so much greenery.

While the menu stays simple, it offers several options ranging from chicken sandwiches to a barbecue sampler to jumbo fried shrimp. Many ingredients are grown on the property, and several others are sourced locally. The beef is local and all natural. Burgers are 6 ounces of fresh ground chuck cooked to a slightly pink interior, unless you request different.

This is a burger of understated elegance. Like a rich person trying to dress down for a casual outing, you can't disguise quality. There's nothing ostentatious yet everything just comes together. It is flawlessly plated. A cup of mustard and one of ketchup fill opposite corners of the dish. Big leaf lettuce, thick slices of red onion, and a sultry tomato that still has garden written all over it, are piled in a careful stack nestling with a pickle spear. The fries are hot and softly plump. I gobble one, admiring its potato goodness. There's still a connection to the soil here.

The hand-formed patty glistens in the filtered sunshine, highlighting color and texture. The lightly toasted bun is golden and tilted back at a jaunty angle, like Sinatra raising the brim of his fedora slightly so he can eye a doll with killer gams.

The first bite is heavenly as a wave of contentment sweeps over me. Primal forces are at work here. This is what I want every burger to be. I sit outdoors in the shade, savoring an exquisite version of a meal I have loved since

Joe's Farm Grill honors the family farm roots of the property while dishing up fresh, exquisite burgers. Courtesy of Rick Mortensen, Phoenix.

childhood. Sometimes lunch is just nutrition. Sometimes it is the silencer of stress and the curator of moods. My search for the perfect burger, I suddenly realize, is actually a search for perfect moments. These are the boots-and-burger days I hold close. I'm immensely grateful to Joe's Farm Grill for a truly special one.

Vegetarian Options: The Farm Veggie Burger is house-made with black beans, brown rice, oats, and 10 fresh vegetables.
Don't Forget: Besides the next-level milkshakes they serve, Joe's Farm Grill also makes their own cheesecake that comes with some lavish sauces.
Details: 3000 E. Ray Rd., (480) 563-4745, www.joesfarmgrill.com.

Wind Cave Trail, Usery Mountain Regional Park

The Usery Mountains rise along the eastern edge of metro Phoenix, the beginning of a mountainous band that includes the Goldfields and the fierce Superstitions. At the geological heart of Usery Mountain Regional Park stands Pass Mountain. Craggy strata of volcanic rock earned the mountain its nickname "Scarface." High up that rocky cliff you'll find an unlikely crisp little hideaway known as the wind cave.

The trail rambles through a pretty patch of desert rising only slightly at first. I was surrounded by a gallery of desert plants so profuse I expected to find a groundskeeping crew nooning in the shade of a palo verde tree. Strategically scattered boulders add a nice bit of texture to the usual suspects of saguaros, chollas, barrels, ocotillos, and creosote.

The only slight distraction is a muffled popping sound. Folks are firing off a few rounds at Usery Mountain Shooting Range. But it's far enough away so it just sounds like I've got some Orville Redenbacher in the microwave. Great. Now I craved popcorn.

Once the trail reaches the base of the mountain it begins climbing in earnest, a steady grade of rocky switchbacks. It is exposed the entire way with the sun just leaning on you. The desert can unleash a withering, angry heat, a heat that stalks you with a knife in its teeth. It is a heat that will make you weep just

Fast Fact: Usery Mountain was named for King Usery, a rancher turned highwayman and horse thief from the area. After his capture he served time in Yuma Territorial Prison.

so it can harvest your tears. It is a great pleasure to reach your destination and slip out of the sun.

The cave is actually a scooped-out alcove atop a ledge of lichen-covered volcanic tuff. It is a long swath of shade—lush sponge cake–like shade—with a cool breeze funneled through. The drop in temperature can be remarkable. Seeping water feeds bunches of rock daisies growing from the walls and ceiling. Bees swarm about, busy like always, but they paid me no mind. It's a sweet spot to relax and enjoy broad vistas across the valley floor.

Some adventurous types like to continue past the cave, climbing a rugged and unmaintained pathway to the top of Pass Mountain. You go ahead. I'll snooze here in the cool, chilled shade.

Where: From Phoenix, go east on US 60 to Ellsworth Rd. Head north on Ellsworth for 6.6 miles to Usery Mountain Regional Park.
Cost: Admission fee.
Difficulty: Moderate.
Length: 3.2 miles round-trip.
Dogs: Yes, on a leash.
Details: (602) 506-2930 ext. 4, www.maricopacountyparks.net.

Matty G's Steakburgers, Mesa

If you want a game to go with your burger, Matty G's is the place for you. The place is loaded with sports memorabilia, more classic era than modern, which is nice, and tables are covered with team logos. So it's a pretty safe bet a game will be airing on the television.

Even the signature burgers bear sports slogan themes. The Field of Dreams brings the heat with two steakburger patties, ghost pepper cheese, pickled jalapeño, sauteed mushrooms, and chipotle aioli. The Triple Crown covers two steakburger patties with Matty G's fry sauce, applewood smoked bacon, and a fried egg. Matty G's fry sauce is a seasoned mayo-ketchup blend made in-house.

Orders are placed at the counter and the food is brought to your table. You can build your own with as many patties as you desire, but I opted for the Photo Finish, two steakburger patties with Swiss cheese, sauteed mushrooms, grilled onions, lettuce, and tomato, with the fry sauce banished.

Even with a tense women's softball game airing, I knew when my order hit the flattop. An aria of hiss and steam enveloped the meat and the fixings. Patties get a quick press, giving them a nice caramelized char. The burger arrived with bun leaning back highlighting the rowdy collision of ingredients that had me almost salivating.

While the beast is definitely a two-hander, it held together well and proved as tasty as it looked. The melted cheese adds a touch of gooey richness as a backdrop. I loved the crispy edges of the patties. The garlic fries, on the other hand, seemed a bit bland. They come with a side of Matty G's fry sauce. In the interest of fairness, I dipped a couple and it really livened them up. While it may not be up my alley, I can imagine it being quite popular.

To put it in the proper parlance, they leave it all on the field at Matty G's.

Sports fans and burger lovers will feel right at home at Matty G's. Courtesy of Rick Mortensen, Phoenix.

Vegetarian Options: The No Hitter is a grilled portobello mushroom, Matty G's fry sauce, Swiss cheese, lettuce, and tomato.

Don't Forget: The menu includes salads, wraps, and foot-long hot dogs.

Details: 1958 E. Brown Rd., (480) 306-7406, www.matty-gs.com.

Siphon Draw Trail, Superstition Mountains

Just when it seems like the Valley of the Sun might go on forever, a dark wall of mountains rise up and civilization crashes and breaks like a wave against the steep ramparts. The Superstitions are fiercely rugged, untamed, and shrouded in legend.

The Siphon Draw Trail provides a good introduction to the Supes without putting you in too much peril. The trail launches from the Saguaro Day-Use Area in Lost Dutchman State Park. At first it follows the easy Discovery Trail dotted with interpretive signs. Soon it turns onto an old mining road pointed toward the sheer-sided front range of the mountains. Other trails branch off at signed junctions but continue to plow ahead. As soon as it enters the Superstition Wilderness Area, the trail turns narrower and steeper.

If you've sworn off switchbacks, you're in luck because there's no weaving or winding here. It's a straight climb up the gullet of these hardscrabble mountains. Carved rock formations close around you as you approach the canyon.

I spotted my first Gila monster on Siphon Draw Trail many years ago. There he was, just below me as I clambered down a slickrock ledge. He looked big enough to ride, even without a saddle but I thought it unwise. Gila monsters are fat, venomous lizards covered with beadlike scales. They look like a poison purse. In all my years of hiking, I've only seen a few, so I'm grateful for each sighting. Gila monsters are a protected species, so if you are fortunate enough to encounter one, treat them with respect, as you do all wildlife you might come across in the backcountry.

Hot Tip: The Superstition Mountain Museum houses an extensive collection that mingles history, folklore, and Hollywood. Multiple structures are spread across the grounds and there is lots of information about the legend of the Lost Dutchman Mine.

The distinctive profile of the Flatiron looms above Siphon Draw Trail. Photo by the author.

The trail continues climbing into a narrowing canyon until you reach a smooth basin of rock. After rains, the water cascades down the steep walls, filling this bowl.

Make this your turnaround spot. A sketchy, treacherous pathway continues up to the top of Flatiron, the prominent outcrop high above, but it should only be attempted by experienced, hardcore, laugh-in-the-face-of-danger hikers. On your return, don't be embarrassed about butt-scooting down the water-polished rock. And keep an eye peeled for my old Gila monster pal.

Where: From Phoenix, drive east on US 60 to Apache Junction. Exit at Idaho Rd., and travel north 5 miles to AZ 88, and bear right. Continue on AZ 88 (Apache Trail) for 5 miles and turn right into Lost Dutchman State Park.

Cost: Admission fee.

Difficulty: Moderate.

Length: 4 miles round-trip.

Dogs: Yes, on a leash.

Details: (480) 982-4485, www.azstateparks.com.

"The half a pound of chopped ground round is still a burger when it goes downtown."
JOHN PRINE

The Chuckbox, Tempe

Gnarled and rickety, The Chuckbox is a burger shack sitting at the edge of Arizona State University, in the shadow of high-rises. The community grew and changed, while The Chuckbox stayed exactly the same. They look like the last holdout—some grouchy old man who refused to sell out so development just sprang up all around, like in a Pixar movie, except nobody wants this little gem to go anywhere.

In 1972 The Chuckbox began feeding hungry students, and then the rest of the city as word of their delicious burgers spread. Decades later they're still winning accolades and awards. Meanwhile, they just keep doing what they do, cranking out delectable, smoky campfire burgers. "Over 278 sold" the sign out front proudly proclaims, which may be a tad low.

Patrons line up at the counter to order, but it moves fast. Study the menu on the wall and then order by size. A Big One is a third-pound patty and a Great Big One is the half-pounder. A Little One is one-fifth of a pound, but pretend it's for your daintiest child if that's all you're going to eat. The grill man slaps patties and rounds of bacon on the grate in a precise sequence. Beneath is a hot bed of mesquite charcoal. Flames rise through the grate, charring patties, crisping bacon, and

Hot Tip: Put your trail-toned leg muscles to use and sign up for Pat's Run held in April. The 4.2-mile run/walk honors Pat Tillman, NFL star turned Army Ranger who died in the line of duty. It winds through downtown Tempe and ends at the 42-yard line of ASU Stadium, paying tribute to Tillman's jersey number. The race raises funds for academic scholarships.

Once patrons have their expertly grilled burgers at The Chuckbox, they can drag them through the lavish toppings bar. Courtesy of Rick Mortensen, Phoenix.

releasing a sizzling aroma—that scent I always remember because it is my first love's perfume.

Beyond ingredients and recipes, a burger is a product of its environment, absorbing the memory of meat gone by, the ghost of ancient grease. This is the terroir of burgers. Each patty stands on the shoulders of burgers that came before. No seasoning compares to a well-used flattop or grill. Burgers at the Chuck are more than a sandwich, they are a beef vintage. The Chuckbox consistently delivers one of the all-time great burgers.

They offer a bacon cheeseburger and a bacon guacamole cheeseburger. The Tijuana Torpedo comes with jalapeño jack cheese blended with the ground beef and adorned with green chiles. But I get mine plain, like most folks do. Because in the middle of the room sits a full topping bar so you can heap on the fixings. The trusting fools. My creation always soars so high I need Sherpas to hoist the final pickles.

Scattered tables fill the dark interior. Tree stumps and wood crates serve as chairs. There's a sliver of porch where I sat and wolfed down my burger. I wondered if folks gazing out of their tall office windows could see how wide my grin was from such a distance. I was eating an Arizona classic.

Vegetarian Options: The menu may be limited but does include a vegetarian garden burger.
Don't Forget: The Chuckbox accepts cash only, no credit cards. There's an ATM on the premises.
Details: 202 E. University Dr., (480) 968-4712, www.thechuckbox.com.

Rain Prayer

On the cusp of monsoon season, when everything seems hot and parched, here's my plea to the Arizona sky . . .

Rain like you love me. Pour out your heart. Shower me with tenderness. Drown me with affection.

Rain like you hate me. Let loose your fury. Bare your wet fangs. Chase me indoors to hide from your pounding savagery.

Rain like we are lost from one another. Help us find our way back to a sense of harmony. Restore the balance that once existed. Bind us together with a veil of pure, clear water.

Rumble at me from a great height. Blot out the light and the sun. Rip open the clouds and empty them. Weep for the land because it is so thirsty. Let your tears put out fires and fill arroyos and push rivers free from their banks. Bring the torrent. Unleash the cascade. Sign your masterpiece with a high arcing rainbow. Perfume the desert.

Please just rain like it does each night in my dreams.

CENTRAL HIGHLANDS

You never know what you might discover exploring this piece of Arizona. It's a land of transition, beyond the grasp of desert but still rugged around the edges. This is where you'll find forests, lakes, crumpled rock formations, wide canyons, and lonely plains with golden grasses bending beneath the breeze. And it's all infused with a large helping of history.

This is where you'll find Whiskey Row, a long ribbon of Route 66, and remnants of the railroad era. Although, come to think of it, people still drink on Prescott's Whiskey Row. And millions of travelers come from across the globe to drive this beloved stretch of Route 66 through Seligman, where the preservation movement began. And the train still chugs out of Williams on its way to the Grand Canyon. Maybe not so much has changed after all. Get out, walk around, and see for yourself.

Weaving among the jumbled boulders of the Granite Dells, the Constellation Trails make for an entertaining adventure. Photo by the author.

Constellation Trails, Prescott

The Granite Dells lie scattered across the slope like the ruins of wounded mountains. They are broken and unruly, an eruption of ancient stone. The coarse-grained granite dates back 1.4 billion years, weathered and worn into rounded boulders and fractured walls, an enticing backdrop for a hike. The Dells creates a distinctive Prescott profile, rising from high grasslands and wrapping around sprawling lakes.

The Constellation Trails are a series of short, quick, interconnected loops exploring the Dells. The trailhead sits right across the highway from the Phippen Museum north of downtown. First up is a commemorative plaque honoring the Navy crewmen of the Air Force Lockheed C-121G Super Constellation who perished when their plane went down nearby in 1959. The cause of the crash is still unknown.

Don't be intimidated by the web of trails. Signs with "you are here" locator maps are posted at each junction and all trail segments together total just over 3 miles as they wind their way through the Granite Dells. Tawny boulder clusters stand tall while rounded rocks lay tumbled about. A scattering of trees and brushy shrubs squeeze among the formations. Dirt paths give way to bare stone adorned with dabs of white paint to guide you.

Most trails are short and easy, with some twisting through rock passageways,

Fast Fact: Most of the thoughtfully designed trails in the Prescott area are the handiwork of the Over the Hill Gang. They are an all-volunteer group dedicated to construction and maintenance of area trails and have created a system of well-signed pathways, including the impressive 54-mile-long Prescott Circle Trail.

providing close encounters with the fabric of the stone. Only a couple of segments like Lost Wall and North 40 offer moderate workouts as they gain enough elevation to offer wide-ranging views.

At one time or another, I've hiked all segments of the Constellation network. Now I choose a different route each visit. Since it's right off the highway, it's a chance to stop and explore these quiet boulders that have been here since the world was young.

Where: From Prescott, head north on AZ 89 for about 6 miles. Trailhead parking is on the west side of the highway, directly across from the Phippen Museum of Western Art.
Cost: Admission fee.
Difficulty: Easy.
Length: 3.5 miles collective.
Dogs: Yes, on a leash.
Details: (928) 777-1121, www.prescotttrails.com.

Brown Bag Burger + Bar, Prescott

Brown Bag Burger started out in a small location in a strip mall. The restaurant had a good run for several years focused mainly on peddling burgers of gargantuan proportions. The concept finally ran out of steam and a new owner took over in 2020. They wisely decided to concentrate on quality, upgrading the menu while downsizing the slabs of beef so they could be managed by human hands. Success quickly followed, and they moved to a larger building in the heart of downtown Prescott and rebranded as Brown Bag Burger + Bar with local brews on tap.

They use a choice ground sirloin/chuck blend from a Scottsdale butcher to make their 7-ounce patties. Each is cooked to order and finished with smoked butter. The chef recommends medium-rare for optimal flavor and tenderness, and I see no flaw in that plan. The hefty patty features a blushing Barbie-pink interior. It's a symphony of beefy flavor, nestled on a fresh-baked bun. This is steak in casual clothes. Brown Bag creates all their sauces and their own seasoning blend that adds a pleasant twist to the fries.

Nearly a dozen signature burgers headline the menu. A popular choice is the

Hot Tip: Prescott retains one of the most distinctive downtowns in Arizona. The stately courthouse and tree-draped lawn form an old-fashioned town square. Surrounding the plaza are galleries, shops, restaurants, and Whiskey Row, a stretch of Montezuma Street once packed shoulder to shoulder with saloons. This was where Wyatt and Virgil Earp, along with Doc Holliday drank and gambled. Still standing is the historic Palace Restaurant and Saloon, Arizona's oldest bar.

Fungus Amongus, topped with sauteed mushrooms, beer battered onion rings, bleu cheese, and steak sauce. DIYers have plenty to work with when starting with a foundation of nearly a half pound of premium meat perfectly cooked. Sandwiches, salads, and rice bowls round out the choices. They also serve breakfast.

Vegetarian Options: Their scratch-made vegan burger is crafted in-house using brown rice, Chinese black forbidden rice, oats, and black beans with a spice blend. It comes with onion jam, lettuce, and tomato. Add vegan cheese if you're feeling daffy.

Don't Forget: They have opened a second Brown Bag Burger location on Route 66 in Flagstaff.

Details: 130 W. Gurley St., (928) 445-3353, www.brownbagburger.com.

Watson Lake Loop, Prescott

This is my favorite hike in Prescott, highlighting the very best of this mountain town. A series of connected trails encircles the sparkling lake, weaving through the Granite Dells, a stony wonderland of massive boulders, weathered and piled into exotic formations—a landscape done in a Neo-Flintstone Revival style.

There are several places to access the loop, but I started in Watson Lake Park. From the parking lot, I turned right on the trail. Some road noise follows you on this segment, but it's still an impressive stretch of lake vistas. Big cottonwood trees cradle the southern toe of the water and wrap around Granite Creek. This verdant spot is Watson Woods Riparian Preserve. The 126-acre preserve harbors the largest and oldest cottonwoods left in Prescott.

After the preserve, it's on to the Peavine, a wide thoroughfare along the eastern bank popular with bikers, joggers, and stroller-pushing moms. The Peavine is part of the Rails-to-Trails Conservancy, a national program converting old railway beds into user-friendly paths. The Peavine continues for a few miles, but turn onto Lakeshore Trail. This dirt singletrack twists among the boulders near the water's edge. A couple of short detours peel off from Lakeshore, Treehouse Loop and Secret Cove. And what hiker can resist invitations like that?

There's an enticing wildness to this side, heaped rock domes accessorized with yuccas and cacti, oaks and pines. Expect to spend plenty of time gawking. Next up, Over the Hill Trail cuts right through the Dells, in and out of rocky gullies until it dips into a marshy patch at the base of Watson Dam. Water gushes from the midsection of the dam creating a corridor of wetlands shaded by cottonwoods and willows. The Northshore Trail clambers up a steep rock face and delivers some of the best lake panoramas. It traces the water's edge back to my starting point.

The Granite Dells rising from the surface makes Watson Lake one of the state's most striking bodies of water. Courtesy of Mike Koopsen, Sedona.

Where: From downtown Prescott, travel north on AZ 89 for approximately 5 miles to Watson Lake Park. Turn right into the park and follow the road until it dead ends.
Cost: Admission fee.
Difficulty: Moderate.
Length: 4.8 miles round-trip.
Dogs: Yes, on a leash.
Details: (928) 777-1121, www.prescotttrails.com.

Sammies Burger Joint, Prescott

I miss walk-up burger shacks. Whatever happened to those? Maybe it's more of a midwestern thing. Ice cream stands, hot dog stands, and hamburger stands all seem more common in that part of the country. Sometimes they're only open in summer. Maybe that's what I love about them—they remind me of lazy carefree days when I had a couple of dollars in my pocket and nothing in the world sounded better than a burger and a shake.

Walking up to a little sliding window to order a burger is one of life's simple pleasures. Sammies Burger Joint lets me relive that. I blame Arizona's car culture on our dearth of walk-ups. Or maybe it's the heat. Everyone is afraid to stand outside for a minute lest the sun beat on their heads with big red fists.

Sammies sits across the traffic roundabout from Watson Lake Park. Last time I decided to eat before my hike and got to Sammies at 9:45 a.m. People were already waiting. We sat patiently in our cars until the window slid open at 10, and then queued up—under a shady awning—to place our orders. Burger joint is right, because Sammies hardly does anything else. They make a pulled pork sandwich, milkshakes, fruit turnovers, and prickly pear lemonade, but that's it.

The rough-hewn burgers are a quarter pound, smashed wider than the soft bun they get from a local bakery. Double it if you want. It comes with grilled onions and pickles, just about my favorite combo. The quality of the beef is unmistakable. It wears a light crust, tattooed from the flattop, still tender inside. A really fine burger that tastes like summer should.

You can also give the M.O.A.B (Mother of All Burgers) treatment to both burgers and fries, piling them with pulled pork, pickled jalapeño, and Sammies special sauce that's sort of a spicy garlic aioli.

There are a few chairs if you want to take a load off while you wait, or go sit in your car. Sammies also has a small inside dining space with mismatched tables. No matter what you choose, your order comes out the same way—in a brown paper bag with someone yelling your name, like mom calling you home for lunch.

Fries are lightly seasoned and you get a ton of them. They spill out of their container filling the bottom of the bag. If you got your order to go, those free-floating bag fries make an irresistible hot, salty snack to gobble on the drive. Once you divvy up the food at home, no one can prove where the missing fries went without forensic analysis of your fingers. It's the perfect summer crime.

Vegetarian Options: Sorry. Come for the fruit turnovers, or milkshakes, or root beer float. Come because you want to support a small local business.
Don't Forget: Don't take too long on your hike. Sammies closes right after lunch.
Details: 2161 E. Hillsdale Rd., (928) 379-5529, www.sammiesburgers.com.

"Everywhere is walking distance if you have the time."
STEVEN WRIGHT

Salida Gulch Trail, Prescott

Pay attention on the Salida Gulch Trail because it traverses an interesting microhabitat through the woods above Lynx Creek, where you'll encounter prickly pear cacti, riparian willows, and tall ponderosa pines all living in harmony.

The hike starts by briefly following Salida Connection. Cross the creek and pass through a gate all within a few hundred yards from the trailhead. Be sure to close all gates behind you. Almost immediately, you'll reach a Y with trail #95 going in both directions That's Salida Gulch. I hung a left, taking this skinny loop clockwise. The first leg traces a riparian strip in a peaceful canyon, cooled by the stream. Old gold mining operations left behind scars along this creek, but you'd never notice now after forest service restoration.

About a half mile in on the left, I spotted panels of intricate rock art carved into a wall of clustered boulders. Renderings of animals, stylized human forms, and geometric shapes spread across the stone face. Look but don't touch. Oils from your skin will degrade these artifacts over time.

I'm always fascinated by these links to a long-vanished civilization. What story do they tell? What kind of day was it when they carved this tight little coil? About 2 miles away, people are in Costco buying olives by the pallet. I'm gazing at ancient carvings and listening to a raven's wing slicing pine-scented air. Sometimes hiking is more than just walking.

A mile past the petroglyphs, the trail banks right and begins a gentle climb up the slope through the timber. Before long I was ambling along the ridgeline through a thin forest fattened by layers of chaparral. The trees break apart, exposing vistas of the

Fast Fact: Founded in 1864, Prescott served as Arizona's first territorial capital.

Petroglyphs etched into rock faces along Salida Gulch Trail offer an intriguing connection to the past. Photo by the author.

Bradshaw Mountains to the south and Granite Mountain to the northwest. Soon the trail drops back down to the gulch, rejoining Salida Connection.

Where: From downtown Prescott, head east on AZ 69 to Walker Rd. Proceed 1.2 miles and turn left on Lynx Creek Rd. (Watch for the sign to Lynx Creek Ruin.) Travel 0.9 miles to a large parking area on the right. Portions of the road are graded dirt, suitable for all vehicles.
Cost: Free.
Difficulty: Moderate.
Length: 4.2 miles round trip.
Dogs: Yes, on a leash.
Details: (928) 443-8000, www.fs.usda.gov/r03/prescott.

Hot Tip: Tucked away in the pine trees, Prescott's Highlands Center for Natural History is an educational venue designed to help everyone appreciate the wonders of nature and become better caretakers of the lands around us. They also have discovery gardens and trails on the property.

Bill's Grill, Prescott

I loved this joint the first time I walked in, and nothing has changed. The whole place is like one big screened-in porch. Plastic tablecloths, sun streaming in, and a full menu of beers and burgers create a most agreeable atmosphere. There's a full bar inside with seating but you can't pry me away from a sunny window. I'm drawn to natural light. If I ever visit your home and disappear, don't worry. I'm not upstairs rooting through your drawers; I'm on the veranda. I'll always be on the veranda. If you don't have a veranda, chances are I won't visit.

Along with the numerous burger options, there are plenty of craft brews to wash them down at Bill's Grill. Photo by the author.

Burgers at Bill's Grill are built from the foundation up. They grind their meat daily, a chuck and brisket blend. Then you choose the style of patty you want—plain, blackened, onion-smashed, or with fresh cracked black pepper. If you're customizing your burger, there's an interesting topping menu, plus 10 different house-made sauces to work with ranging from curry honey mustard to Thai peanut.

Specialty burgers include the Portlander with ham, bacon, caramelized onions, a fried egg, cheddar, and goop sauce. My favorite is the Bill's Smashed Burger with an intriguing blend of flavors. The earthiness of the crimini mushrooms, the snap of fresh-cracked peppercorns, the sweetness of caramelized onions, and smoothness of aged Swiss cheese create a harmonious sandwich with a distinctive viewpoint. I practically inhale the tender bundle.

Vegetarian Options: Black bean or vegan patties can be used for any burger. They even offer a couple of specialties like the Guacamole Black Bean Burger, made with roasted bell peppers, guac, and pepper jack cheese.
Don't Forget: The menu extends far beyond burgers and many patrons come in just for the fish and chips.

Details: 333 S. Montezuma St., (928) 237-9138, www.billsgrillprescott.com.

Hot Tip: Sharlot Hall Museum is built around the site of the First Territorial Governor's Mansion, with other historic buildings scattered across beautifully landscaped grounds. Sharlot Hall was a poet, journalist, historian, and the first woman to hold public office in the territory. Her personal collection of artifacts served as the foundation to this extraordinary museum.

Sycamore Rim Trail, Williams

I'm not sure why this trail with its panoramas of Sycamore Canyon isn't more popular. It swings a wide, mostly level circle through forests and meadows, while knitting together an idyllic day of springs, ponds, cliffs, and canyons all garnished with bouquets of water lilies. What's not to love?

There are five major trailheads for Sycamore Rim and I started from the most accessible, off Forest Road 56. Take the trail clockwise heading toward Dow Spring. Cut across a deep grass meadow ringed by ponderosa pines. You soon pass the ruins of a century-old sawmill and Dow Spring. Remnants of a few cabins can still be seen, and though it is hard to imagine in this lonely spot, the community once had its own post office.

Past the cabins, the trail drops into a shallow canyon filled with small spring-fed pools that in summer hold water lilies. I spend a lot of time hiking Arizona trails, and trust me when I say that water lilies are few and far between. I tend to linger here at water's edge awhile, gazing at the floating flowers, like little boats of joy. I like to keep track of small miracles—sort of life's scorecard.

Expect different looks over the next couple of miles—copses of oaks, then ponderosa pine forests, and swatches of rippling prairie. Near the halfway point of Vista Point, you can scan the dense woods cloaking Sycamore Canyon below. Soon afterward, you arrive at Sycamore Falls. During spring snowmelt and following summer storms you'll sometimes find water tumbling. But more often you'll see rock climbers making their ascent on the perpendicular walls, and hopefully no tumbling is involved.

The trail veers away from

Fast Fact: At 20 miles long and 7 miles wide, Sycamore is the second largest canyon in the state. If you're curious as to the biggest, it's the one we call Grand.

Pronghorns gallop through a meadow along the Sycamore Rim Trail. Photo by the author.

the canyon and rambles through Pomeroy Tanks, lovely perennial pools in another shallow canyon. From here you climb KA Hill, the only serious workout of the journey. Crossing the 7,287-foot summit, you'll have views all the way to the San Francisco Peaks. After that, switchbacks twist down the slope, a mile back to the trailhead.

Where: From Flagstaff, travel west on I-40 nearly 30 miles. Take exit 167 (Garland Prairie Rd.) and turn south on Forest Road 141. Roughly 12 miles from the interstate, turn right on FR 56. Follow FR 56 for 1.5 miles to the signed trailhead. The dirt roads can be managed in a sedan.

Cost: Free.

Difficulty: Easy.

Length: 11 miles round-trip.

Dogs: Yes, on a leash.

Details: (928) 635-5600, www.fs.usda.gov/r03/kaibab.

Hot Tip: Grand Canyon Railway still delivers passengers to the South Rim of the Grand Canyon. Along the ride through pine forests, musicians wander through the cars performing songs. On the return trip, the train is "robbed" by the Cataract Creek Gang. Steam engines are used a few days each year, and during the holiday season, the train transforms into the Polar Express.

Cruiser's Route 66 Café, Williams

Welcome to the Mother Road's porch. This is where travelers on the historic highway hang out. It's a classic diner with a big patio, great music, and half-pound burgers landing on your table.

Cruiser's Route 66 Café is a mainstay in downtown Williams. Ribs are always slow-cooking on a custom-made wood-burning smoker. They cunningly keep the big metal contraption on the patio near the entrance so the perfume of burning mesquite captures your attention as you walk past. You stand there haunted by a fragrance as the guy playing guitar on the patio launches into a John Prine song, and your decision is made. "Let's eat here," you announce. And that's a good call.

A gas station in the 1930s, the building fell on hard times after Route 66 was decommissioned. Cruiser's Café opened in 1988 and is filled with neon,

Burgers, beer, neon, and live music make Cruiser's a popular stop for Route 66 travelers. Photo by the author.

antique pumps, and vintage signs. Sit inside or, better still, outdoors where they have live music almost daily through the summer.

Burgers are Angus beef served with lettuce, tomato, onion, and a choice of cheese on a brioche bun. Extra toppings are available, or try a signature offering like the Smoked Longhorn Burger, covered with smoked brisket, barbecue sauce, homemade coleslaw, and cheddar cheese. Wash it down with one of the local craft brews on tap. It especially hits the spot on a summer evening, beneath the glow of neon, while listening to the soundtrack of your youth as traffic slow rumbles down Route 66. As you relax, it becomes easy to lose track of the decades here.

Vegetarian Options: A candied walnut and cranberry salad makes a light alternative.
Don't Forget: Browse their gift shop, overflowing with Route 66 memorabilia.
Details: 233 W. Route 66, (928) 635-2445.

Hot Tip: Visitors can explore Bearizona Wildlife Park from the comfort of their vehicles, aboard a shuttle bus, or on foot to see a variety of animals in natural habitats. The park also offers educational programs emphasizing the importance of conservation.

Stone to Steel Dam Trail, Ash Fork

Here's a weird engineering tidbit: The first large steel dam in the world was built in Ash Fork. This trail takes you to it, starting from another historic dam.

In 1898, the Ashfork Bainbridge Steel Dam was constructed in remote Johnson Canyon to supply water for the railroad. While the steel dam proved to be cheap and fast to build, there were concerns about how it would hold up for the long haul. So, in 1911, a traditional masonry dam was built from precision-cut stone blocks less than a mile upstream. If the steel dam failed, water would still be available for steam locomotives. Those fears proved groundless.

Only three steel dams went up in this country, and the only one still serving its original purpose is here. Both dams back up small lakes, now managed as recreational reservoirs. This easy path (0.85 miles) starts from the stone dam and rambles along the edge of Johnson Canyon through a scrub forest of juniper and pine to reach the steel dam. Nearly 50 feet tall, the dam was constructed out of 24 curved steel plates, giving it a scalloped appearance.

Pulling off to take this short hike offers a crash course in transportation across the Southwest. You arrive via the smooth, comfortable interstate. Then you bounce down a couple of miles of old crumbling Route 66, the iconic Mother Road, to reach the spot where steam locomotives once huffed across the high plains. The one replaced the other that had replaced the other. And they all followed the original line carved by the Beale Wagon Road, which lies just to the north. Built in 1857 by Lieutenant Edward Beale leading a group of men, horses, and camels, this was the primary route for western travelers until the steel rails of track were laid in the 1880s.

The lake behind the stone dam is stocked with trout and bass and is a popular spot with anglers looking for a little solitude. Or maybe they just like fishing in the shadow of so much history.

Where: From Ash Fork, travel east on I-40 for 6 miles to exit 151 (Welch Road). Travel north for a few hundred feet and then turn right on FR 6. Follow this dirt road for 0.5 miles and at a T junction make a hard left turn onto an orphaned segment of historic Route 66. This stretch of dilapidated pavement is signed FR 6E. Continue west for about 3 miles and turn right at the turnoff for Ash Fork Stone Dam. The trailhead is located at the end of this half-mile dirt road. Be aware that the access road can deteriorate quickly. There's a parking apron for fishing access at 0.2 miles. Depending on your vehicle, it may be wise to park here and continue on foot.
Cost: Free.
Difficulty: Easy.
Length: 1.7 miles round-trip.
Dogs: Yes, on a leash.
Details: (928) 635-5600, www.fs.usda.gov/r03/kaibab.

"Looking hard for a drive-in,
searching for a corner café,
where hamburgers sizzle on an
open grill night and day."
CHUCK BERRY

Delgadillo's Snow Cap Drive-In, Seligman

Bite into a piece of history at Delgadillo's Snow Cap Drive-In. This Route 66 icon opened in Seligman in 1953. It was built by Juan Delgadillo out of scrap lumber collected from the railroad. Juan specialized in serving good food with a side of goofy humor, making this a beloved stop for generations.

The Delgadillo family have deep roots in Seligman and it was Angel Delgadillo, the town barber, along with his brother Juan, who spearheaded the preservation movement that saved Route 66. Be sure to bring the kids. Seligman was the inspiration for the town of Radiator Springs in the Pixar movie *Cars*. Both Angel and Juan are thanked at the end of the movie. Sadly, Juan passed away in 2004, but his family keeps the traditions going—tasty grub and lots of laughs.

Step inside (if you can figure out which is the right doorknob) and it's like entering a carnival funhouse, although it smells a whole lot better. The menu is a series of running jokes (Dead Chicken and Cheeseburger with Cheese)

Since 1953, the iconic Delgadillo's Snow Cap has been dishing up food and laughs along Route 66, America's Main Street. Photo by the author.

and the place is wallpapered with gags, business cards, and currency. "Sorry, We're Open" proclaims one sign. The goofiness continues out back in Juan's Garden with a collection of kitsch and old automobiles.

But just because they're quick with a joke doesn't mean they don't know their way around the kitchen. Order at the counter then grab a picnic table under the shady awning. They dish up good old-fashioned road food like burgers, corn dogs, and tacos. The Chorizo Burger has some kick to it.

The Snow Cap is also in *Guinness World Records* for the largest display of milkshake flavors. They concocted 266 different flavors of shake, including some bizarre combinations such as chocolate fudge mustard hot dog, and creamy avocado cod filet. Don't worry. The permanent shake menu trends more traditional. Still, those bizarre combos were pretty funny, and I'll bet that somewhere Juan Delgadillo was smiling.

Vegetarian Options: They have a veggie burger on the menu.
Don't Forget: The Snow Cap closes for the winter, shutting down in November and reopening at the beginning of March.
Details: 22235 Old Highway 66, (928) 422-3291.

Hot Tip: Starting from Seligman, the Annual Historic Route 66 Fun Run takes place the first weekend in May. Hundreds of classic cars, hot rods, street rods, muscle cars, jalopies, motorcycles, and a few vehicles that defy description make a 140-mile drive to Kingman and finally to Topock. It's a rolling party with live music, barbecues, dances, and car shows all along the way.

Rattlesnake Rendezvous

Throughout my years of hiking, I've encountered dozens of rattlesnakes. They're fascinating creatures and I'm generally delighted to see them. I've only had one close encounter.

I was hiking one of my regular trails in Dead Horse Ranch State Park on a warm May morning. The trail becomes a sandy path leading down to a wash. Just above the wash where the sand is heaviest, a row of rocks lines the edge of the path, providing firmer footing. Soon as I stepped on the rocks, a rattle exploded beneath my feet. Fortunately, momentum was on my side and I hit the wash in a long stride.

When I looked around, the snake was pulling back so I knew it had taken a swipe at me from the path. It came sidewinding down the trail, mad as can be, then slithered off down the wash, rattling the whole time. But I couldn't understand how I had missed seeing a snake on an exposed trail.

It only took a brief examination to figure it out. The stones are packed in sand, no room under them. But the second rock jutted out a bit and with the way the hill sloped down, there was a slender strip not visible from a hiker's angle. The rattler must have been lying there snugged up against the rocks, completely out of sight. As I approached, it stayed motionless, hoping not to be seen, which is always their first reaction. Then, rudely, I almost stomped its head. No wonder it was perturbed.

All in all, this was a good reminder. I'm alert when hiking but, despite that, I had a brush with danger because of one tiny blind spot. Now I know to watch for similar situations.

I love all of Arizona and that includes rattlesnakes, Gila monsters, cactus spines, and mesquite thorns. A little danger adds spice to the beauty. Get outside and experience it for yourself. But leave the earbuds at home. If I had been listening to music, I could not have immediately identified the location of the rattle and would have come to a stop and almost certainly been bitten.

SEDONA AND THE VERDE VALLEY

Nestled at the mouth of Oak Creek Canyon and surrounded by a sea of red sandstone, Sedona exists at an impossible intersection: a real-life getaway and fantasyland escape. The scenery bites your heart in half.

Multi-hued stone formations jut upward from the high desert floor and create a vivid, mesmerizing setting that changes hourly with the light. Surrounded by 1.8 million acres of national forest land, visitors have instant access to recreational activities. Trails for hiking and biking weave among the bristling forest of pinnacles, spires, buttes, and domes. Yet you're never far from the indulgences of town. Sedona is equal parts rugged and resort.

The surrounding Verde Valley was named by early Spanish explorers surprised to discover such a verdant landscape. Bordered by the Mogollon Rim and Sedona's red rocks on one side and the long line of the Black Hills and Mingus Mountain on the other, the valley is nourished by the crucial watershed of the Verde River and its many tributaries, attracting wildlife and people. Although the mines of Jerome have long fallen silent, this is still a thriving agricultural area and has grown into a popular wine destination filled with vineyards and tasting rooms.

The Ground Control Trail crosses the high sandstone shoulder of the Cockscomb formation as part of a scenic loop. Courtesy of Mike Koopsen, Sedona.

Cockscomb–Ground Control Loop, Sedona

Combine three trails in West Sedona to create a lively interactive adventure. This memorable route delivers outsized panoramas and slickrock thrills. Ground Control Trail is the centerpiece of a high-flying loop that scrambles up the shoulder of the Cockscomb, a distinctive formation rising in the Dry Creek area.

It's all part of the Western Gateway Trails system. From the Aerie Trailhead set out on Cockscomb Trail for about a mile as it rambles across open country. You'll pass a junction with Outer Limits, but keep going. That will be your return route. Hang a right on Ground Control at the base of the Cockscomb formation. The trail slants uphill in a modest ascent at first before turning spicy.

Ground Control becomes a slender snake as it slithers up the flank of Cockscomb and clings to the curving sandstone. Edgy and ledgy, the narrow passage hugs the cliff face 300 feet above the valley floor. Views are dramatic crossing the open slickrock shelf, but watch your step. Red cliffs rise overhead and it always intrigues me to see how these formations appear when I'm not gazing at them from a distance but creeping among their nooks and crannies. They seem more personal, more vulnerable when I can touch their scars.

Through here it felt like a slow-motion carnival ride as I light-footed along the dips and twists. The path curls beneath the bristling columns that give Cockscomb its name and then drops steeply over the side. Watch for sightings of Sedona icons Courthouse Butte and Cathedral Rock. While Ground Control never feels dangerous, there is some exposure on the upper ledges, so keep that in mind if heights make you nervous.

Outer Limits is waiting once you touch down, so hang a right as it meanders through groves of ocotillos and makes its way back to Cockscomb Trail. Turn left to reach the trailhead.

Where: From the traffic circle of AZ 179/89A, drive west on 89A for 3.2 miles, then turn right on Dry Creek Road. Proceed 2.9 miles to a T. Turn left on Boynton Pass Road and continue 1.6 miles to another T. Turn left and go 1.4 miles to Aerie Road. Turn left on Aerie and drive to the trailhead approximately a half mile on the right.
Cost: Free.
Difficulty: Moderate.
Length: 3.2 miles round-trip.
Dogs: Yes, on a leash.
Details: (928) 203-2900, www.fs.usda.gov/r03/coconino.

Hot Tip: The focus of Sedona Heritage Museum is split between exhibits on apple growing, cowboys, and movies. This was cowboy country, although early settlers thrived along Oak Creek by growing apples and peaches. And nearly 100 feature films were shot in Sedona, so the movie room features photo stills, posters, storyboards, and a loop of Sedona-based flicks. The setting, a peaceful homestead and orchard in Jordan Historical Park, alone is worth a visit.

Nick's on the West Side, Sedona

Sedona tends toward the swanky, with world-class resorts and high-end properties catering to well-heeled tourists. Amid the ethereal beauty and mystical surroundings, unassuming joints geared toward locals are rare indeed. When you find one, it's important to support them just to maintain a sense of balance. Especially when they sling the grub like Nick's on the West Side.

Long a mainstay of West Sedona, Nick's specializes in a range of comfort food. They serve breakfast all day, do scratch-made Mexican dishes, and smoke barbecue in-house. New owners took over in 2024. Hailing from Louisiana, they'll sometimes throw a Cajun recipe into the mix.

Then there are the burgers. Build your own or choose a house specialty. I opted for their popular Guiness Burger, wearing an assemblage of mushrooms, grilled onions, and a thick piece of Guiness cheddar cheese. It arrived open-face with leaf lettuce, ripe tomato, and a pickle spear on the side. Putting it all together created a hefty, busy sandwich. But I liked the harmony of the flavors with the beery cheese adding a little smooth maltiness. Despite the crush of yummy toppings, the sturdy bun held the parcel together while I chomped my way through.

Maybe in the future they'll throw some Cajun spice on the slightly timid fries to give them a kick in the pants.

The friendly staff at Nick's makes everybody feel welcome. Although some more than others. When a family with a baby slid into the next booth, the waitress hurried over to coo and fuss over the baby, commenting on his big blue eyes. Yet during my entire meal, not a single mention was made regarding my peepers, which, for the record, are green.

Vegetarian Options: There's a vegetarian burger, salads, and Mexican and breakfast selections.

Don't Forget: They serve a popular brisket sandwich that's slow roasted for 17 hours.

Details: 2920 AZ 89A, (928) 204-2088, www.nickswestside.com.

Hot Tip: The Amitabha Stupa and Peace Park is a quiet spot at the base of Thunder Mountain in West Sedona. The free site is open from dawn to dusk for visitors of all faiths for prayer, healing, and meditation. The stupa, a Buddhist structure, is one of the oldest forms of sacred architecture on earth.

Hangover Trail, Sedona

This trail falls outside standard ratings of easy, moderate, or strenuous. Hangover should be listed as scary. The incline is moderate but the exposures and drop-offs up the ante into a realm of butt-puckering tenseness. If there is such a thing as technical walking, this is it. Welcome to slickrock hiking.

For a town built on sandstone, Sedona remains downright miserly regarding the slickrock experience. Several trails cross patches of slickrock, but not in a large expanse like in southern Utah's canyon country. There is no hiking I enjoy more than hoofing across the slant and slope of petrified waves. I love the hard lines, the clean definition, the ancient power I feel under my feet as I touch the bones of the land. Slickrock is a general term used for any bare, exposed sandstone level enough for walking or riding. The Hangover barely qualifies, because level is not its strong suit. The hike

The Hangover Trail plunges into Sedona's red rock backcountry. Courtesy of Mike Koopsen, Sedona.

involves lots of climbing and descending sandstone slopes with nothing but open space on all sides.

If you have a high-clearance 4WD vehicle, then start on Cow Pies Trail just off rough and rutted Schnebly Hill Road. It's an easy path cutting through scrubby woodlands. Where Cow Pies branches off, continue toward Mitten Ridge.

I'm reminded of the Fred Astaire movie *Royal Wedding*, where he's dancing like mad, then taps his way up the walls and onto the ceiling. I was walking through the forest toward a cliff of sandstone, then boom! I walked straight up the wall.

This is the magic of slickrock hiking, requiring good grippy soles on your boots, a little faith, and careful foot placement. I pursued a curving route marked by white painted hexagons as it flowed across the contours of rock toward a saddle separating the Bear Wallow and Oak Creek drainages.

Views here are profound. Just make sure you come to a complete stop to savor them. This is not a course you want to stray from. Keep your footing precise as the sandstone slopes to the sides toward long perilous drop-offs. It's a trail that will sober you up fast. If you're balance-challenged or prone to vertigo, steer clear of this outing.

This trail mixes just the right combination of madness and beauty. I crossed the saddle and dropped into a nifty little bowl, then latched onto a thin ribbon of a path clinging to the slope as it passes beneath protrusions of overhanging rock. This section prompted the trail name. From here, I was treated to sensational views of Midgely Bridge swarming with ant-sized tourists. I crossed one final saddle and eased down the ridge to circle back toward the trailhead.

Don't attempt Schnebly Hill Road without 4WD, even if you've done so in the past. The road has seriously deteriorated. Another way to hike the

Fast Fact: As crazy as it seems, this trail is used by hardcore mountain bikers. Hangover is rated double black diamond, which translates to a big skull and crossbones and should only be attempted by experienced, slightly unhinged bikers.

Hangover Trail is to start out on Munds Wagon Trail. Use the Huckaby/ Margs Draw Trailhead, which is located on the lower paved portion of Schnebly Hill Road. Follow Munds Wagon Trail for 2.5 miles to Cow Pies, and complete the loop.

Where: From the traffic circle of AZ 179/89A, take 179 south 0.3 miles. Turn left on Schnebly Hill Road and drive 3.5 miles to the signed parking area. The last 2.5 miles is a rugged dirt road requiring high clearance 4WD. Passenger vehicles should park at the Huckaby Trailhead right before Schnebly Hill Road turns to dirt.
Cost: Free from Cow Pies, admission fee if starting from Huckaby/Margs Draw Trailhead.
Difficulty: Moderate.
Length: 4.8 miles round-trip from Cow Pies, 9 miles round-trip by adding Munds Wagon Trail.
Dogs: Yes, on a leash.
Details: (928) 203-2900, www.fs.usda.gov/r03/coconino.

Fast Fact: The town of Sedona was named by its first postmaster, T. C. Schnebly. His original suggestions of Oak Creek Crossing and Schnebly's Station were rejected by the postmaster general as being too long, so T. C. simply named the community after his lovely wife, Sedona.

Dellepiane, Sedona

The people in Argentina certainly know their way around a quality cut of beef. They also have a reputation for their love of eating. Dellepiane, opened in 2017, celebrates that cuisine and culture while also delving deep into plant-based vegetarian and vegan options. A sustainable restaurant, they emphasize locally grown and seasonal produce.

The wood floors, simple tables, and bright flags strung along ceiling beams create an international flair. One wall bears a mural of a Buenos Aires street scene, the location of the original restaurant. Big cuts of meat line the shelves of dry-aging cabinets in the back for steaks, sandwiches, and empanadas, which are pockets of flaky dough stuffed with a litany of ingredients.

Dellepiane serves only grass-fed Niman Ranch beef. All burger patties are 6 ounces, smashed and cooked to medium-well. The namesake Dellepiane burger comes crowned with pecan-smoked bacon, grilled provolone, cheddar, caramelized onions, barbecue sauce, and chimichurri-based house sauce. The Surf n' Turf is crowned with plump shrimp, mango chutney, tomato, jalapeño, and cilantro.

It felt like I sat in a farmhouse in the Argentinian countryside as my burger was served on a wooden plank sided by a metal tub filled with rich, rustic fries. It was a sight for sore eyes and empty stomach. The vegetables tasted garden fresh and blended perfectly with the supple savoriness of the beef. The succulent package proved utterly satisfying, held together by a soft sesame seed bun. From a land of steaks and barbecue, this burger wore a regal pedigree.

Vegetarian Options: A big chunk of the innovative menu is dedicated to vegetarian and vegan choices. Along with an Impossible burger and an Impossible vegan burger, there are Impossible kebabs, vegan beef lasagna,

Dellepiane emphasizes locally grown and seasonal produce and uses grass-fed Niman Ranch beef for their delicious burgers. Photo by the author.

plant-based fried chickn, a flight of empanadas, a Thai chile burger, and plenty more.

Don't Forget: Peruse the dessert case for a selection of homemade American and Argentine sweet treats.

Details: 7000 AZ 179, (928) 862-4129, www.dellepianeburger.com.

"There are always flowers for those who want to see them."
HENRI MATISSE

Hiline Trail, Sedona

This trail is like a Sedona highlight reel. It showcases incredible panoramas, good slickrock hiking, and even offers an option for a dip in Oak Creek. Hiline shares similar parentage as the Hangover. Another stunning trail with outlandish views built by bikers and adopted by the forest service. This one also earns a double black diamond rating for spoke-jockeys but is more heavily trafficked. Hiline, Hangover, and their ilk have turned Sedona into a primo mountain biking destination.

From the trailhead at Yavapai Vista, a knot of short connector trails branches off, but maps are posted at each junction. Follow Kaibab Trail to Slim Shady and then bear left to Hiline.

Hiline wiggles up a narrow gulley to a rocky slope and then tilts upward, an eyebrow of a trail pasted against the tall promontory known as the Pedestal. The climb was steady, but I never noticed as I stopped every few feet to close my gaping jaw. Lavish vistas of multiple formations included Bell Rock, Courthouse Butte, and Cathedral Rock.

Make the mesa top your picnic/turnaround spot if you don't want to do a full 7 miles. The trail tumbles off the backside, dropping in a series of red rock ledges providing various angles of Cathedral along the way. Keep an eye peeled for bikers hurtling through here. Over bare rock, just follow the dabs of white paint.

The trail finally levels off, entering a dry streambed flanked by sun-dappled woodlands. Hiline junctions with the Baldwin Trail after 3.5 miles. If you've come this far, there's no need to hurry right back. I hung a right on Baldwin and a half mile later was under a dense canopy of cottonwoods and sycamores, on the edge of silver-tongued Oak Creek. This is a Tom Sawyer–quality hooky spot, perfect for fishing or snoozing the afternoon away. I chose the latter.

The Hiline Trail puts Cathedral Rock on display for hikers and mountain bikers. Courtesy of Mike Koopsen, Sedona.

Where: From the traffic circle of AZ 179/AZ 89A, take 179 south 5.5 miles to Yavapai Vista Trailhead. Yavapai Vista can only be accessed via southbound AZ 179.

Cost: Admission fee.

Difficulty: Moderate.

Length: 7 miles round-trip, 8 if continuing to the creek.

Dogs: Yes, on a leash.

Details: (928) 203-2900, www.fs.usda.gov/r03/coconino.

PJ's Village Pub, Sedona

At some point—and I can't say exactly when it happened—PJ's Village Pub changed. Not in a bad way. It's still a dyed-in-the-wool sports bar, the kind you're more likely to find in your hometown rather than on the tourist-filled streets of Sedona. Walls are adorned with sports memorabilia, neon signs, and more televisions than Best Buy has on display. Same well-stocked bar, same friendly atmosphere.

It's just that somewhere along the way they got serious about food. They always made a good burger but they've also upped their game with an expanded menu and more wide-ranging specials. You can order steak tacos or a half rack of barbecued ribs. And of course, they couldn't even call themselves a sports bar without crispy, juicy wings.

But let's get back to those burgers. They start with a half pound of prime Angus beef cooked to order. They dish up a tender Red Wine Burger, cooked in vino with caramelized onions, sauteed mushrooms, lettuce, bleu cheese crumbles, and port wine mayo. Their signature burger is the Boomer, topped with an international layer of cheeses—American and Swiss—hot pastrami, mustard, and mayo.

As I have stated previously—and which will likely be carved on my tombstone—I avoid mayo in every situation. So I will never experience the full execution of this burger. But I can't imagine that adding a dollop of white goop to such a carefully crafted burger does anything to enhance what is a sharp flavor profile. It would seem to distract from the very notes you want out front.

Oh well. It's a very popular burger as it stands, so I know I'm in the minority. Burgers are meant to be enjoyed however you see fit. There is no wrong way to eat a burger. It's just that my way is more right.

Vegetarian Options: They offer a grilled portobello burger, or you can substitute the big mushroom slab for any of their signature burgers.
Don't Forget: With trivia nights, karaoke, live music, and dance parties, PJ's is always jumping. Oh yeah, they've even been known to air sporting events on their multitude of television devices.
Details: 40 W. Cortez Dr., (928) 284-2250, pjsvillagepub.co.

Margs Draw Trail, Sedona

Some people play hooky, but not me. I take hooky very seriously.

Certain days demand you slip free of small responsibilities. Days like this—winter on the cusp of spring, but balmy enough for shorts and T-shirt, with a sky belligerently blue. I couldn't slump in front of the computer a minute longer as March tapped on the window with soft primrose knuckles. I'm only flesh and blood.

Margs Draw, named for a mule owned by one of the area's first pioneers, makes the perfect escape. According to local lore, Marg the mule, used to hide out in this scenic area to avoid work. To celebrate that irrepressible spirit, I followed in Marg's hoofsteps.

The trail starts from the parking lot at the end of the pavement on Schnebly Hill Road. This also serves as trailhead for the Huckaby and Munds Wagon Trails. A Red Rock Pass or equivalent is required and can be purchased at an on-site kiosk.

Margs Draw crosses the road and disappears into the woods. This easy hike carves out a path through Munds Mountain Wilderness, edging along the Copper Cliffs and offering the best views of Snoopy Rock, a prominent formation visible from Uptown Sedona. It doesn't take much imagination to spot the beloved beagle lying atop his doghouse with little bird pal Woodstock sitting on his nose. Look close and you can even find Lucy seated nearby.

Near the midway point, about a mile into the hike, you'll pass the junction for the Sombart Lane Trailhead. This provides a nice option when you need a shorter hike. Much of Margs Draw lies a mere crystal's throw from civilization, yet the surrounding forest provides a

Fast Fact: Surprisingly, Snoopy Rock was not named by Sedona's early pioneers. It was originally called Saddle Back Rock.

Snoopy Rock snoozes above Margs Draw. Courtesy of Mike Koopsen, Sedona.

genuine backcountry experience. Instant access to hidden wonders is one of Sedona's many charms.

The path crosses the draw at a lovely dry waterfall and then angles downhill to its end point at Broken Arrow Trailhead, which connects to a whole new network of trails. Turn around here and retrace your steps for a tidy 4-miler. Or keep going to explore the red rock delights along the Broken Arrow Trail. I guess you just have to ask yourself, what would Marg do?

Where: From the traffic circle of AZ 179/89A, take 179 south 0.3 miles. Turn left on Schnebly Hill Road and drive 0.8 miles to the signed parking area.
Cost: Admission fee.
Difficulty: Easy.
Length: 4 miles round-trip.
Dogs: Yes, on a leash.
Details: (928) 203-2900, www.fs.usda.gov/r03/coconino.

Hot Tip: Sedona's most famous piece of architecture is the Chapel of the Holy Cross, completed in 1957. The slender church was built between two burly pillars of rock with high cliffs forming the backdrop. The interior is simple and unadorned. A few benches, some tapestries, and flickering candles create a meditative oasis, while sunlight streams through the floor-to-ceiling window. It's open to the public.

Butterfly Burger, Sedona

Exuding a cosmopolitan air, Butterfly Burger would not be mistaken for your typical burger stand. With its soft lighting, sleek marble bar, stylish décor, and busy open kitchen the restaurant conveys the distinctive vision of award-winning chef Lisa Dahl. She's been elevating Sedona cuisine since the 1990s with a collection of acclaimed dining establishments.

Yet here the menu remains laser-focused on burgers, albeit with a gourmet twist. And you might find me happily eating at a corner table. So in that way, it really is a typical burger stand.

While the word "butterfly" may conjure up something ethereal, imagine them bulked-up. Big burly butterflies although still colorful and complex. That complexity is a signature of the restaurant with each burger carefully constructed, revealing a rhapsody of flavor in each bite. Among the specialty burgers are the Funghi Supreme, smothered in sauteed mushrooms, imported truffle gouda, and house dijonnaise on a soft artisan bun, locally sourced. The namesake Butterfly Burger comes adorned with Manchego cheese, a meaty peppered bacon, guacamole, and chipotle aioli.

Imaginative side dishes range far beyond typical fries and include potato salad, three-seed coleslaw, and plump butter beans. They also offer salads, soups, and some shared plate starters like their amped-up street tots. These plush little potato puffs are smothered in fresh pico, cotija cheese, and a queso-chorizo fundido sauce.

For boring traditionalists like me, their classic burger highlights the quality of the fresh meat and ingredients, and the careful preparation that goes into each order. While I've enjoyed their more innovative creations, an elegant and fundamentally sound burger is all I really need. These are glorious bun-clad beef planets that pull me into their rotation.

Gourmet burgers, upscale sides, and stylish décor define Butterfly Burger. Courtesy of Mike Koopsen, Sedona.

Vegetarian Options: Noncarnivores are made most welcome here. The Hipster is a lentil-walnut sofrito vegan burger finished with oven-roasted Campari tomato jam and pimentón aioli. Or the Primo Portobello is grilled and marinated, topped with caramelized onion, Manchego cheese, shredded romaine, and chipotle aioli.
Don't Forget: The gourmet milkshakes are seriously indulgent and can be boozed up if you like.
Details: 6657 AZ 179, (928) 862-4448, www.butterflyburger.com.

Sketch–Ridge Loop, Sedona

With the trailhead tucked away on Chavez Ranch Road, this moderate loop is seldom crowded despite revealing some dramatic views of Sedona's red rock country. At less than 3 miles with a nice remote feel it's really an ideal hike for most. But if you have a genuine fear of heights, consider sitting this one out.

From the parking area, walk back down the road to Ridge Trail, turning right to amble uphill. Veer off on Sketch Trail as it enters from the left. Then hold on to your hat.

While Ridge Trail climbs across the middle of the plateau, Sketch pushes out to the edge. The early portion of Sketch hugs the eastern rim of Carroll Canyon, an exposed path threading its way among ledges, boulders, and a few scraggly trees fighting to hang on. The trail is a skinny singletrack but not quite as sketchy as the name implies—unless a mountain biker suddenly comes hurtling downhill at you as they are wont to do. Just stay alert.

With nothing but air on one side, views turn epic. I especially enjoyed the looks at triangular Pyramid, one of Sedona's lesser-known formations. Sketch follows the contours of the rim, and soon the drop-offs become less severe. As the trail curves east, I was treated to a broad panorama of Thunder Mountain and Coffee Pot Rock. This perspective provides an intriguing overview of the area. Soon Sketch reaches the second junction with Ridge Trail. Turn south on Ridge as it meanders through scrubby woodland and then drops downhill while offering looks at Cathedral Rock and the Oak Creek floodplain.

Where: From the traffic circle of AZ 179/89A, travel west on 89A (toward Cottonwood) for 4.2 miles to Upper Red Rock Loop Rd. Turn left and go 1.5 miles to Chavez Ranch Rd. Turn left and proceed 1 mile to the locked

Hikers enjoy a red rock panorama on the Sketch and Ridge Trails. Courtesy of Mike Koopsen, Sedona.

gate where you'll find several parking spaces. Walk back 200 yards the way you came on Chavez Ranch Rd. to Ridge Trail and head up the hill.

Cost: Free.

Difficulty: Moderate.

Length: 2.7 miles round-trip.

Dogs: Yes, on a leash.

Details: (928) 203-2900, www.fs.usda.gov/r03/coconino.

Outlaw Grille, Sedona

Tucked just off the main drag of Uptown Sedona, Outlaw Grille is a secret hiding in plain sight. Order at the walk-up window of this small place and grab one of the tables lining the covered breezeway between shops. Anyone who loves good food knows you should always scour the nooks, crannies, and alleys of a town. This is where you'll often find some intriguing haunts.

Burgers here are big and beefy, no punches pulled. A half pound of certified Angus beef is a sandwich to be reckoned with. These will keep you in the saddle all day. If you walk away hungry, have yourself checked for a tapeworm.

The Ace High comes mounded with bacon, bleu cheese crumbles, grilled onion, and mushroom. That's just a devastating combination. The Morning After lands on your table with a bang because it's wearing a melted slice of cheddar cheese, fried egg, crispy bacon, and grilled jalapeño. That will pop your eyes open no matter what kind of fun/rowdy/wild/lost/embarrassing adventures you had the night before.

Plenty of folks come for Outlaw Grille's tender ribs. They're hickory smoked with their house-made rub and then finished on the grill. Wings, chicken fingers, sandwiches, and salads round out the menu.

Vegetarian Options: Veggie burgers are available, and they make a Caesar salad. If you're looking for an interesting appetizer, the Bull Whips are battered green beans served with wasabi ranch.

Don't Forget: Be aware that all burgers are cooked medium-well unless otherwise requested.

Details: 250 Jordan Rd., (928) 862-4085, www.outlawgrille.com.

West Fork Trail, Sedona

This creekside walk into a high-walled, forested gorge is considered by many to be the most beautiful hike in Arizona. And in a state with the Grand Canyon, that says plenty.

The Call of the Canyon Picnic Site includes restrooms and picnic tables. A paved path leads past informational signs to an arched footbridge. After crossing the bridge, the trail reverts to dirt and rambles through an old orchard. Beyond the trees, the ruins of the Mayhew Lodge are tucked among the brush.

From here, the path traces a stream into a narrow defile guarded by soaring cliffs. It's a mesmerizing combination of soft forest and sheer stone, intimacy and dizzying drama. The maintained trail is 3 miles long and includes a dozen creek crossings, so a sturdy walking stick makes a good companion.

This was a trail I hiked often back in the day when it was less accessible. No signs and no parking kept most folks away. Much more popular today, it's still a trail not to be missed. Echoes of birdsong and the splashy stream fill the canyon. The trail parallels the meandering creek the whole way. Crossings generally involve a short hop over strategically positioned rocks, but wear shoes you don't mind getting wet. And be sure you know how to identify

Fast Fact: While staying in the cabins at the head of West Fork that would become Mayhew Lodge, western writer Zane Grey penned the words to The Call of the Canyon. It was the first of his novels snapped up by Hollywood. At Grey's insistence, the filmmakers shot the 1923 silent movie on location, the first of many to use Sedona's red rocks as a backdrop.

Autumn leaves add a touch of drama to the already spectacular West Fork Trail. Courtesy of Mike Koopsen, Sedona.

poison ivy because it is plentiful along the water, growing among grapevines, sumac, and Virginia creeper.

The erosion-scarred sandstone creates unique ledges and overhangs that kids love. And to be honest, so do us well-seasoned mugs. I still like to visit on summer weekdays, climb on a rock, and luxuriate in this loamy stream-fed woodland wrapped in red sandstone. The maintained portion of the trail ends at a wide pool framed by towering cliffs. This is the normal turnaround spot. However, you can continue an additional 11 miles if you don't mind wading, bushwhacking, and swimming.

Spectacular in any season, West Fork's fall color displays are legendary. The October chill transforms the woodlands into a tapestry of yellow, orange, and red beneath a sky achingly blue. It is stunning, which is why this trail is always jam-packed in autumn.

Where: Trailhead is at Call of the Canyon Picnic Site, 9.5 miles north of Sedona on AZ 89A.
Cost: Admission fee.
Difficulty: Easy.
Length: 6 miles round-trip.
Dogs: Yes, on a leash.
Details: (928) 203-2900, www.fs.usda.gov/r03/coconino.

Indian Gardens Café & Market, Sedona

This is the country market that all country markets aspire to become. Eclectic, historic, and hidden away in the scenic heart of Oak Creek Canyon, it seems more oasis than retailer. Indian Gardens first opened in the 1940s as a general store, selling goods and gasoline through the decades. Recently, the building with the stone façade and gorgeous setting transitioned into more of a traditional cafe.

There's still a market side if you need supplies for a picnic by the creek. But most people come for the gourmet coffee and food. The menu emphasizes locally grown and organic products, honoring the long agricultural past of this location. Pastries are baked in-house and Indian Gardens is known for serving hearty and healthful breakfasts. Despite the road through Oak Creek Canyon being a thoroughfare of tourists, lots of locals make the drive to support this significant eatery and community gathering spot.

For lunch the focus stays on sandwiches and salads. The creative sandwiches go well beyond standard lunch meat and cheese duets. The Ferrari comes with roasted garlic, fresh mozzarella, basil pesto, arugula, sliced Roma tomato, roasted red pepper, red onion, and balsamic glaze on a toasted ciabatta. It's an intriguing mix of flavors, like a naughty caprese salad—a caprese salad that's turned to a life of petty crime.

And while the seating inside is nice; do not miss the tree-swaddled patio out back. It's an enchanted garden beneath a leafy canopy abutting sandstone cliffs. A

Fast Fact: This is where Sedona got started. Jim Thompson, the area's first white settler, built a cabin here in 1876 or 1877. He began cultivating the gardens of the Native people who had been growing corn and squash alongside the creek.

Indian Gardens offers good food and drink, deep within scenic Oak Creek Canyon. Courtesy of Mike Koopsen, Sedona.

visit during the changing leaves of autumn will nourish your soul, not just your body. This is spectacular alfresco dining, even by Sedona standards.

Vegetarian Options: A large portion of the menu is vegetarian, including the Beet and Bleu salad with organic spring mix, red and gold beets, apples, beet vinaigrette, toasted almonds, and bleu cheese.
Don't Forget: They serve locally roasted coffee.
Details: 3951 N. AZ 89A, (928) 282-7702, www.indiangardens.com.

Cornville Trail System, Cornville

If the Backbone Trail seems fairly smooth and straight, well it should. It mostly follows an old stage road as it cuts across grassy plains. Backbone stretches for nearly 5 miles as it flows through pasture but also crosses a few washes. Fairly smooth, I said. At least by hiking standards. In a wagon or stagecoach it would make for a much bumpier ride. This is part of the Cornville Trail System, a series of interconnected trails for nonmotorized vehicles, helping to connect the communities of the Verde Valley.

Don't expect to find much corn growing in Cornville. The name was a result of sloppy handwriting, poor eyesight, or some other mix-up. The town requested the name of "Cohnville" honoring a pioneer family from the postmaster general's office. Or maybe "Coaneville" or "Coneville," depending on what account you read. But the application was misread and the name Cornville was assigned. No one felt like battling the bureaucracy, so Cornville it stayed.

Even though the town sits along the banks of Oak Creek, you won't have a riparian experience on the current system of trails that includes a few separate loops attached to Backbone and some additional connectors. Although the hope is to continue to expand. Currently Backbone connects Bridgeport (at the edge of Cottonwood) to Cornville.

I wholeheartedly support urban trail systems, especially when they're in my own backyard. This is how we preserve more green space and protect wildlife corridors. Hiking here you'll see rooftops and farmhouses, but you'll also quickly find yourself in open country, among rolling grasslands sprinkled with creosote, junipers, and ocotillos. The tall Black Hills, dominated by Mingus Mountain, fill one horizon (can you spot Jerome up on the slope?) and the red waves of Sedona rise on the other side.

Look at a map to choose your route. All trails are easy with a few moderate stretches. The main segments are well-signed, but look out for social paths coming from surrounding neighborhoods. Backbone Trail roughly parallels Cornville Road. The two main trailheads are on Zalesky Road in Bridgeport, and on Tissaw Road in Verde Santa Fe, a planned community surrounding a golf course.

If you start Backbone from the Zalesky trailhead, you'll quickly reach the short Zalesky Loop (0.4 miles) that wraps around a small hill then rejoins Backbone. The main stem drops through a deep-cut wash and skirts past the homes of Verde Santa Fe. The 2-mile Side Oats Loop makes an interesting ramble if you're so inclined.

Starting from Tissaw Road puts you into open country a little quicker and provides access to Creosote Loop (1 mile) and Black Grama Loop, a slightly wilder 2.1-mile option. Don't be surprised to encounter cows because this is open range country. Also don't be surprised to encounter me because this is open range country.

Where: Start in Cottonwood from the AZ 89A/AZ 260 junction. For Zalesky Road Trailhead: Drive east on 89A for 0.8 miles. Turn right on Zalesky Rd. and drive 300 feet to the parking area. For Tissaw Road Trailhead: Drive east on AZ 89A for 1.8 miles. Turn right on Cornville Rd. and drive 1.1 miles. Turn right on Tissaw Rd. and continue 0.7 miles to trailhead parking on the left.
Cost: Free.
Difficulty: Easy/moderate.
Length: 12 miles total.
Dogs: Yes, on a leash.
Details: (928) 203-2900, www.fs.usda.gov/r03/coconino.

"Please, if it's not too late, make it a cheeseburger."
LYLE LOVETT

G's Burgers, Cornville

Grapes and burgers. That's what the bustling metropolis of Cornville is known for. The vineyards and wineries set on the sloping hills above Oak Creek just outside of town are the foundation of the Verde Valley American Viticultural Area. The entire region is now a wine destination.

Cornville is also becoming a burger destination because of this eatery next to a gas station. G's Burgers opened in 2015 and sports a rustic industrial interior with a large fully stocked bar and tractor seats serving as barstools. A few tables line the walls and more are outside on the skinny patio. Order at the bar once you've sorted through the lengthy slate of always fresh Angus chuck burgers. There are 15 on the menu plus a special burger of the week for those regulars who like to walk on the wild side.

One comes roofed with a brick of mac and cheese. The Verde Valley

G's Burgers in Cornville draws hungry folks from all over the Verde Valley. Courtesy of Mike Koopsen, Sedona.

packs a little heat with fire-roasted green chiles and pepper jack cheese. I'm partial to the Steakhouse, which features an artfully designed collection of ingredients—bleu cheese crumbles, bacon, tomato, arugula, onion twigs, and steakhouse mayo. Naturally, I declined the latter and the burger doesn't miss a beat. It was juicy without being sloppy.

The sharpness of the bleu cheese leads off but never gets too far in front. There's a harmony to the burger with everything working together and the bacon and onion twigs adding a satisfying crunch. The brioche bun, wearing a little "G" brand on top is soft but stable, holding the concoction together until the very last bite.

Vegetarian Options: There's a veggie burger, a couple of salads, and some munchies like fried zucchini and spicy fried green beans.
Don't Forget: If you're not in town for the wine, G's Burgers carries an impressive selection of whiskey.
Details: 1220 S. Eastern Dr., (928) 634-2867, www.gsburgersaz.com.

Hot Tip: Housed in a refurbished century-old school, Clemenceau Heritage Museum is one of those great small-town museums full of charm and model railroads. The nonprofit facility is operated by volunteers and gives a nice glimpse at life in the valley through exhibits and artifacts. They have a whole model train room that recreates the complex rail network that once serviced the communities. It's a must for any railroad buff, and kids of all ages.

Jail Trail, Cottonwood

A small river rock building sits at the head of this trail, prompting the name. This was the Cottonwood jail constructed in 1929. As I walked past on a summer morning I felt pity for its former occupants. You're really doing hard time locked inside a little sunbaked oven so close to the river you could smell it, close enough to hear leaves rustling on big shady cottonwoods.

The Jail Trail starts as a wide path but narrows as it slips under the trees. Cross a small bridge and the pathway bears right, wandering through this riparian forest. Cottonwood is named for these big trees guarding the Verde River. While it may seem peaceful here along this slender oasis, this is actually a busy throughfare for migrating species. The rufous hummingbird, the common black hawk, and monarch butterfly are just a few species utilizing this watery route on their journeys.

Watch for deer in the meadows and beavers, river otters, bald eagles, and great blue herons around the water. As you wander through the riparian zone, small side trails lead to the Verde. The Jail Trail goes under the bridge and finally ends after a mile in the woodsy brush of a disc golf course on the edge of Riverfront Park. You can also cross the bridge to enter Dead Horse Ranch State Park, which is a fee area. Bring your state park pass.

Each season adds a different flavor to this easy hike. In autumn, I cheer for the soft-lit rage of golden leaves. On summer mornings, I like to watch the dawn push through the willow branches like they are lace curtains, knowing a long-lost love waits on the other side.

It's a popular escape for birders, dog owners, and parents with kids. If it had been around a century ago, I'm sure it would have been a dreamed-about escape for bootleggers, ruffians, and other scoundrels gazing through the tiny barred windows of the Cottonwood hoosegow at a cool, shady oasis.

Here's an added bonus. Once you're back at the trailhead, you can walk to your burger joint waiting at the other end of Old Town. And since Prohibition is over, feel free to stop and sample local wines at the tasting rooms you'll pass on the way.

Where: Trailhead is at 1101 N. Main Street. The parking lot sits at the north end of Old Town beneath the archway proclaiming "Gateway to the Verde River."
Cost: Free.
Difficulty: Easy.
Length: 2 miles round-trip.
Dogs: Yes, on a leash.
Details: (928) 639-3200.

Bing's Burger Station, Cottonwood

Occupying a prime corner in Old Town Cottonwood, Bing's is a vintage gas station disguised as—wait for it—a vintage gas station. At least from the outside where a bright orange 1950 Plymouth Special Deluxe sits beside antique pumps as if waiting for one last fill-up. Inside you'll find a stylish diner with shiny booths, counter seating, and a wall of license plates.

Grab an order slip and pencil when you walk in. Fill it out but take your time because you've got lots of options to ponder. Check off the items you want, along with toppings, condiments, sauces, and beverages. You even choose the mix-ins for your milkshake. In addition to burgers, Bing's dishes up sandwiches, hot dogs, salads, chili, and soup.

I always feel at home at Bing's. Maybe because my first actual job was working as a pump jockey at a neighborhood gas station. Long before self-serve became the norm, guys like me came out to pump the petrol and wash the windshield. I was 15. The owner was a man named Tater, a burly guy with a walrus mustache, a booming laugh, and a generous heart. He knew everyone in the community from cops to preachers to hookers to the lady who smoked incredible ribs in her backyard. Everyone brought their cars to Tater's. For a wide-eyed aspiring writer, it was quite the education.

Of course, those station days are long gone at Bing's too. Now hand-formed patties sizzle on the flattop. The burgers emerge lightly crusted and sweetly juicy. The shoestring fries are cut fresh daily and pack a

Hot Tip: At the center of the Verde Valley American Viticultural Area are the numerous wine tasting rooms set among the shops, restaurants, and hotels in picturesque Old Town Cottonwood. Check into your lodgings and then start swilling the grape juice.

Bing's Burger Station celebrates its service station roots. Courtesy of Mike Koopsen, Sedona.

potatoey punch. Complete the trifecta with a creamy milkshake made with real ice cream for a complete balanced meal. Bing's also stocks classic bottled sodas.

Vegetarian Options: A garden burger is on the menu, or one made from quinoa and roasted garlic. Grilled cheese and salads are other options.

Don't Forget: Bring the pooches because they will love the big shady patio.

Details: 794 N. Main St., (928) 852-0109, www.bingsburgers.com.

Hot Tip: The hard part about writing this kind of book is that I don't have nearly enough room to include all the good burgers out there. For example, Acme Pizzaria in Cottonwood is a locally owned, community-minded eatery. Despite their focus on pizza, they make good sandwiches including a very nicely executed burger, juicy and flavorful. You just never know where you might discover an honest burger until you hit the road and start stuffing them in your face.

Thumper Loop, Cottonwood

While it may not be as dazzling as trails at the Grand Canyon or even nearby Sedona, this is my home field. Located just minutes from my house, I have logged more miles on the dirt paths in Dead Horse Ranch State Park than anywhere else in Arizona. By far.

Perched on the Verde River and sheltering a rare cottonwood and willow riparian forest, Dead Horse is a crown jewel in the Arizona state park system. The Thumper Loop consists of three trails: Lower Raptor Hill, Thumper, and Lime Kiln. And it is a rare week when I'm not hiking one portion or another. The trail is always there for me. It soothes me during hard times, celebrates my victories, gives me a quiet place to think, entertains me, inspires me, keeps me healthy, and most of all, vanishes me.

Minutes after leaving home, I'm gone. I'm solid gone, baby. I'm on a fast orbit into the backcountry above the river. I'm untethered and free. No one can find me unless I want to be found. That's the magic of a trail.

Many burger calories have been walked off by the author on the trails of Dead Horse Ranch State Park. Photo by the author.

Mountain bikers generally tackle the loop clockwise climbing Raptor Hill. For me, I like to start at Lime Kiln with parking at the lagoons that often bustle with activity. Ducks drift across the water, redwing blackbirds chatter in the cattails, and gangly great blue herons stand on the shore, all legs and curious necks. Watch for our nesting pair of bald eagles that are often seen, especially in spring.

The trail traces a limestone ridge past the remains of an old kiln. After a short, steep climb known as the Stairs, the route levels off and slices through hills, dotted with junipers, yuccas, cliffrose, and crucifixion thorns. Big sky and sweet views all the way. After a couple of miles, hang a left onto Thumper. This is a lovely segment, rambling across rolling plateaus, dipping in and out of shallow ravines. After 2.2 miles on Thumper, turn left on Lower Raptor Hill.

You begin a gradual descent dropping via terraced ridges. Along the way you're treated to sprawling views of Cottonwood, Clarkdale, and the pueblo at Tuzigoot National Monument, a prehistoric site perched dramatically above a bend in the Verde River. The trail ends at a campground, and a series of pathways leads back to the lagoons where your vehicle is parked. The loop is 7.2 miles but you'll total close to 8 by the time you reach your ride.

Where: From Cottonwood, drive northwest on Main St. following the signs to Dead Horse Ranch State Park.

Cost: Admission fee.

Difficulty: Moderate.

Length: 8 miles round-trip.

Dogs: Yes, on a leash.

Details: (928) 634-5283, www.azstateparks.com.

Fast Fact: In the late 1940s the Ireys family looked at ranches in Cottonwood, including one with a deceased equine. When the father asked which property they liked, the kids said, "The one with the dead horse." They christened their new home Dead Horse Ranch, and in 1973 when it was sold to Arizona State Parks, the Ireys made retaining the name a condition of the sale.

Verde Lea Market Deli & Grill, Cottonwood

It would be easy to drive right past Verde Lea Market without a second glance unless you happened to notice all the vehicles in the parking lot during lunch time. The little neighborhood grocery store has long been part of the community and feeds work crews from all over the Verde Valley.

Shelves with groceries line one wall, and big refrigerated cases for beverages stretch along the back. Small tables fill the middle of the room as folks order at the deli counter. Verde Lea specializes in big sandwiches from both sides of the border. Tortas stuffed with carne asada or crispy pork carnitas are on the menu along with tacos and burritos. There's a full lineup of hot sandwiches including cheese steaks, po' boys, and cold subs. Everything is made fresh when ordering, even the salads.

Diners, shoppers, and hungry work crews stream into Verde Lea Market Deli & Grill. Photo by the author.

Among the specialties is the Arizona Burger, a one-third-pound patty topped with bacon, onion ring, pepperjack cheese, and homemade prickly pear barbecue sauce. I like the flavors of the Big Boy. It makes a hefty meal with two patties covered with a heaping assortment of sauteed mushrooms, grilled onions, big roasted green chiles, and cheddar cheese melted like a schoolgirl's heart on prom night. Served piping hot off the flattop on a toasted bun, everything meshes combining a smoky sweetness with a flavorful spice.

Vegetarian Options: There's a veggie burger, a veggie sub, salads, and bean and cheese burrito.
Don't Forget: After your meal you can get a little shopping out of the way. Grab cereal, chips, toothpaste, and other necessities.
Details: 516 N. Main St., (928) 634-8731, www.verdeleaaz.com.

Parsons Trail, Clarkdale

Water and woods and red rock cliffs—there's just so much to love about this trail that is all kinds of spectacular. It pulls you from scrubby desert grasslands into a jungle-like oasis that stretches for miles. Imagine the towering red buttes of Oak Creek Canyon but with no roads or resorts, no homes or hotels. You've just conjured up an image of adjacent Sycamore Canyon. Parsons Trail provides the easiest access to this rugged wilderness area.

At the beginning, the trail scrambles 200 feet down the canyon wall to the creek bed. From there, it's a gentle meander through a tunnel of leafy shade alongside Sycamore Creek. Fed by several springs, pools form along the way, rippled mirrors reflecting the lush canopy of treetops and high cliffs that surround you.

The path is generally easy to follow, drifting from one side of the stream to the other about a half dozen times. Sometimes I walked in sand, other times crossed stone ledges at the water's edge. Flash floods occasionally roar through to realign the route, but you should have no real problem. Just remember to never stray far from the creek.

During spring, wildflowers brighten an already cheerful wood. That's my favorite time to visit, when trees erupt in sudden greenery, their new leaves still lacy and damp, unfurling like tiny parasols opening in unison. The woods take on that musky fragrance with a nursery of young plants rising to meet the sun, and the air is as sweet and delicate as a butterfly liqueur. Since the water is too chilly for swimming, I often have the trail to myself.

Summer months brings crowds as the larger pools turn into excellent swimming holes. In Arizona, swimming holes are our watery cathedrals. They are revered. Unfortunately, they are not always treated with the respect they deserve by everybody. Always remember to practice Leave No Trace principles and pack out everything you pack in.

After about 4 miles, you reach Parsons Spring, a wide marshy area. This

The Parsons Trail chases a creek into peaceful Sycamore Canyon. Photo by the author.

marks the end of the trail and the end of reliable water in Sycamore Canyon. The rest of the vast canyon is a scenic but mostly parched wilderness.

Where: From Cottonwood, drive northwest on Main St., following signs to Tuzigoot National Monument. Turn right on Tuzigoot Rd., cross the Verde River, and turn left on Sycamore Canyon Rd. (FR 131). Drive about 11 miles to the trailhead. The dirt road has a couple of rough spots but can usually be managed in a sedan.
Cost: Free.
Difficulty: Easy.
Length: 8 miles round-trip.
Dogs: Yes, on a leash.
Details: (928) 203-2900, www.fs.usda.gov/r03/coconino.

Hot Tip: Nothing is as scenic as a gentle train ride into a high-walled canyon. Verde Canyon Railroad chugs out of Clarkdale for the ghost ranch of Perkinsville and returns. The route follows a winding river and travels past ancient ruins, rocky formations, and eagle nests. Along the way, I'll blab at you through the speakers as the train's narrator. They offer several specialty outings through the year including Ales on Rails and Summer Starlight Rides.

Haunted Hamburger, Jerome

Going to Jerome and not eating at the Haunted Hamburger is like going to the Grand Canyon and never looking down. The restaurant has a complete menu that includes fish and chips, ribs, and a legendary stuffed meatloaf. But anyone who can saunter into a place called Haunted Hamburger and *not* order a burger possesses either an abundance of willpower or a lack of common sense.

This former boardinghouse nestles on the side of the mountain, one of the many historic buildings that line the steep, narrow streets of Jerome. A gang of skeletons cling to the outside walls. And yes, the restaurant has a resident ghost.

The dining room of Haunted Hamburger sports a big picture window, but nearly everyone gravitates to the covered deck that feels like a sacred space, a place to relax far from the mundane woes of day-to-day life. They also have the cozy View Bar on the back side of the restaurant. Vistas roll across the Verde Valley to the red cliffs of Sedona and the San Francisco Peaks beyond. Even if you're a local, for a moment it feels like you're on vacation.

The Haunted Hamburger is a must-stop destination for the great food and the views when visiting Jerome. Courtesy of Mike Koopsen, Sedona.

Expect a generous wheel of tender, flavorful beef cradled on a cushiony bun that's baked fresh on the premises. The Haunted Burger is their signature, a big sloppy behemoth heaped with cheddar, Swiss, bacon, mushrooms, green chiles, grilled onions, and a fat dollop of guacamole. Fans of drippy burgers will be in heaven. More than a dozen specialty burgers fill one column of the menu, including a Bourbon Jalapeño Bacon Bison Burger, which is just as big and complex as it sounds.

Haunted Hamburger opened in 1994, shortly before I moved to the Verde Valley, so it has been sort of my local place. The Haunted Group has since expanded and now includes several excellent restaurants and a hotel in the area. While I don't want to take credit for their success, being a burger joint just a few miles from my house has its advantages. It practically guarantees any bank loan they want gets fast tracked. In the burger world, I am rock solid collateral, baby.

Vegetarian Options: They serve a chipotle black bean patty. There's also a veggie wrap, and fork-and-knife Caesar salad.
Don't Forget: Haunted merch is for sale inside their souvenir store. Take a little bit of that Jerome spirit home with you.
Details: 410 N. Clark St., (928) 634-0554, www.thehauntedhamburger.com.

Hot Tip: The Jerome Art & Wine Walk takes place on the first Saturday of each month with shops and galleries extending their hours into the evening. Special exhibits, artists at work, and show openings create a lively atmosphere through the town. Enjoy wine tastings, good food, and live music. There's usually a free shuttle running.

My 12 Favorite Westerns Filmed in Arizona

1. *Stagecoach* (1939)
2. *Rio Bravo*
3. *Angel and the Badman*
4. *3:10 to Yuma* (1957)
5. *Broken Arrow*
6. *Winchester '73*
7. *Hombre*
8. *Posse* (1975)
9. *Monte Walsh*
10. *Joe Kidd*
11. *The Outlaw Josey Wales*
12. *Tombstone*

FLAGSTAFF

The San Francisco Peaks, which form a scenic backdrop for the town of Flagstaff, are the hulking remains of an eroded stratovolcano. They're part of a volcanic belt stretching for 50 miles. In the 1500s, Spanish conquistadors roaming the land in a quest for gold named them *Sierra Sinagua*, meaning Mountains Without Water, because no rivers or streams flowed down the slopes.

A century later, Franciscan friars doing missionary work with the Indigenous people bestowed the name San Francisco to the mountains in honor of St. Francis of Assisi. As a freshman at Northern Arizona University, I was told the mountains acquired their name because you could see the lights of San Francisco from the summit. I was also warned that on cold nights packs of wolves loped down from the heights and prowled the streets in search of meat. Neither statement was true. But to a gullible Ohio boy who had seen little beyond flat fields and farmlands, anything seemed possible in this dramatic landscape.

"Climb the mountains and get their good tidings."
JOHN MUIR

The trail to Humphreys Peak crosses a stark landscape of windswept tundra. Courtesy of Mike Koopsen, Sedona.

Humphreys Peak Trail, Flagstaff

Humphreys Peak tops out at 12,633 feet, the highest point in the state. Other hiking guidebooks tout the spectacular views from the summit—and they are pretty eye-poppingly yowza. But I'll level with you. This is not a hike you take for pure pleasure. It's a long, hard climb at high altitude across exposed ridges raked by wind and cold. You hike this trail because you have a screw loose—because some crazy notion compels you to climb to the roof of Arizona.

If you're a hiker, you want to face that challenge. It's like a double-dog dare.

From the trailhead, the route cuts across a meadow and enters a dense forest of spruce, fir, and aspen. The tangled canopy creates a tunnel effect, so don't expect big panoramas early. The ascent isn't steep at first, just relentless. At 11,400 feet there's a sign warning that camping is not permitted beyond this point. And who other than Yeti would seriously consider it? Things start getting serious now. Switchbacks tighten, the grade sharpens, and the forest breaks apart in pieces. Soon nothing is left but gnarled, twisted bristlecone pines. They're the toughest tree in the world, surviving in impossibly harsh conditions, but soon even they say, "Screw it. You go ahead, we'll wait here."

At 11,800 feet you reach the saddle connecting Humphreys and Agassiz, Arizona's second tallest peak. From this high perch there's a spectacular view into a rough valley filled with crumbling cliffs and scraps of forest. A little more climbing and I was above the tree line completely.

Fast Fact: Humphreys Peak and Agassiz Peak (12,356 feet) are the southernmost mountains above 12,000 feet in the continental United States.

All that remains is a lung-squeezing slog across a raggedy ridge of alpine tundra, the only tundra in Arizona. Tundra ecosystems are treeless regions found in the Arctic and at high elevations where the climate is cold and windy. Moonscape-stark up here amid a jumble of dark rocks, only a few shriveled plants grow in sheltered crannies. I always pause for a moment to ponder the startling diversity of Arizona. I'm hiking in tundra—tundra, for crying out loud. Two hours south of me, the Sonoran Desert sizzles beneath a withering sun.

As I crossed this barren spine, the wind battered and clawed me. Remember that you are completely exposed here. Temperatures are much colder than at the trailhead. Snow is possible any month of the year, and lightning is an extreme danger. The air is thin and unreliable, like an undertaker's smile.

Expect a couple of false summits—oh, cruel mockery—before bagging Humphreys. A parapet of lava rocks is stacked on the summit, allowing me a chance to hunker out of the wind and appreciate the fact that I am now the tallest person in Arizona. Views stretch to the colorful gash of the Grand Canyon, the Hopi Mesas, and the pastel cliffs of the Painted Desert.

Where: From Flagstaff, drive 7 miles northwest on US 180, and turn right on Snowbowl Rd. Follow the road up the mountain about 7.4 miles to the ski area. Turn into the first parking area on the left.
Cost: Free.
Difficulty: Strenuous.
Length: 9.6 miles round-trip.
Dogs: Yes, on a leash.
Details: (928) 526-0866, www.fs.usda.gov/r03/coconino.

Miz Zip's, Flagstaff

Here's my theory: The guy who started the Cracker Barrel chain first hatched the idea while eating at Miz Zip's.

Mind you, I have no corroborating evidence to back this up. It's just a hunch. Because if you're looking for comfortable and down-home, you hit paydirt walking into this little Route 66 café. The front room includes a worn, scuffed checkerboard floor, a few booths, and a small horseshoe counter ringed by chrome bar stools. The main dining room looks like the back of an antique store with old kitchen utensils dangling from wagon wheel fixtures, a rustic cupboard in the corner, and wooden walls adorned with vintage photos and signs. The best part is that the food matches the comfort of the setting.

The menu stays mostly in a diner groove, starting with big breakfast spreads, and mixing in several Mexican dishes. They make their slow cooked beef birria in house. Seven specialty burgers are available including the Chorizo Beer Cheese Burger, which sounds tempting. But I stick with an old friend. My Hatch Burger turns out to be a triumph of earthy sweet heat that highlights the tender juiciness of the beef. The craggy edges of the burger are like a halo of smoky caramel. It's complemented by some unique fries, real skin-on potatoes cut into thin wide planks and nicely seasoned. I gobble everything in sight.

The only downside was that Miz Zip's had already sold out of their delicious homemade pie for the day. And I arrived pretty early, too. Curse that gluttonous breakfast crowd!

Vegetarian Options: Along with all the breakfast items, there is a nice selection of salads and a few mac and cheese varieties.
Don't Forget: You can purchase a whole pie with 24-hour advance notice. Imagine what your day would be like with an entire pie to call your own.
Details: 2924 E. Route 66, (928) 526-0104, www.mizzips.com.

Veit Springs Loop, Flagstaff

Veit Springs is my oldest Arizona friend. It's the first trail I ever hiked in the state. As a freshman at Northern Arizona University in Flagstaff, I was on my way to English class one October morning when I glanced toward the San Francisco Peaks banded with yellow. Suddenly, nothing else mattered. Not Faulkner, not Kerouac, not even Twain. The aspens had turned.

I rounded up two like-minded scofflaws and we headed for Veit Springs, a short loop curling through lavish groves of the white-trunked aspens and their canopy of heart-shaped leaves. Past a historic cabin and gurgling springs, at the foot of a basalt cliff adorned with pictographs, sits a field of sprawl-friendly boulders. For the rest of the afternoon, we draped atop those rocks like cheese slices melted on burgers. Shafts of sunlight streamed through the rustling patchwork of lemon and saffron above us and every breeze triggered the soft fireworks of fluttering golden leaves.

The trail begins as a gentle climb along an old jeep road to a small preserve. This 160-acre tract was homesteaded in 1892 by Charles Ludwig Veit. It's now managed by Arizona Game and Fish Department and is known as the Lamar Haines Memorial Wildlife Area. Elk and deer are common sights mornings and evenings. The road narrows to a path and reaches a fork at 0.2 miles. Take the loop counterclockwise.

At the plaque honoring Haines, a Flagstaff educator and environmentalist, look to the left for short spur trails that walk you through the area's history. Here you'll find the tumbledown remains of Veit's cabin. During my earliest visits, the cabin still

Fast Fact: Pictographs are images painted on rocks, not to be confused with petroglyphs, which are etched into the surface of a rock. Pictographs are much rarer.

A rock-walled spring house is tucked amid the aspens on the Veit Springs Trail. Courtesy of Mike Koopsen, Sedona.

retained an upright shape, but time has taken a toll, as it has on me. Now we're both weathered ruins.

Two small springhouses are tucked against the cliff, and nearby is a grassy bog. Veit Springs makes a good kid-friendly hike with easy walking and plenty of nooks and crannies to explore. Follow the cliff around to the left to discover a few red-orange pictographs, estimated to be more than 1,000 years old. Tall ferns line the path in summer, and autumn brings a showy display of colorful leaves.

Just below the rock art is that collection of big comfortable boulders. If you see an old guy stretched out atop one of these hooky recliners, pay him no mind. He might be a beloved Arizona author hard at work.

Where: From Flagstaff, drive north on US 180 to Snowbowl Rd. and turn right. Travel 4.2 miles and watch for a small parking area on the right.
Cost: Free.
Difficulty: Easy.
Length: 1.6-mile round-trip.
Dogs: Yes, on a leash.
Details: (928) 774-5045, www.azgfd.gov.

"I still love making hamburgers on the grill. I guess whenever I eat them, childhood memories come up for me."
BOBBY FLAY

Mama B's, Flagstaff

It's called the M.O.A.B—Mother of All Burgers—and it's been a mainstay of Mama B's. Originally opened as Mama Burger in 2009, the cozy eatery developed a loyal following for their fresh smashburgers, hand-cut fries, and thick, straw-collapsing shakes. When they closed in 2022 for extensive remodeling, residents of Flagstaff did everything but don burger-shaped black armbands. Their mourning period lasted 18 months, until the restaurant reopened with the new name, new design, but still serving the same delicious food.

Mama B's has garnered a loyal Flagstaff following for their smashburgers, innovative shakes, and tasty papas (fries and tots). Photo by the author.

Customers clamor for the M.O.A.B., which features two patties crowded with mustard, mayo, pickles, diced jalapeños, grilled onions, fries, American cheese, bacon, lettuce, and tomato. It's a lot to handle. Another intriguing option is the Scheppy Burger, with sweet onions shaved thin and smashed into the beef, then crowned with mustard, American cheese, and pickles or diced jalapeños—a tribute to the Depression-era onion-fried burgers of Oklahoma.

The build-your-own version offers plenty of construction materials to create intriguing combinations. You don't find many places offering diced jalapeños among their toppings and that's just a spicy party waiting to happen. The fries are radiant with a zesty spud flavor, and mix-ins are available for the milkshakes. Hey, when it comes to good home cooking, no one does it like Mama.

Vegetarian Options: A veggie patty can be substituted for any burger.
Don't Forget: Every month, there's a new featured burger and a shake.
Details: 991 N. Fort Valley Rd., (928) 226-0616, www.mamabs.com.

Hot Tip: At the Museum of Northern Arizona, the entire history of the immense Colorado Plateau, from its geologic creation to the peoples who have populated it, is explored. The museum maintains five permanent galleries and three rotating ones and serves as a repository with over 600,000 artifacts on hand, such as pottery, jewelry, stone tools, baskets, and weavings.

Red Mountain Trail, Flagstaff

I love the fantasyland aspect of Red Mountain and the sudden jangly weirdness of it. The short, easy trail travels through scenic woodlands before plunging into the mystical gullet of a volcano.

Red Mountain is one of hundreds of cinder cones poking through every pore in the volcanic landscape surrounding Flagstaff. But unlike most symmetrical cones, Red Mountain is a haphazard U shape, with an amphitheater carved from the northeast flank. "Carved" may be misleading; it looks like some giant cosmic being took a chomp, leaving behind a raggedy assortment of hoodoos and a labyrinth of mini canyons.

The trail rises gently through a forest of junipers and piñon pines. Dipping into a sandy wash it continues toward the base of Red Mountain, towering 1,000 feet overhead. About a mile from the trailhead, things take a freaky turn.

Experience a volcanic wonderland on the Red Mountain Trail. Courtesy of Mike Koopsen, Sedona.

Walls of black cinder rise up, flanking the streambed with a few lonely ponderosa pines growing from the desolation. The trail squeezes between dark towers of volcanic tuff (ash that's been cemented by the ages). A 6-foot ladder climbs over a stone wall and suddenly you're engulfed in an arena of gnawed spires, twisted pillars, and hard-edged badlands. The reds of Red Mountain are not the saucy, seductive hues of Sedona or Monument Valley. They're more earthy tones, ochre and orange dressed for a dance.

The inner basin spreads out among the clustered hoodoos that beg for a little exploration. The surface makes for good bouldering. It's a hobbit-sized Bryce Canyon, vivid and entertaining. Yank the kids off the swing set and let them explore a natural playground for a change.

Where: From Flagstaff, drive northwest on US 180 for 25 miles. Near milepost 247, turn left at the forest service sign. Take the dirt road a quarter mile to the parking area.

Cost: Free.

Difficulty: Easy.

Length: 3 miles round-trip.

Dogs: Yes, on a leash.

Details: (928) 526-0866, www.fs.usda.gov/r03/coconino.

Satchmo's, Flagstaff

Barbecue and Cajun food seem like such a natural combination, it's a wonder there isn't a Satchmo's in every town. They started in 2009, slinging grub from a tiny shack. The down-home cooking and authentic flavors quickly caught on, leading to this crowded eatery in East Flag. Ultimately, Cajun, Creole, and barbecue are all comfort food with deep southern roots. But Satchmo's puts their own signature on each dish.

Grab a menu when you walk in and order at the counter before taking a seat. There's a nice walled patio for those mild summer days at 7,000 feet. It's no surprise that house specialties include a bold jambalaya and slow-smoked pork ribs.

Mouthwatering sandwiches make up a big chunk of the menu. Pulled pork, chicken breast, and beef brisket represent the 'cue. Or try the po' boys like andouille sausage or catfish, blackened or fried and served on toasted bread with a blend of tomatoes, slaw, and house-made remoulade. The seasoned tater tots and smoked beans are not to be missed. While I have a weakness for barbecue, I seem to stray more to the Cajun side of the menu, savoring those good earthy spices.

The cast-iron cornbread is made in-house daily. Sauces and rubs are made from scratch. They even keep a variety of woods stacked out back so that different meats can be smoked to perfection with the right combination of fuel.

Vegetarian Options: Satchmo's offers a vegetarian po' boy and plenty of delicious sides.
Don't Forget: They also offer catering, so if you've got an event coming up, your worries are over. Hire Satchmo's to do your wedding and I'll gladly show up as a plus one, officiant, best man, bridesmaid, whatever you need.
Details: 2320 N. Fourth St., (928) 774-7292, www.satchmosaz.com.

Sandys Canyon Trail, Flagstaff

Surprises lurk in this slender gorge just off Lake Mary Road. The trail traces the rim of Walnut Canyon before dropping through mixed forest in a short but mildly steep descent. After reaching the canyon floor the hike stays level passing through the defile.

Grassy meadows are enveloped by walls of towering stone and pine-clad slopes. During summer months, monsoon-inspired wildflowers add colorful seasoning to the quiet little gulch. Further along you'll find cross-bedded cliffs in intricate designs. These petrified sand dunes add a touch of the exotic in this intimate place. After a mile you'll reach a junction with the Arizona Trail, so theoretically you could tack on an extra 800 miles if you felt feisty.

Or just bite off a small portion. Head north on the Arizona Trail to Fisher Point, an enormous jutting wall of rock that pushes its way into the canyon.

A hiker admires the cross-bedded cliffs of Fisher Point along the Sandys Canyon Trail. Photo by the author.

with a shallow cave carved out at the base. The cave provides a nice dollop of shade on a sunny day if you need the respite.

Plenty of Flagstaff trails go winding up mountain slopes with distant panoramas peeking through the forest. Maybe that's why I like this simple hike on which the focus stays close at hand. Textures of the scarred rock, the breeze across the grasses, and the cheerful blooms of the wildflowers are all welcome companions on a summer day in this cozy space.

Fisher Point makes a good turnaround point, although there is a larger, deeper cave farther along on the right. Make sure you have a good light source before entering. The trail continues into Walnut Canyon but becomes narrower and steeper and can be overgrown. If you're looking for steep hikes, Flag has plenty of those. I'm content to keep Sandys Canyon as a simple, sweet outing.

Where: Drive southeast out of Flagstaff 5.5 miles on Lake Mary Rd. Follow the signs for Sandys Canyon Trailhead.
Cost: Free.
Difficulty: Easy.
Length: 3 miles round-trip to Fisher Point.
Dogs: Yes, on a leash.
Details: (928) 526-0866, www.fs.usda.gov/r03/coconino.

Hot Tip: Lowell Observatory was established in 1894, making it one of the oldest in the country. The dwarf planet Pluto was discovered from this high perch. Visitors can enjoy interactive exhibits, take historic tours, view the sun through a specially equipped telescope, attend science talks, and stargaze.

Tiki Grill, Flagstaff

Turn your meal into a mini vacation at this tropical hideaway tucked in a strip mall. Tiki Grill is a happy place with a laid-back island vibe and flavors so authentic you'll swear you can smell an ocean breeze. Diners enjoy a delicious blend of scratch-made mainland and seafood dishes. Fish and shrimp tacos can be grilled, blackened, or fried, and they offer a variety of sandwiches. For me, the light char of the blackened catfish perfectly emphasizes the delicate flavor of the tender flesh.

But all the proteins are represented here, where they emphasize comfort food and cocktails. The burgers start with 6 ounces of fresh hand-formed Angus chuck. Mine arrived a hot glistening circle of well-seasoned and juicy beef. Along with the standard model that can be bolstered with add-ons, they dish up a couple of surprise burgers. For the Tiki Loco Moco, the grilled patty is served over garden rice with pork belly gravy and a fried egg.

The popular Pittsburger was inspired by the legendary sandwiches created

With its beachy theme, good seafood, and tasty burgers, Tiki Grill is full of surprises in this mountain town. Photo by the author.

by the Primanti brothers. The burger comes piled with fries, coleslaw, cheese, and tomato, just like the original sandwich invented during the Great Depression by Joe Primanti. He slapped together the comfort feast to feed truck drivers in Pittsburgh's industrial Strip District so they could eat an entire meal with one hand while steering with the other.

Stop by Tiki Grill on Thursdays for creative burger specials whipped up as late-in-the-week treats. A stream of regulars stops in to sample the goods. And don't miss the Cajun fries, coated with a lightly spiced house-made seasoning rub. They actually bring a little bayou authenticity to the table. Too many places store their potatoes near a bottle of paprika and try to pass them off as Cajun fries. These are the real deal.

Vegetarian Options: They make their own black bean burger with quinoa and mashed sweet potatoes.
Don't Forget: For dessert, the ooey-gooey butter bars are made in-house, a cross between a brownie and a cake.
Details: 1509 S. Milton Rd., (928) 440-3693, www.tikigrill.live.

Fast Fact: According to most historians, the cheeseburger was invented by Lionel Sternberger in 1924 while working at his father's hamburger stand in Pasadena, California. As the story goes, the 16-year-old burned one side of a burger and to conceal his mistake, draped a piece of cheese over it.

Kachina Trail, Flagstaff

This high-country ramble delivers a big mountain experience without much climbing, bless its woodsy heart. Kachina follows a rolling course across a high shoulder of the San Francisco Peaks. It passes through groves of conifers and huddled aspens and meadows filled with waist-high bracken ferns.

The trail stretches 5 miles, descending 700 feet from the upper end at 9,500 feet to its terminus in the mouth of Weatherford Canyon. Limber pine and Douglas fir dominate old-growth forests at the highest elevations along with a dense understory of aspens. As the trail drops to the south-facing slopes of Agassiz and Fremont Peaks, our old friends the ponderosa pines rise up in welcome.

Although popular, the trail seldom feels overrun. Everyone seems to find a

A lush carpet of ferns spreads beneath the aspen trees of the Kachina Trail. Courtesy of Mike Koopsen, Sedona.

comfortable pace and strings out among the trees. Clusters of andesite boulders, remnants of an ancient lava flow are scattered through the timber. This now peaceful landscape was born of fire, yet the river of lava that once scoured these slopes has been embraced by the forest, which seems to bear no grudge. Big boulders are sprinkled with soil, leaves, and debris, and trees grow from their very pores.

Crossing shallow drainages and skirting small cliffs, I wound around the rising bulk of the peaks. On the second half of the hike, the pastures widen, exposing lovely views of mountaintops above and towns, buttes, and hills far below. When the Kachina junctions with the Weatherford Trail, about-face it and return to your car.

What I said about the trail not feeling crowded doesn't apply during the first half of October. That's when the leaf peepers come out to see Kachina transformed into a corridor of gold. Expect plenty of company then.

Where: From Flagstaff, drive 7 miles northwest on US 180, and turn right on Snowbowl Rd. Follow the road up the mountain about 7.4 miles to the ski area. Turn into the first parking area on the right.
Cost: Free.
Difficulty: Easy/moderate.
Length: 10 miles round-trip.
Dogs: Yes, on a leash.
Details: (928) 526-0866, www.fs.usda.gov/r03/coconino.

Hot Tip: Get your thrills at Extreme Adventure Course, where families can conquer rope swings, climbing walls, hanging nets, wobbly bridges, and ziplines. There are multiple circuits on the adult playground, and one course designed just for children.

Diablo Burger, Flagstaff

Stop here for the flavors of Arizona. At Diablo Burger, Arizona grass and sunshine come in a tender package. All beef is from the ranches of Diablo Trust, raised on open range and free of growth hormones and antibiotics. Operating southeast of Flagstaff, Diablo Trust supports the stewardship of nearly a half million acres of a local ecosystem. This helps preserve open spaces and restores healthy watersheds. In fact, Diablo Burger sources almost everything they can within a 250-mile radius, guaranteeing freshness and sustainability.

The restaurant is tucked into a corner of Heritage Square in downtown Flag. It's hidden away behind a curved wall mural with seating inside and on the patio. The building is actually the underside of a garage parking ramp, and I love that. Far as I'm concerned, burger joints should open in every abandoned structure available, no matter how small, funky, or curiously shaped.

Not only does Diablo Burger serve excellent food, the restaurant also strives to be as local and sustainable as possible. Photo by the author.

Since the beef is about 95 percent lean, try the burgers medium-rare. The richness of the burger is unmistakable, and the freshness of all the ingredients creates a vivid medley of flavors. But here's where Diablo Burger and I diverge. Burgers are served on a handmade preservative-free English muffin. It adds a little crunch and most people seem to love the uniqueness of it. From my perspective, it slightly muffles the vibrancy of an absolutely exquisite burger. But since Diablo Burger continues to be named one of the top burger joints in the nation, I am obviously in the minority, as I so often am.

Along with the 10 or so signature burgers listed, there's usually a blackboard special, or you can pick and choose from toppings, almost all grown nearby. I heartily applaud their efforts to protect and sustain Arizona resources.

Vegetarian Options: The Beaut—that's the name of their meatless burger made from whole fresh vegetables, millet, beans, and spices. They also have a house salad and an uptown grilled cheese.
Don't Forget: DB Frites are Belgian-style fries, and always fresh. The method means the slightly thick-cut potatoes are fried, cooled, and fried again, and lightly seasoned with herbs. They come with your choice of dipping sauces.
Details: 120 N. Leroux St., (928) 774-3274, www.diabloburger.com.

The First Hamburger Chain

The world's first fast food hamburger chain was White Castle. They were founded in Wichita, Kansas, in 1921 and soon spread to other cities and states, concentrated mostly in the Midwest. Their small beef patties steam-cooked on a bed of onions have become iconic and are little changed over the past century. In 2014, *Time Magazine* called it "the most influential burger of all time."

These are the original sliders. All small burgers that show up as sliders on menus now—occasionally topped with hoity-toity add-ons like pork belly, caviar, or Pop Tart crumbles—are following in the slippery, oniony footprints left by White Castle. The company is now based in Columbus, Ohio.

White Castle was one of those Midwestern flavors I always tried to sample when I would return to Cincinnati for a family visit. The first White Castle in Arizona finally opened in 2019, and it was the world's largest at the time. But mostly I preferred them as an Ohio indulgence.

Toward the end of her life, my mother suffered from dementia. She had mobility issues and was losing her ability to communicate. Getting her to eat was sometimes a challenge. But during those times, surprisingly, she never passed up a trip to White Castle.

I don't think she had been in years and it was rarely a spot my parents visited. But while we were there, Dad would reminisce about how White Castle was one of their earliest date nights when they were newlyweds and money was

Fast Fact: It was a Cincinnati White Castle operator named Earl Howell who introduced the idea of adding five holes to the small patties in 1947, helping them to cook faster and absorb more flavor.

tight. You could get two sliders for a quarter so they could live it up on just a few dollars.

More than six decades later, Mom and Dad were back at White Castle. Almost all my mother's memories had been stolen by then, but there she sat, eating one slider and then another, reaching for the fries. Dad fairly beamed as he ate, thrilled, I think, to once again be out on a date night with his best girl.

GRAND CANYON

No matter how you steel yourself, nothing prepares you for the cosmic thunderbolt of the Grand Canyon. That first glimpse is so beyond scope and precedent, it devastates you. Yet the whole structure stays hidden from view, sheltered by a thin screen of forest, until you're practically on top of it. You know you're getting close as you approach. The trees waver and then break apart against a wall of sky as the world abruptly ends.

Standing at the high crest of an overlook, a collapsed mosaic of terraces and buttes spreads below in intricate patterns that go on forever, finally dissolving into a lavender haze. There should be a state law that says every Arizona resident must visit the Grand Canyon at least once. It will be the first piece of legislation I enact when I'm elected governor.

Hikers traverse the long, beautiful, sun-blasted South Kaibab Trail. Courtesy of Mike Koopsen, Sedona.

South Kaibab–Tonto–Bright Angel Loop, South Rim

Nobody in their right mind should even consider this entire route as a day hike. This is by far the hardest outing in this book and should not be attempted unless you're physically fit, experienced, and acclimated to the Grand Canyon. It is extremely difficult and potentially dangerous. Try short hikes down the Bright Angel to develop your canyon legs first. Then explore the South Kaibab. Only after you've made multiple forays below the rim and know the terrain and your capabilities should you plan to tackle the Tonto Loop. But I warn you; dipping your toes into the Big Ditch can be extremely addictive.

The best time to attempt this long, arduous loop is in the spring or fall. The easiest route (13.6 miles) is to descend on the South Kaibab, cut across the Tonto Trail, and climb out on Bright Angel.

Screamingly steep, shadeless, and sunbeaten may not sound like endorsements, but it's what makes the South Kaibab astounding. Most canyon trails follow fault lines limiting your range of vision. But the Kaibab only briefly hugs the upper cliffs before breaking free. At 0.9 miles it elbows into the canyon at aptly named Ooh Aah Point. From here the trail skitters down a narrow ridge and offers virtually unobstructed views.

After 1.5 miles, you reach a comfy plateau called Cedar Ridge, complete with vault toilets and scraps of shade. Most day-trippers will rest a bit and then wisely turn around here. Think about it.

Dropping, the trail

Fast Fact: Every year more than 250 people have to be rescued from the Grand Canyon. Also, every year people die hiking in the canyon. Do not be a casualty.

curves past O'Neill Butte and approaches Skeleton Point, a jut of stone atop the Redwall Limestone. At Skeleton Point, 3 miles from the trailhead, you get your first glimpse of the Colorado River. You'll find an excellent perch on the western side of the promontory. This is your last chance to turn back for a rugged but still manageable 6-mile day hike. It's a hike I've done often, a favorite way to sample the canyon's special beauty.

Continuing beyond Skeleton Point means a serious commitment. Because from here the trail drops through a natural break in the Redwall Limestone layer in a series of sheer switchbacks, depositing you on the scrubby Tonto Platform. Known as the Tipoff, there's another toilet here and emergency telephone, just past the junction of the Tonto Trail.

Turn west on the Tonto, following the rangy benchland through the belly of the canyon. The Tonto Platform hangs on the rim of the Inner Gorge and is a place of immense peace and solitude. This is one of my happiest trails. I'm a speck amid the vastness, but a mighty speck drunk on panoramas of towers and temples, with the Colorado River crashing far below.

For 95 miles this trans-canyon route parallels the course of the river. Less traveled sections are sometimes overgrown, but the 4.6-mile link between South Kaibab and Bright Angel is clearly defined. The trail undulates in and out of washes and skirts the edges of deep box canyons. It's such a pleasure hiking on a canyon trail that's not pointed steeply down or up. You get to just walk and celebrate the wonder.

A smattering of trees marks two trickling stream crossings at Burro Springs and Pipe Creek. Otherwise, expect a sunbaked landscape of blackbrush, bunch grass, and tumbled boulders. You'll also see fresh geometric patterns to the canyon, a tapestry of strata, and tall buttes and mesas. Instead of gazing at it from the safe distance of the rim, you're striding among it.

Tonto connects with Bright Angel Trail amid a grove of cottonwood trees below the spring-fed oasis of Havasupai Gardens. Drinking water, privies, and picnic tables make this a welcome rest stop. But after the solitude of the Tonto, you'll

Fast Fact: The Grand Canyon is 277 miles long, up to 18 miles wide, and over a mile deep.

encounter a jarring amount of humanity. Campers, backpackers, and mule riders will be enjoying the same amenities.

Leaving Havasupai Gardens, you'll have about a half mile of Bright Angel Trail tilted gently uphill and just as you start thinking this won't be so bad, you bang into Jacob's Ladder, a series of steep and seemingly endless switchbacks.

Three Mile Resthouse perches atop the Redwall, where there is another chance for a bathroom break, and water is available in the summer months. The same goes for Mile-and-a-Half Resthouse farther up the trail. The last miles are exhausting. Take your time, rest often, stay hydrated, and grind it out. Bright Angel emerges next to Kolb Studio in Grand Canyon Village.

Congratulations! You just had a day that few people in this world will ever experience.

Where: Trailhead is south of Yaki Point, off Desert View Drive. The road is closed to private vehicles. Free shuttle buses and a hiker shuttle provides access.
Cost: Admission fee.
Difficulty: Strenuous.
Length: 13.6 miles round-trip.
Dogs: No.
Details: (928) 638-7888, www.nps.gov/grca.

Hot Tip: Anyone who spends time staring into the world's most glorious wound and doesn't have a few geology questions isn't paying attention. The exhibits at Yavapai Geology Museum provide the answers, as panoramas fill the broad windows. Located near Yavapai Point in Grand Canyon Village.

Bright Angel Fountain, South Rim

Look, if you just hiked double-digit miles into and out of the Grand Canyon, then you've earned whatever your stomach desires. Chow down at El Tovar Hotel's fancy dining room overlooking the canyon. Or one of the many other South Rim eateries. Charter a private plane from Tusayan to whisk you away to Vegas where you can hire one showgirl to cut up your porterhouse steak and another to feed it to you.

My traditional stop is not so elaborate. I walk out of the canyon, straight to the soda fountain and luncheonette attached to the back of historic Bright Angel Lodge. I'm hot, tired, covered with trail dust, and I got no time to coordinate with showgirl schedules. This little spot waits for me like a culinary oasis selling sandwiches, hot dogs, potato chips, cold drinks, and ice cream. No seating inside, just shuffle through and grab what you need.

I snagged a couple of Nathan's hot dogs. There's really nothing special about them, but trust me, find a shady spot to sit by the rim and take that first bite, and these dogs will taste like you're sitting behind the dugout during the late innings of the seventh game of the World Series with your team up by six.

Vegetarian Options: Pastries, bagels, fruit, egg salad sandwich, and don't forget big scoops of ice cream.
Don't Forget: Did I mention ice cream?
Details: 9 Village Loop Dr., (928) 638-2631.

Fast Fact: The Bright Angel Trail was once operated as a private toll road.

Grandview Trail, South Rim

Here's something I've done several times over the years: I get up early on a summer morning and drive to the Grand Canyon. I hike a few miles down into the gorge, find a comfortable spot, and eat lunch. Then I hike back out and drive home in time for dinner. Know why I do it?

Because I can!

That is a privilege granted only to Arizonans and I never want to lose sight of how special it is to have a world wonder for a backyard.

One of the trails I use for my summer getaways is the Grandview. In the 1890s, when Pete Berry discovered copper on Horseshoe Mesa, he needed a way to haul it out. He began work on a seemingly impossible design, attaching the skeleton of a route to sheer rock walls. Upper sections of the very steep Grandview are still braced by logs and steel rods. You'll be hugging limestone in places where the trail squeezes skinny. Footing is occasionally tricky over segments of cobbled rock, but the views, as advertised, are quite tasty. The steep grade eases slightly after the first mile to the point where it's only insanely steep, switchbacking through layers of sandstone and shale.

Soon you cross a saddle between Hance and Grapevine Canyons. You reach Horseshoe Mesa atop the Redwall in 3 miles to find remnants of Berry's Last Chance Mine, which operated until 1907. Rocky ruins of the old cookhouse and a few artifacts are scattered about. Please leave everything undisturbed for

Hot Tip: There are 11 tribes that have historic connections to the lands and resources now found within Grand Canyon National Park. Cultural demonstrations from affiliated tribes are held several days a week, spring through fall, at Desert View Watchtower on the eastern edge of the South Rim.

The Grandview Trail delivers just what the name promises. Courtesy of Mike Koopsen, Sedona.

others to enjoy. Camping is allowed on the Mesa with a backcountry permit. There's also an eco-friendly and very exposed toilet if needed.

You may notice trails dropping over the edge through the Redwall Limestone to connect with the Tonto Trail or Cottonwood Creek hundreds of feet below. Day hikers should stay atop the mesa. You may want to follow a rocky path along the western arm until it dead-ends dramatically 2,000 feet above the Colorado River. There's a piñon-shaded ledge where you can ponder the unleashed joy of magnificent solitude.

But if you find me there eating lunch, scram. Go discover your own spot and start your own tradition.

Where: Grandview Point is off Desert View Drive, 12 miles east of Grand Canyon Village.
Cost: Admission fee.
Difficulty: Strenuous.
Length: 6 miles round-trip to Horseshoe Mesa.
Dogs: No.
Details: (928) 638-7888, www.nps.gov/grca.

"In the Grand Canyon, Arizona has a natural wonder which is in kind absolutely unparalleled throughout the rest of the world."
THEODORE ROOSEVELT

North Kaibab Trail, North Rim

If you've only visited the South Rim don't be alarmed by the lack of crowds here. A blanketing serenity is normal on this side of the trench, which receives a fraction of the visitors the South Rim does. Only 10 miles apart as the raven flies, it's a 215-mile drive from rim to rim. Rising 1,000 feet higher than its southern counterpart, the North Rim sits atop the Kaibab Plateau and is crowned with mixed conifer forest and lush grassy meadows.

The North Kaibab Trail plunges steeply from the start, dropping from big timber and twisting through Roaring Springs Canyon. At 1.7 miles you'll reach Supai Tunnel to find restrooms and water. This makes a good turn-around point if your time is limited or your knees are grouchy. You'll glide down the switchbacks, but they'll be waiting for you and they somehow quadruple in number on the return trip.

I loved zigzagging down the Redwall Limestone, a lightning bolt of trail clinging to sheer cliffs. The trees have dispersed, and this section offers incredible views and thrilling exposure. Much of this corridor has been blasted from solid rock. This feels like a classic Grand Canyon experience, scrambling along a steep trail of remarkable engineering amid a soul-freeing backdrop.

You'll hear Roaring Springs before you see it, a frothy geyser bursting from the cliffs and cascading downhill to form Bright Angel Creek. The water source for all Grand Canyon National Park, Roaring Springs is absolutely the end of the line as a day hike. A 0.25-mile spur trail descends to picnic tables and restrooms tucked beneath a clutch of cottonwoods that thrive in this riparian setting formed by the springs. Make this a leisurely pit stop because

Fast Fact: North Rim services are closed from mid-October through mid-May.

Launching from the North Rim, the North Kaibab Trail twists down the walls of Roaring Springs Canyon. Courtesy of Mike Koopsen, Sedona.

you'll need to marshal your resources for the 5-mile climb back to the trailhead.

For those doing a rim-to-rim hike, or backpacking to Cottonwood Camp, push on. You'll chase Bright Angel Creek all the way to the Colorado River. Be sure to make the short detour to Ribbon Falls, a magical oasis that looks like it was plucked from a tropical island. The silvery spray of water tumbles down rock walls in a picturesque grotto. It's another 2.5 miles to Cottonwood Camp and 9.4 to Phantom Ranch.

Where: From Grand Canyon Lodge, drive 2 miles north to the trailhead.
Cost: Admission fee.
Difficulty: Strenuous.
Length: 10 miles round-trip to Roaring Springs.
Dogs: No.
Details: (928) 638-7888, www.nps.gov.grca.

IN MEMORIAM
Grand Canyon Lodge, North Rim

In July 2025, just before this book reached the layout and design phase, calamity struck. The Dragon Bravo fire at the North Rim burned through thousands of acres and destroyed dozens of buildings, including the iconic Grand Canyon Lodge.

When the news went out that the lodge was gone, hearts broke all across the state and around the world, mine among them. Over the years, I was a regular visitor. I slept in the cabins, relaxed on the patio (one of the greatest in the history of patios), and ate in the restaurant behind a wall of windows. Built right on the edge of the abyss in 1937, using native limestone and ponderosa timbers, it should come as no surprise that Grand Canyon Lodge was a featured eatery in this book. They served a mighty fine burger.

No doubt the next Grand Canyon Lodge will be spectacular as well. The new one will be the third. The original lodge was built in the 1920s but burned down in 1932. Life goes on. Fortunately, memories are calamity-proof. We who spent time there will carry those cherished moments to the end of our days.

Consider this a reminder not to postpone life. If there are places you want to go, things you want to see, don't put it off. The world changes; things disappear. Don't miss out on opportunities. I'm grateful for the time I had at Grand Canyon Lodge but I always expected to return for more adventures. No one gets a peek at the cosmic calendar. Seize your days, whenever you can.

10 Easy Grand Canyon Adventures

1. Climb into the saddle and ride a mule along the rim of the canyon. For the rest of the day, call everyone you meet "partner."
2. Pack a lunch and walk along the Rim Trail until you find a quiet spot in the pine forest filled with birdsong overlooking the Grand Canyon. Think you will ever forget that picnic?
3. Attend a park ranger talk. Don't be afraid to ask questions.
4. Rediscover the genius of architect Mary Colter with a historic walking tour of Grand Canyon Village.
5. Rent a bike at Bright Angel Bicycles and tour the South Rim in style.
6. Take a class with the Grand Canyon Field Institute.
7. Learn to identify five plants growing at the canyon that you didn't already know.
8. Have a late afternoon drink on the patio of the El Tovar, because a view like this guarantees the happiest of happy hours.
9. Study the Fred Kabotie murals at Desert View Watchtower. Ponder their meaning.
10. Find a comfortable seat near the canyon rim, turn off your phone for 60 minutes and count all California condors that fly past. If none do, you have just spent an hour doing nothing but gazing across the Grand Canyon. You are that kind of person now. Way to go.

ARIZONA STRIP AND NAVAJO NATION

For one unforgettable adventure after another, visit the distant northern edge of Arizona. High atop the Colorado Plateau, everything feels vast and spread wide. Roads are rare, people are few and widely scattered. Solitude is rich here and the scenery astounds me still, after all these decades. This is where I come to lose myself for a while.

The Navajo Nation and Hopi Reservation blanket Arizona's northeast quadrant. The Arizona Strip is that part of the state that lies north of the Colorado River, a land cut off by impenetrable canyons. In between them, Page perches on the slickrock mesa at the edge of Lake Powell, a final speck of civilization amid a lonely landscape.

In this quiet terrain, tall skylines of stone rise like lost cities. Sagebrush flats stretch away toward dreamy, distant horizons. And a river flows ever onward, carving canyons like nowhere else on earth.

Swirls of undulating sandstone have prompted some to refer to the Beehive Trail as the New Wave. Photo by the author.

Beehive Trail, Page

Traversing a large patch of swirling, swooping sandstone, this trail has emerged as a popular option for folks unable to score a coveted permit to the Wave, an iconic formation in the nearby Vermilion Cliffs National Monument. In fact, it's frequently called the New Wave Trail. Beehive is part of the Glen Canyon National Recreation Area and makes a family-friendly outing with views of Lake Powell along the route. That's something the Wave doesn't do.

No matter what you call it, this is a fun hike across a humped island of sandstone. The trail starts from a gravel turnaround, directly across from the Beehives Campground. Use the big brown Park Rules sign as a place marker. You'll spot a pathway lined by rocks and a small trail sign leading up the slope.

The trail flows nicely over the undulating landscape, never steep, never too edgy, but offering a taste of the slanted walking that comes with traversing slickrock. I moved across the ripples of the rock admiring the ridges and mounds, the beehives and scoops, that rose all around me. So much texture here. Upon reaching a Y, I swung to the left.

Soon afterward, a short side trail points toward a viewpoint, and that's an offer I never can resist. This one leads up a slope of bare rock, squeezing through a small cleft in the swirls of sandstone. I followed an angled ridgeline that showcased wide views of broken plateau country all the way. Time well spent.

Back on the main trail, it hugs a shoulder of stone as it circles a large outcrop formation. Ancient winds have left fingerprints all over this trail, sculpting long curving lines through the slickrock. No doubt that hypnotic pattern of swoops and swirls invites comparison to the original and more elusive Wave.

I certainly understand that. But the Beehive Trail easily stands on its own merits. Instead of trying to create a comparison to generate more social media buzz, embrace it for what it offers—easy access to a rarefied world of wind-sculpted stone, a masterpiece of time and erosion.

Where: From Page, drive north on US 89 to just past the Carl Hayden Visitor Center. Turn left onto a dirt road leading to the Beehives Campground (just before the south entrance to Wahweap Marina). Trailhead parking is on the left side of the road directly across from the Beehives campsites.
Cost: Although this trail is within Glen Canyon National Recreation Area, no admission fee is required.
Difficulty: Easy.
Length: 1.5 miles round-trip, 2 miles if you include the side trip.
Dogs: Yes, on a leash.
Details: (928) 608-6200, www.nps.gov/glca.

R.D.'s Drive-In, Page

Every town needs a mom-and-pop drive-in. After a summer day at the pool, the beach, or the trail, these were the kind of places where you stopped. Hit the drive-thru for refreshing dipped cones, tacos, corndogs, or, oh yeah, a burger, fries, and shake. Now that sounds like a heck of a combination.

R.D.'s Drive-In offers all those things and more. They maintain an extensive menu, including breakfast. But there is no dining area. Everything flies out the window for two drive-thru lanes that see a steady stream of customers. R.D.'s has a longtime rep in Page. They've been open for decades, so all the kids who used to scream for ice cream from the back seat now drive their own kids there—and no doubt plead with their progeny not to drip or spill on the upholstery, just like their parents once did. Karma, am I right?

The burgers here exude a vintage charm. There's a little Americana in every bite. Patties are thin but the burger is carefully constructed to deliver the correct proportion of flavors. Burger architecture is more complex than people realize. At R.D.'s they understand the proper technique for organizing and stacking the toppings to deliver the right balance. The quarter-pound single is full of flavor. More ravenous appetites can double or triple the patties.

Vegetarian Options: After a bean and cheese burrito, there's a whole bunch of shakes, cones, sundaes, and banana splits to consider.
Don't Forget: You can grab a cream soda at R.D.'s. When was the last time you had one of those?
Details: 143 S. Lake Powell Blvd., (928) 640-3972, www.rdsdrivein.shop.

River Trail, Lees Ferry

This short hike offers a fascinating history lesson paired with exquisite scenery. I consider it one of the most beautiful and under-appreciated hikes in the state. The River Trail is located in Lees Ferry, part of the Glen Canyon National Recreation Area. When John Lee started his ferry service in 1873, this became the only Colorado River crossing in hundreds of miles. So of course this became a hub of Western history.

This is also the put-in place for rafters beginning their river trip through the Grand Canyon. The ramp is often astir with people loading boats and basting themselves in sunscreen, eager to get underway. Yet sandal-wearing river rats show little interest in hiking, so the River Trail itself stays generally deserted.

Fast Fact: When Navajo Bridge was completed in 1929, it offered the only direct access across the Colorado River between Arizona and Utah. In 1995, the original bridge was replaced by one similar in design just downstream, and now the twin spans stretch across Marble Canyon. The old bridge is only open to pedestrians. It provides river views and is a good spot to watch for endangered California condors.

You'll find the trailhead at the far end of the parking area for the launch ramp. Just walk past the parked buses. Up first are two small stone buildings, a fort that was never attacked and a post office that never sent mail. Well, hardly ever. It just speaks to the isolation of this remote settlement.

The level path continues on a bench above the river past old buildings and rusted pieces of

The gentle River Trail at Lees Ferry offers a quiet respite in a place of rare beauty. Photo by the author.

mining equipment. Well-placed signs provide a surprisingly detailed account of life on the frontier here that included Mormon pioneers and hopeful speculators. There are some stories about Charles Spencer, a prospector who arrived in 1910 and tried desperately but unsuccessfully to strike it rich. Many ruins and remnants can be traced back to him.

Meanwhile, the scenery steals your breath. The river shimmers in the sun, blue, then green, then melancholy and moody as cloud shadows sweep overhead. Banks are fringed with grasses and scrubby trees, as colorful hills slant down toward the water. The Spencer Trail branches off to the left, an old pack mule route hacked from the cliffs. The Spencer Trail is short but brutal, climbing 1,500 feet in a mile. But it's worth scrambling uphill for just a level or two to admire the elevated vistas.

Past the trail junction, the hull of Spencer's old steamboat lies submerged in the river, a ghost of failed schemes. The trail officially ends after 1 mile at the ruins of an old cabin once available to overnight travelers. But feel free to continue. A clear path, created by fishermen, traces the riverbank and it just seemed to pull me along. With the history lesson behind me, I marveled at the array of colors surrounding this mighty river that continues to chisel away at the tall cliffs of the Colorado Plateau. It's stunning here in this intimate space. And I've heard that the erosion work is even more impressive in some kind of canyon just downstream. Wonder if those rafters know anything about that.

Where: Lees Ferry (and entrance to Glen Canyon National Recreation Area) is located in Marble Canyon just west of Navajo Bridge Interpretive Center off US 89A. Follow the paved road 5 miles until it ends at the launch ramp.

Cost: Admission fee.

Difficulty: Easy.

Length: 2 miles round-trip.

Dogs: Yes, on a leash.

Details: (928) 608-6200, www.nps.gov/glca.

Hot Tip: Be sure to visit Lonely Dell Ranch, the former homestead built by John D. Lee and the families that came later to operate the ferry. Historic buildings still stand, flanked by rocky cliffs and surrounded by orchards planted long ago. Munch a piece of ripe fruit from the branches as you ponder what life here was once like.

Cliff Dwellers Restaurant, Marble Canyon

How I love a middle-of-nowhere burger. They appear like a mirage, glistening with juiciness, beyond civilization, almost beyond hope. These are small beefy miracles on the raggedy edge of the frontier. You'll find no better example than Cliff Dwellers Restaurant, a culinary outpost on the Arizona Strip.

Is it weird that I drive hours to reach one of my favorite burgers? What does that say about me?

Cliff Dwellers sits 9 miles west of Navajo Bridge, at the base of the Vermilion Cliffs. It is the last vestige of humanity before plunging into the sagebrush hinterlands. A rustic place that's surrounded by hotel rooms, it's the kind of isolated eatery where you just hope the food is edible. To find a menu that is varied, scratch-made, and delicious in such a distant hideaway, where they also sell gas and bait, is one of the ultimate joys of travel.

Perched on the Arizona Strip, Cliff Dwellers Restaurant is a culinary oasis in a far-flung and lonely spot. Photo by the author.

The little settlement of Cliff Dwellers includes a line of motel rooms, a small store with gas pumps, and fishing supplies. They also offer guide services for fly fishermen and rent and haul kayaks for those looking to explore the flat water stretch of Colorado River from Glen Canyon Dam to Lees Ferry, including Horseshoe Bend.

You can sit inside because they have a few tables. But I never do. Not when there's a porch and a covered rock-walled patio with roll-up garage doors available. I like to sit in the open air, gazing at angular cliffs swabbed in sunset hues as I count down the seconds until my burger arrives.

Small though the restaurant may be, they employ skilled chefs. Every meal I've had here has been excellent, including breakfasts, but I always return to the burgers. Each is a design-your-own affair, starting with the usual selection of fresh produce, and allowing you to expand from there. Expect a half pound of well-seasoned beef, cooked to order and full of flavor. An absolutely splendid burger that resonates with the fine spice of remoteness.

Vegetarian Options: A veggie burger is on the menu along with a large garden salad and Southwest-style Caesar salad.

Don't Forget: The original homesteaders opened a trading post in the 1920s. The curious stone house they built utilized big boulders and prompted the name cliff dwellers. Those ruins can still be seen at the end of the property.

Details: Milepost 547 US 89A, (928) 355-2237, www.cliffdwellerslodge.com.

Fast Fact: Jimmy Buffett wrote the song "Cheeseburger in Paradise" after a particularly rough boat trip. Following days at sea with provisions running low, Buffett yearned for a cheeseburger. He was thrilled when he reached the island of Tortola and found a cheeseburger on the restaurant menu.

Wildcat Trail, Monument Valley Tribal Park

There are many ways to explore the radiant desolation of Monument Valley, but if you want a piece of it all to yourself, there's no better experience than hiking the Wildcat Trail. It brushes so close to the iconic formations known as the Mittens, you can feel them gently holding you.

Start by signing the trail register inside the information center. Then walk down the parking lot toward the graveled scenic road. Watch for signs as the trail briefly follows this dirt road, then crosses it at the first curve and angles down a sandy hill to the valley floor.

This feels like the beating heart of the West. Blocky towers vault from the sand and sagebrush to pierce a tall sky. It is hauntingly quiet here in the brittle afternoon light. I walked into the expanse gazing at monoliths stranded like shipwrecks washed up on an ancient shore.

Curving through the gnarled scrub and wind-bent juniper trees, Wildcat loops around West Mitten. This is one of the three prominent formations that form the core of Monument Valley, along with East Mitten and Merrick Butte between them.

The Navajos, or Diné, which means "the people," have occupied these lands for centuries. And dozens of Diné families still live within the tribal park. I have seen sheep herds and, on more than one occasion, horses grazing. If you don't think those were special

Hot Tip: Park visitors can drive their vehicles on a rough, 17-mile dirt road through the heart of the park. Better still, Navajo-led tours are available and well worth the cost. It's a chance to learn more about Diné culture and explore portions of the park that are off-limits to non-Navajos.

The Wildcat Trail delivers Monument Valley in the most intimate way possible. Courtesy of Mike Koopsen, Sedona.

moments—me and a horse, alone in Monument Valley—then the power of this landscape somehow eludes you.

Sporadic trail markers keep you on the right path through the gently rolling terrain, scarred with washes and narrow ravines. Summer storms can quickly chew through this landscape. Stay on the trail to limit erosion. Other signs identify plants and animals that eke out a living here. Swinging around the backside of West Mitten, I gazed toward the broad wall of Sentinel Mesa flanked by formations like Big Chief, Castle Butte, and the Bear and the Rabbit.

The sky is velvet, set against the hard skin of the monoliths. It shifts and flows, and presses ever down. Cloud shadows caress the sandstone like a mother comforting a sleeping child.

Many beautiful places in Arizona are a furious clutter of formations but this is not one of them. Here the stones maintain a comfortable distance from each other. They are separate and distinct, respecting personal boundaries. Yet they share equal billing with slices of sky that fall in between, the plump planets of clouds wafting overhead, and long shadows that dance in when nobody is looking. I come to Monument Valley to witness the slow-motion eruption of the earth. But it's the sky that steals my heart.

Where: From Kayenta, drive north on US 163 for 23 miles and turn right into Monument Valley Tribal Park. Trail begins 0.4 miles north of visitor center from the campground.
Cost: Admission fee.
Difficulty: Moderate.
Length: 3.8 miles.
Dogs: Yes, on a leash.
Details: (435) 727-5870, www.navajonationparks.org.

Fast Fact: Unlike the rest of Arizona, the Navajo Nation observes Daylight Saving Time.

Amigo Café, Kayenta

Driving through Kayenta, travelers may only notice a sprinkling of fast-food restaurants. But pay attention because as soon as you turn north on US 163 heading for Monument Valley, you might spot a little building surrounded by cars, often spilling into the adjacent lot. Seems like everyone in town eats at Amigo Café.

Established in 1983, this cozy café dishes up authentic Mexican and Navajo dishes, while also offering wholesome and health-some options. Everything is made from scratch and artfully executed. They offer some intriguing burgers, including a classic Navajo burger nestled on fry bread. One of these days,

The Navajo tacos at Amigo's Café are served on a puffy, doughy circle of fry bread. Photo by the author.

I need to try them. But I'm still working my way through creative Mexican and Native dishes. The Three Sisters Burrito pays homage to the foundation of traditional agriculture with corn, beans, and squash as well as other goodies wrapped in a flour tortilla and slathered with a rich pumpkin mole sauce.

Of course, it's always hard to resist their Navajo taco. For the uninitiated, Navajo tacos are served open-face using fry bread as a base buried under a landslide of beans or beef, lettuce, tomatoes, cheese, and more. The fry bread at Amigo Café is a golden wheel of dough, puffy in the middle and crispy on the skin—a flavor not easily forgotten.

Vegetarian Options: Along with the Three Sisters Burrito, they serve chile rellenos, a cheese enchilada combination plate, and more.
Don't Forget: Amigo Café is also a full-on coffee bar, offering a variety of fresh-brewed java, specialty blends, and seasonal selections.
Details: US 163 (just north of US 160), (928) 697-8448, www.amigocafekayenta.com.

"I wish for infinity hamburgers."
HOMER SIMPSON

Let Me Finish

So I will tell you how the dawn breaks like a piñata filled with showery golden light above the tablelands of the Colorado Plateau. And I will tell you how the clear water of a mountain stream tinkles like a chorus of bells as it spills over rocks in a pine forest.

I will tell you about the morning meadow where a hummingbird stared long and deep into my eyes while hovering in front of me wrapped in a gauzy blur of wings. It wanted me to know something, and I still regret not following when it finally flew away.

I will tell you about the cactus that jumps and the horned lizard that shoots blood from its eye and the big wasp that haunts tarantula dreams. I will tell you about standing in a rainy aspen grove listening to wolves howl from the ridge above. And I will tell you about the bear that followed me, and the owl that scared the absolute bejeebers out of me as it swooped silently past like a dragon shadow in dusky woods. I will tell you about hiking among saguaros in the middle of summer where the sun lands on my head like a freshly microwaved cinderblock.

And I will tell you about scandalous sunsets, as bloody as a revolution, yet soft as angel skin collapsing into the arms of the horizon, time and time again. I will tell you about a canyon so wide and so deep you can peer at the earth's insides and listen to its beating heart. I will tell you how my boots make music on every trail surface, a melody of crunches and scrapes and whispers. I will tell you what I dream when I snooze in the shade. I will tell you about the stillness only I get to experience. And I will tell you about stormy skies, cool breezes, fragrant forests, windswept plains, and endless fields of bright, cheery wildflowers unfurling satin petals in welcome. I will tell you about the miles and the memories.

But first, just let me finish my burger.

Acknowledgments

I wish to express my profound gratitude to several people. At the top of the list are those that work so hard to build, maintain, and protect the incredible system of trails that help make Arizona such a recreational paradise. That includes government employees, park staff, trail organizations, maintenance crews, search and rescue groups, trail stewards, mountain bikers, equestrians, hikers, and a veritable army of volunteers across the state who create and care for the pathways that guide us all back to nature.

I am always grateful to those in the food service industry, from the folks who open restaurants to those that keep them running, along with the staff cooking and serving the food and to those cleaning up afterward—especially the cooks and chefs on the business end of a spatula standing watch over my burgers. It's an incredibly hard job and often a thankless one. Just know that you fill my stomach with food and my heart with joy. I'm probably not the only one.

My heartfelt thanks go out to two talented photographers, Rick Mortensen and Mike Koopsen, who make writing these books so much more enjoyable. Their interest, enthusiasm, and skill help bring each project to fruition. Working with them has been a privilege. Thanks also to Ken Lapides, who uses his considerable skills to make everything look better in the end. I am forever in Jill Cassidy's debt. She allowed me to somehow carve out a career as an Arizona travel writer by continuing to splash my words across the pages of the *Arizona Republic* since 2007. Thanks to Peter Aleshire, who gave me a start at *Arizona Highways*, but even more importantly, who first took me to Harvey's Wineburger. Of course, I owe everything to my wife, Michele, my sweetheart, my soulmate, my best friend, the vegetarian love of my life.

And a final thanks to Bill, of Bill's Sandwich Shop. He knew elementary students weren't supposed to be there during school hours, so he had every right to kick my skinny law-breaking butt out, but instead he willingly made himself an accessory to my crime spree, feeding me again and again. The man made a most memorable burger.

About the Author

Roger Naylor is an award-winning Arizona travel writer and author. He has been swoony in love with Arizona since arriving as a wide-eyed college student. For decades he has explored his adopted state while writing about his discoveries. He specializes in national and state parks, lonely hiking trails, twisting back roads, diners with burgers sizzling on the grill, small towns, ghost towns, and pie. Naylor's work has appeared in the *Arizona Republic*, *USA Today*, *The Guardian*, *Country Magazine*, *Arizona Highways*, and dozens more. He was inducted into the Arizona Tourism Hall of Fame in 2018. He is also the narrator of the Verde Canyon Railroad.

Naylor has authored several books including *Arizona National Parks and Monuments*, *Awesome Arizona: 200 Amazing Facts about the Grand Canyon State*, *Arizona's Scenic Roads and Hikes*, *Arizona State Parks*, *The Amazing Kolb Brothers of Grand Canyon*, *Arizona Kicks on Route 66*, and *Crazy for the Heat: Arizona Tales of Ghosts, Gumshoes, and Bigfoot*. For more information, visit www.rogernaylor.com.

The Southwest Adventure Series

ASHLEY M. BIGGERS, SERIES EDITOR

The Southwest Adventure Series provides practical how-to guidebooks for readers seeking authentic outdoor and cultural excursions that highlight the unique landscapes of the American Southwest. Books in the series feature the best ecotourism adventures, world-class outdoor recreation sites, back-road points of interest, and culturally significant archaeological sites, as well as lead readers to the best sustainable accommodations and farm-to-table restaurants in Arizona, Colorado, Nevada, New Mexico, Utah, and Southern California.

Also available in the Southwest Adventure Series:

Arizona National Parks and Monuments: Scenic Wonders and Cultural Treasures of the Grand Canyon State by Roger Naylor
Slow Travel New Mexico: Unforgettable Personal Experiences in the Land of Enchantment by Judith Fein
Arizona Family Outdoor Adventure: An All-Ages Guide to Hiking, Camping, and Getting Outside by Chels Knorr
Colorado Family Outdoor Adventure: An All-Ages Guide to Hiking, Camping, and Getting Outside by Heather Mundt
New Mexico Family Outdoor Adventure: An All-Ages Guide to Hiking, Camping, and Getting Outside by Christina M. Selby
South Mountain Park and Preserve: A Guide to the Trails, Plants, and Animals in Phoenix's Most Popular City Park by Andrew Lenartz
New Mexico Food Trails: A Road Tripper's Guide to Hot Chile, Cold Brews, and Classic Dishes from the Land of Enchantment by Carolyn Graham
Arizona's Scenic Roads and Hikes: Unforgettable Journeys in the Grand Canyon State by Roger Naylor
Arizona State Parks: A Guide to Amazing Places in the Grand Canyon State by Roger Naylor
Eco-Travel New Mexico: 86 Natural Destinations, Green Hotels, and Sustainable Adventures by Ashley M. Biggers